# Training Plans
# for Multisport
# ATHLETES

# Training Plans
# for Multisport
# ATHLETES

## Second Edition

## Gale Bernhardt

BOULDER, COLORADO USA

VeloPress®
1830 North 55th Street
Boulder, Colorado 80301-2700 USA
303/440-0601 · Fax 303/444-6788 · E-mail velopress@insideinc.com

Library of Congress Cataloging-in-Publication Data

Bernhardt, Gale, 1958-
 Training plans for multisport athletes / Gale Bernhardt. — 2nd ed.
     p. cm.
 Includes bibliographical references and index.
 ISBN 1-931382-92-1 (alk. paper)
 1. Triathlon—Training. 2. Physical education and training. I. Title.
 GV1060.73.B465 2006
 796.42'57—dc22

                                          2006031705

Cover design by Stephanie Goralnick
Cover photo by Chris Milliman
Back cover photos by Timothy Carlson (left) and Don Karle
Interior design by Nicola Ferguson

For information on purchasing VeloPress books, please call 800/234-8356 or visit www.velopress.com.

10 9 8 7 6 5 4 3 2 1

*To Delbert:*
*I cannot find enough words to express*
*my gratitude for your support.*
*Thank you.*

# CONTENTS

# CONTENTS

# FOREWORD

I met Gale Bernhardt for the first time when I rejoined the USA Triathlon National Coaching Commission (NCC) in 2000. At the time, the NCC consisted of a collection of experts in various aspects of sports science and coaching who were struggling to put together a coherent coaching certification program. Upon assuming the chair's position not long after, Gale stepped into the fray and used her considerable organizational and communication skills to move us forward efficiently toward completion of the task at hand.

She brings the same skills to the task of coaching triathletes. Her *Training Plans for Multisport Athletes* distills the essence of what is known from both sports science and practical sports experience into a relatively simple and effective approach to preparing for triathlon competitions. She addresses all major elements of this preparation in a way that allows the average person to quickly and simply incorporate them into a usable training plan. She has further developed specific plans for the wide variety of triathlons at various distances and in differing combinations. Beyond this, she introduces advanced concepts and methodology only commonly utilized at the very top performance levels in the sport. She does all this in a way that allows even the rawest beginner to quickly absorb and make practical use of the information to train effectively.

When I was asked to write the foreword for this book, I was quite pleased to do so. It goes without saying that Gale's positive, organized approach to both coaching and writing has moved innumerable individual triathletes forward more rapidly than they could ever have hoped to do on their own. Even more significantly, her tremendous commitment to the sport and her work with USA Triathlon in both the coaching certification program and elite team development have moved the entire sport forward in dramatic ways. As I write this, Gale continues to give of herself in this way—benefiting those of us around her as well as continuing to expand her own knowledge base. I would strongly suggest taking advantage of the opportunity to gain the benefit of her vast experience yourself by purchasing and reading her newest edition of *Training Plans for Multisport Athletes*. I wish you health and success in triathlon.

—George M. Dallam, PhD

*Associate Professor of Exercise Science and*

   *Health Promotion, Colorado State University, Pueblo*

*USA Triathlon National Teams Coach, 1996–1997*

*USA Triathlon Selection for U.S. Olympic Committee*

*2005 National Coach of the Year*

*2004 Doc Counsilman Science in Coaching award winner*

*Longtime coach of Hunter Kemper*

# PREFACE TO
# THE SECOND EDITION

It has been a wonderful journey from the first edition of *Training Plans for Multisport Athletes* to this new and improved second edition, filled with new experiences and greater knowledge. I am happy that many athletes have dropped me notes to tell me that they have found success using the first book as their guide. These athletes have contributed to the second edition with their thoughtful feedback, questions, and encouraging comments.

This edition contains updates, new research, and the addition of one of my most popular plans, "13 Weeks to a Sub-13-Hour Ironman." I have also expanded on the concept of periodization, and the training plans in Chapters 4 through 17 are all periodization plans. For some plans, the depth of fitness will be enough for "survival." For other plans, the depth of fitness will be geared toward increasing speed on an already established base.

I hope you enjoy your multisport journey as much as I've enjoyed mine.

# PREFACE TO THE FIRST EDITION

My younger brother Jerry was my first multisport training partner. In our preteen years we could be found at the pool nearly every day of summer vacation. Before we knew what goggles were, we swam until our bloodshot, tearing eyes demanded a time-out. The play continued as we rode our bicycles everywhere, on- and off-road. Jerry was the champ at off-road maneuvers. On the bike or running, my brother could really sprint. More often than not, the sprint concerned an argument, so sprint training usually turned into strength training—wrestling until one of us was pinned, both of us refusing to beg for mercy. Our family fitness carried over into neighborhood activities like baseball, football, ice skating, and other assorted sports. We both understood that being strong and fast had advantages.

As a preteen I noticed fitness in other people, particularly adults. One adult role model was Susie Poeschal. Susie taught swimming lessons and held the glorious job of lifeguard. At twelve years old I thought, "I want to grow up to be a lifeguard." Between the ages of twelve and eighteen, I continued to marvel at Susie's fitness. I noticed she could do fun things other adults had long since given up, like hiking mountain trails and riding her bicycle long distances. I recall listening as she told us she rode her bike fifteen miles and that it was pretty easy. What a feat, considering she was almost thirty years old! I wanted to be that fit when I got older.

Susie influenced my desire to remain fit and teach sporting activities, and Dick Hewson influenced my desire to coach. Dick coached the Loveland Swim Club and made certain that all of the kids had a chance to participate and reach their personal best performances. As I continued into high school, Dick remained my swim coach. He coached in a manner that made people *want* to swim fast, as opposed to driving their performance with fear and intimidation. I recognized that difference in coaching techniques early on and wanted to find out how to help people want to reach beyond what they think is possible.

Throughout high school, college, and into my early twenties, I was able to maintain some level of fitness, and I also taught or coached various sports. In 1987, after entering the "real world," I met Joyce Friel. She knew I taught aerobics, biked to work, and ran enough to complete a race now and then. She also knew of my previous swimming background. She insisted I try a triathlon. "A what?" I wondered.

Swimming, biking, and running all combined into one event for time, she explained; changing clothes was timed as well. It sounded like fun, but I recall that my biggest concerns were mascara and contacts. At that time in my life, I was not seen in public without mascara—which I am happy to say is no longer the case. I was also worried about losing my contacts in the swimming pool—then how would I see anything on the bike ride?

I managed to overcome these two weighty issues, and with six weeks of swim training, I did the Fort Collins Triathlon, a sprint event. The event was great fun and inspired a new concern—"How do I go faster and get better?" I read everything on triathlon training. Joyce told me that her husband Joe coached triathletes and that he could help me get faster. A triathlon coach? I was just an age-group athlete, with no delusions of getting paid to do this fun sport. Did I really need a coach? As it turns out, hiring Joe as my coach was an excellent decision. His structure and guidance helped me tremendously.

My experience in coaching individual athletes led to a column in the 1995 issue of *Triathlete* magazine. The column, "Going from One to Du," instructed runners and cyclists on how to become duathletes. Readers were excited to have a daily guide to help them train and they continued to request specific training plans to guide their multisport journeys. Each column seemed to generate requests for more plans. Over time, I realized that it was difficult to offer detailed, advanced training plans tailored to every athlete in the magazine format, and the idea for this book was conceived.

# ACKNOWLEDGMENTS

I must thank *Triathlete* magazine, editors, and staff for their column request in 1995. That June column was the seed for this book. John Duke, Christina Gandolfo, T. J. Murphy, Lisa Park, Cameron Elford, Rebecca Roozen, and the team at *Triathlete* have been instrumental in publishing my training materials for their readers.

After the first edition of this book was written, the popularity of the Internet absolutely exploded. I am grateful to the team at the Active Network for including my training columns in their publications, which I believe has contributed to more athletes migrating to triathlon and multisport. The list of Active Network people involved in supporting my work is very, very long. You know who you are, as I have dropped you a personal thank-you somewhere along the way.

Both Active Trainer and TrainingPeaks carry online versions of some of the training plans in this book. Partnered with the supporting information in this book, these interactive systems make modifying the training plans and logging your success very easy.

I would like to thank VeloPress and all its editors who contributed expertise to this book. Thank you as well to all the athletes who took the time to provide their insightful comments.

I am quite indebted to my immediate and extended family and friends for their support and encouragement. I cannot begin to inscribe this extensive list.

Joe Friel, Cathy Sloan, and Tom Manzi gave generously of their time and suggestions to improve the first edition's content. Joe also influenced the text in the first edition as one of the early experts in endurance sport training. In addition to offering editing suggestions, Cathy helped keep me sane by assisting in my business. Her value as a training partner, buddy, and Buffy No. 1 makes her irreplaceable. Tom offered fresh perspective in the first edition and provided plenty of entertainment at those early coaching clinics.

Chris Book, a registered dietitian, was a tremendous help in the transformation of my own diet and furnished a good deal of information for the nutrition chapter of this book. Athletes and nonathletes alike value her expertise. Dr. Deborah Shulman, registered dietitian, exercise physiologist, and elite-distance runner, reviewed the majority of data in the nutrition chapter. She supplied useful information based on firsthand experience and her work with endurance athletes.

In 1996 I had a major shift in my training philosophy concerning periodization concepts as applied to endurance athletes. Fran Bell, Brian Quale, and Greg Jensen, with the Colorado Acceleration Program, were instrumental in that change. They taught me the value of overspeed training on the treadmill, plyometrics, and power training. Together we figured out how to apply those training tools to endurance athletes, some of which are reflected in this book.

Nick Hansen not only improved my personal swim times, but also made significant contributions to Chapter 19. A small taste of his extensive knowledge and experience is in the sample workouts in Appendix E. He is also the coauthor of two of the Workouts in a Binder® books for swimmers. Plan to see more from this excellent coach in the future.

The first edition of this project would not have been possible without Amy Rinehart. She supported the concept for the book and managed the publication process. Clancy Drake edited what I meant to say into readable text, Lori Hobkirk kept the project moving forward, and Paulette Livers Lambert provided book design expertise.

The second edition was made possible by Renee Jardine. She is a brilliant editor who made suggestions that significantly improved the first edition. She is also one of my favorite people to enjoy a long conversation with. She's just a good person.

Jill Amack copyedited this edition, which was no easy task. Chapters were rearranged, new material was added, and the chapters ebbed and flowed. Her patience and expertise are priceless.

Iris Llewellyn was the extremely valuable managing editor on this second edition. She oversaw the entire editing process, working with designers, freelancers, and me. A tough job for sure.

I am grateful to all the athletes who have allowed me into their lives and allowed me to influence their athletic endeavors. Without them, neither edition would have been possible. A word of thanks must also go to all the athletes who contributed quotations to the beginning of each chapter.

Finally, I must mention Shelby, and her new dog-sister Meeka, who relieved all episodes of writer's block with timely urgings to go for a run. Their constant companionship provides security from all things scary, allowing my mind to wander in peace.

# INTRODUCTION

*Getting faster is a matter of wisely investing time,*
*not simply spending more time.*

When I began to train for my first triathlon, I searched the bookstores for a text with a plan. I had roughly six weeks to get ready for my first race and I wanted a guide to help me prepare. What I found were books explaining what the sport was, what equipment was necessary and how to find it, the physiology of endurance training, and lots of sample weeks or sample training workouts. But I wanted a plan—the whole enchilada. What should I be doing every day between the start of training and race day? And for how long? How fast? I was busy, so what was the minimum training necessary? What I wanted—a detailed, progressive plan—was not available.

If you're searching for a book with training plans, you are in the right place. This tome contains fifteen plans to guide the training of multisport athletes, from novices to experts. Each plan details specific workouts, with each workout's time and intensity placed within an organizational structure for the plan as a whole. Some athletes will use the plans verbatim. For others, the plans may require small changes to fit personal needs. The ability to see each plan in its entirety, along with knowledge of your personal schedule and level of fitness, allows you to make calculated modifications to any of the plans.

To begin using this manual, read Part I, which contains information that is vital to all of the training plans. It covers the concepts of training and racing periodization and intensity, the limits of the notion that "one plan fits all," and a nutrition primer. Once training intensities are grasped in the opening sections, the workout codes detailed in Part VI have more meaning. There are codes for swimming, cycling, running, and strength-training workouts, and each code and its respective sport are also covered in separate chapters within Part VI. These codes are referenced in nearly every plan, though not all of them are used in each plan. Defining every workout of value with a handful of codes is an attempt to carefully monitor variety and progression. Hence, every plan also includes special instructions for some of the workouts within the text of its accompanying chapter.

If you thumb through the book to find the training plans, you may find the code-filled columns and rows a little overwhelming. Take a deep breath and look at only one week at a time. Each plan has an underlying logic and a pattern that repeats. The pattern may vary a bit from phase to phase on the longer plans, but it remains a pattern as well as a progression. On the longer plans, it may be helpful to use a highlighter to define three- to four-week training blocks. This visual separation helps to break the whole plan into smaller segments of accomplishment.

Each of the chapters that feature plans begins with an athlete profile, which describes the person for whom the plan was designed and the goal to be accomplished at the end of the plan. The goals for the plans in Part II are accomplished in six to thirteen weeks. These plans are written for athletes with limited training time, limited experience, limited fitness, or some combination of those circumstances. These early plans contain stashes of information useful to athletes of all experience levels. In fact, I recommend skimming the text for all plans, as each chapter contains useful tips not repeated elsewhere in the book.

The plans in Part III are for duathlon, XTERRA®, and general multisport fitness training. The plans in Part IV are for athletes looking for improved performance in sprint triathlon, Olympic triathlon, duathlon, or a sub-13-hour Ironman®.

Part V is for long-term training. There is a half-year plan for both half-Ironman and Ironman racing. This part also contains a yearlong plan for an Olympic-distance race; a full fifty-two weeks long, if completed, this plan would be challenging to many seasoned triathletes.

Whether the plan you choose spans a few months or an entire year, there will more than likely need to be modifications. After all, real life doesn't always stick to a schedule. Tips for modification are also included with each plan. If you decide to attempt the design of your own plan, *The Triathlete's Training Bible* by Joe Friel, also available from VeloPress, is a good resource.

The plans within this book are intentionally different in design. I have yet to discover a single training plan that fits everyone's needs. The only standard used in all the plans is the principle of periodization—adding increments of training volume or intensity followed by rest, in a structured format, to achieve athletic improvement. For some this means having the fitness to comfortably survive an event, while for others it entails pushing the limits of speed. For still others, it means maintaining a fitness level that allows participation in a variety of sports, including triathlon. No matter which description fits you, I hope the book is a valuable training tool, one that you'll refer to time and time again.

# WORKOUT CODES
# QUICK REFERENCE

*Refer to Chapters 19, 20, and 21 for further details on each of these workout codes.*

## Cycling

*A1a—Easy Group Ride.* Ride with a group and stay mostly in Zones 1 to 3.

*A1b—Faster-paced Group Ride.* Ride with a group and stay mostly in Zones 1 to 4.

*A1c—Fast, Aggressive Group Ride.* Ride with a group and ride in all zones.

*A1d—Ride as You Feel.* If you are feeling great, ride aggressively with some time in all zones; if tired, take it easy.

*A2 (5bZ)—Speed Endurance Intervals.* Warm up well on a mostly flat course, then do the specified number of intervals, allowing heart rate to climb into Zone 5b.

*A6 (5b–cZ)—Hill Reps.* Warm up well, then ride up a hill with a 6 to 8 percent grade, and complete the specified number of hill repetitions.

*A7—Taper Intervals.* Warm up well, then complete the specified number of 90-second accelerations, getting your heart rate into Zone 3, 4, or 5a as specified on the plan.

*E1.* Ride in the small chainring on a flat course, keeping your heart rate in Zone 1.

*E2.* Ride a rolling course in Zones 1 to 2.

*E3.* Ride a rolling course in Zones 1 to 3.

*E4.* Ride a hilly course at all intensities. Begin conservatively, and then steadily increase time spent in high-intensity zones.

*Form.* Select from workouts S1, S2, S3, S4, or S5.

*M1—Tempo.* Warm up on a mostly flat course, then ride in Zone 3 for the time indicated on the plan, e.g., M1 (15) means ride at a steady pace for 15 minutes in Zone 3.

*M2 (3Z)—Cruise Intervals.* On a mostly flat course or indoor trainer, complete the number of intervals given on the plan, allowing your heart rate to rise into Zone 3 over the course of each interval.

*M2 (4–5aZ)—Cruise Intervals.* On a mostly flat course or indoor trainer, complete the number of intervals shown on the plan, allowing your heart rate to rise into Zones 4 to 5a over the course of each interval.

*M3 (3Z)—Hill Cruise Intervals.* Same workout as M2 (3Z) but adding a long hill with a 2 to 4 percent grade.

*M3 (4Z)—Hill Cruise Intervals.* Same as M2(4–5aZ) but adding a long hill with a 2 to 4 percent grade.

*M4—Crisscross Threshold.* Crisscross from low Zone 4 to high Zone 5a for the time specified on the plan.

*M5—Tempo.* Warm up on a mostly flat course, then ride in Zones 4 to 5a for the time indicated on the plan.

*S1—Spin Step-ups.* Warm up 15 to 20 minutes, then increase cadence to 100 rpm for 3 minutes, followed by 110 rpm for 2 minutes and 120-plus rpm for 1 minute. Repeat as time and experience allow.

*S2—Isolated Leg.* Warm up on an indoor trainer with light resistance, then do 100 percent of the work with one leg while the other leg rests on a stool. Begin conservatively, and then steadily increase the isolation time. (Workout can be done outdoors by relaxing one leg and letting the other do 90 percent of the work.)

*S3—Accelerations.* Warm up well, then complete the specified number of 30-second accelerations, spinning easy for 2 minutes and 30 seconds (2' 30") between accelerations.

*S4—Fartlek.* Ride mostly in Zones 1 to 2, adding a few 10- to 20-second accelerations throughout the ride.

*S5—Cadence.* Ride the entire workout at 90 rpm or greater, keeping your heart rate in Zones 1 to 2.

*T1 (5), T1 (8), T1 (10)—Aerobic Time Trial (ATT).* Warm up, then ride 5, 8, or 10 miles with your heart rate 9 to 11 beats below your lactate threshold heart rate.

*T2—As-fast-as-you-can-go Time Trial (TT).* Warm up 15 to 30 minutes, then complete a 5- to 8-mile time trial as fast as you can possibly ride.

*XT.* Your option to crosstrain, using aerobics, cross-country skiing, rollerblading, or another activity of your choice to work out.

## Running

*A1a—Easy Group Run.* Run with a group and stay in Zones 1 to 3.

*A1b—Faster-paced Group Run.* Run with a group and stay in Zones 1 to 4. Time spent in Zone 5 should be minimal.

*A1c—Fast, Aggressive Group Run or Race.* Run with a group in all zones.

*A1d—Run as You Feel.* If you are feeling great, run aggressively with some time in all zones; if tired, take it easy.

*A2 (5bZ)—Speed Endurance Intervals.* Complete the specified number of intervals, allowing heart rate to climb into Zone 5b.

*A6 (5b–cZ)—Hill Reps.* Warm up well, then run up a hill with a 6 to 8 percent grade and complete the specified number of hill repetitions.

*A7—Taper Intervals.* Warm up well, then do the specified number of 90-second accelerations, getting heart rate into Zones 4 to 5a. Take 3 full minutes to recover between intervals.

*E1.* Run on a flat course—ideally on a soft surface like grass, dirt, or a treadmill—keeping heart rate in Zone 1.

*E2.* Run, keeping your heart rate primarily in Zones 1 to 2. Can be on a rolling course.

*E3.* Run a rolling or hilly course in Zones 1 to 3.

*E4.* Run a hilly course, allowing heart rate to rise into all zones. Begin conservatively, then steadily increase the amount of time spent in high-intensity zones.

*M1—Tempo.* Warm up, then run on a mostly flat course in Zone 3 for the time indicated on the plan. For example, M1 (15) means run at a steady pace for 15 minutes in Zone 3.

*M2 (3Z)—Cruise Intervals.* Complete the number of intervals given on the plan, doing so on a mostly flat course or treadmill. Allow heart rate to rise into Zone 3 over the course of each interval.

*M2 (4–5aZ)—Cruise Intervals.* Complete the number of intervals given on the plan, doing so on a mostly flat course or treadmill. Allow heart rate to rise into Zones 4 and 5a over the course of each interval.

*M3(3Z)—Hill Cruise Intervals.* Same workout as M2 (3Z) but on a long hill with a 2 to 4 percent grade.

*M3(4Z)—Hill Cruise Intervals.* Same workout as M2 (4–5aZ) but on a long hill with a 2 to 4 percent grade.

*M5—Tempo.* Warm up on a mostly flat course, then run in Zones 4 to 5a for the time indicated on the plan.

*S1—Strides.* Warm up 15 to 20 minutes, then do 20- to 30-second fast run segments on a soft, flat surface, such as a grassy park or football field. Walk or slowly jog back to the start position, taking 1 to 2 minutes to do so.

*S2—Pick-ups.* Start by running in mostly Zones 1 to 2, then insert several 20- to 30-second accelerations. Jog easy for 2 or more minutes between accelerations.

*S3—Cadence.* Run on a flat to gently rolling course in Zones 1 to 2 and check your leg speed a few times during the run by counting left-foot strikes for 15 seconds. Aim for a cadence of 21-plus strikes.

*T1—Aerobic Time Trial (ATT).* Warm up, then run 1 to 3 miles with your heart rate 9 to 11 beats below your lactate threshold heart rate.

*T2—As-fast-as-you-can-go Time Trial (TT).* Warm up 15 to 30 minutes, then complete a 1.5-mile time trial as fast as you can.

*TT.* Length of time trial designated within each plan.

*XT.* Your option to crosstrain, using aerobics, cross-country skiing, roller-blading, or another activity of your choice to work out.

## Swimming

*A.* Swim all out in the main set—no conserving, just go for it.

*A (Form).* Include swims faster than T1 pace in the main set, adding form work at the beginning or end of the workout.

*E1.* Control the intensity of the workout, keeping RPE in Zone 1.

*E2.* Control the intensity of the workout, keeping RPE in Zones 1 to 2.

*E3.* Control the intensity of the workout, keeping RPE in Zones 2 to 3.

*E (Form).* Include form work at the beginning or end of the workout.

*E (OW).* Swim for a designated time in open water.

*E (Speed).* Include some very fast 25s or 50s, emphasizing high-speed arm turnover.

*Force (Form).* Include paddles in the main set and begin or end the workout with form work.

*Force (Speed).* Include paddles in the main set and end the workout with some very fast 25s or 50s, emphasizing high-speed arm turnover.

*M.* Combine the main set into distances lasting 20 to 40 minutes, keeping a good portion of the set at T1 pace or slightly faster, i.e., by two to five seconds.

*M (Form).* Keep main set at T1 pace, and include form work at the beginning or end of the workout.

*M (OW).* Swim for the designated time in open water at race pace.

*M (Speed).* Include swims at T1 pace in the main set and end the workout with very fast 25s or 50s, emphasizing high-speed arm turnover.

*T1.* Swim 3 × 100 with 20 seconds rest between 100s.

*T1b.* Swim 3 × 300 with 30 seconds rest between 100s.

# PART I

# Multisport Basics

Before you dig right into a training plan, it is advantageous to read the first three chapters. Chapter 1 discusses the factors that influence individual performance—some of which we can control, others of which we can't. Those factors mean that there are benefits and limitations to any generic training plan. As we all know, one size does not fit all—but several sizes can fit many quite well, with a few alterations.

Chapter 2 covers the concepts of training periodization and intensity. It reviews the body's means of energy production and discusses how to establish training zones through the single or combined use of a heart rate monitor and the Borg scale, both of which measure your rate of perceived exertion (RPE). This chapter, along with the text accompanying each plan, will help you tailor your training to fit you.

Chapter 3 deals with nutrition; a faulty nutrition plan can derail even the best athlete. Good athletes need to be as intentional about fueling and hydration as they are about training.

# 1

# CAN ONE PLAN FIT ALL?

*Gale has painstakingly gone through the literature and applied scientific theory to sound coaching practice. This is what the multi-sport world has needed for years.*

—JAMES M. GREEN

In all the years I've been coaching individual athletes, I've never written two training plans exactly the same—even if two athletes had the same race schedule. This is because there are sundry elements that enter into creating a training plan, including the athlete's work schedule, family obligations, ability to recover from training and racing, individual fitness areas that limit performance, experience level, desire, nutrition, and genetics, for example. But just how much of our performance can we control, and how much is fate?

## FACTORS THAT INFLUENCE TRAINING

### GENETICS

Sometimes parents are blamed for an athlete's endurance performance. Your parents *are* responsible—for a portion of your performance. Several scientific studies have been conducted to determine if genetics are responsible for great athletic performances. Claude Bouchard, PhD, and a team of researchers at Laval University in Québec looked at identical twins and put a group of 20 (i.e., 10 pairs) on a 20-week training program. The twins trained four to five times per week for 45 minutes each session, at an average intensity of roughly 80 percent of maximum heart rate. The result? Identical twins did in fact respond nearly identically to the training program. One pair gained 10 and 11 percent respectively on their $VO_2$max, or aerobic capacity, while a second pair gained 22 and 25 percent. Most of the variation in performance gains was among individuals who were not related, not between genetically identical twins.

Although this study of twins revealed that 82 percent of the variation in $VO_2$max was due to genetics, it also revealed that only 33 percent of the differences found in ventilatory threshold (another benchmark of improvement) were attributable to genetics. This is important because ventilatory threshold—and the closely related lactate threshold—are frequently found to be the best predictors of actual performance. This is good news for all of us, because lactate threshold tends to be more trainable than $VO_2$max.

The researchers at Laval conducted further studies, concluding that genetic factors account for only 20 percent of the variation in the performance of endurance athletes. Nongenetic factors, however, were found to influence 40 percent of the variation. Nongenetic factors include nutrition, lifestyle, past exercise patterns, age, socioeconomic status, and mental skills, to name a few. Gender differences accounted for 10 percent. The final 30 percent of variation was due to how a particular set of genes reacted to a particular training program. That is, some people respond to one training program, but not to another.

So what's the bottom line? First, you can control around 70 percent of your performance, and second, what works for you won't necessarily work as well for the multisport athlete next to you.

## TRAINING RESPONSE RATES

Speaking of that person next to you, what about the differences between athletes using the same program? The researchers at Laval conducted another study to determine how much variation there would be in fitness gain if people followed the same training program. In this study, 24 similar subjects (initially sedentary) followed the same training program for 20 weeks. After 20 weeks, there were some big changes. The average gain in $VO_2max$ was 33 percent, and one person in the group gained a whopping 88 percent! Unfortunately, another individual sweating on the same plan increased $VO_2max$ by a mere 5 percent.

In the same study, scientists measured power output on a bicycle ergometer, on which subjects pedaled away for 90 minutes. Their average power output was measured before the training program began and again at the completion of the 20 weeks. The average power improvement was a nice 51 percent. One happy person gained a gigantic 97 percent, while another gained only 16 percent.

Why do some people seem to make big gains while others make minimal gains? And do their gains happen at even rates? The studies at Laval led researchers to believe people can be divided into "responders" and "nonresponders." Those who are considered responders make big improvements in aerobic capacity and power as a result of their training, while nonresponders barely show a gain, even after 20 weeks of hard work. The scientists estimate that around 5 percent of us are high responders who can make improvements over 60 percent, while about the same number are low responders and may only expect a 5 percent improvement.

In addition to identifying responders and nonresponders, the studies revealed a scale of responsiveness. Some people made solid gains after just four to six weeks of training, but seemed to plateau and made minimal gains in weeks seven to twenty. Others were late bloomers who were at a standstill for six to ten weeks, but then improved their aerobic capacities by 20 to 25 percent after ten weeks of additional training.

## HOW TO MODIFY TRAINING PLANS

Given any single training program, not all individuals will react exactly the same. Some people will make big gains while others may make marginal gains. Some will make their gains quickly, while others do so after more time has passed. Learning how your body responds to training and how to make adjustments will help you optimize your performance.

While there are limitations to using a generic training program, I've found that a good number of athletes have been quite successful using my plans as a guide. Some are versions of plans I've written for *Triathlete* and other magazines over the years. They are a combination of several individual training plans that have been tested and tweaked by many athletes.

At the beginning of each plan in this book is an athlete profile describing the person the plan is written for, a goal, and what the athlete should expect if he or she follows the plan. Each chapter in the second edition has been bolstered with even more tips on how to modify the particular training plan featured in that chapter. For additional help in modifying the plans, I'm including a list of common questions raised by athletes looking to tailor a training plan to their needs. Many of these questions and answers will make more sense after you choose a training plan and more thoroughly review the weekly workouts.

# GENERAL QUESTIONS AND ANSWERS

## TRAINING VOLUME

**Q:** Should I always shoot for the longer workout when a range is given?

**A:** No. A range is given on some workouts to allow you to customize the workout according to how you feel. Also, if you are in a time crunch and you have to cut the workout short, do fewer repetitions.

**Q:** If a bike workout prescribes two hours and I am feeling great, can I just go ahead and ride three hours?

**A:** Generally speaking, on two-hour rides, try not to go over or under more than about 15 minutes. On three-hour and longer rides, shoot for plus or minus 20 to 30 minutes. On shorter weekday rides, try to stay within around 10 minutes of the recommended duration.

Q: What happens if I get in a real time crunch and can only do 30 minutes of a 60-minute workout or I have to skip it altogether?

A: Realistically, you will probably miss a few workouts. If you need to skip a workout, try to make it an E1 workout that is one hour or less. The priority workouts are usually the long weekend workouts that continuously build volume, weekday intervals, and strength sessions.

Q: Is race performance related to training volume? In other words, if I use the training plan with the highest volume, will I be faster?

A: You will be faster only if your body can handle the training load and recover from that load. Know that the highest training volume does not always correlate to podium performance. Do the least amount of training that gives you continuous improvement.

## TRAINING SCHEDULE

Q: Can I rearrange the workouts within the week? I work weekends.

A: Rearranging the workouts is fine, with a few guidelines:

- *Allow at least 48 hours between strength training sessions.*
- *Breakthrough workout sessions should be 48 hours apart unless the original plan states otherwise.*
- *Do not try to make up missed weekday workouts on the weekend. In other words, don't try to ride for six hours on Saturday if you missed three one-hour workouts during the week and you have a three-hour Saturday ride scheduled.*

Q: If a swim, then a run, is shown on a particular day, do they have to be done in that order?

A: No. If your masters swimming group meets in the evening and you run in the morning, that's fine.

Q: If I miss a Thursday run or bike and Friday is shown as a day off, can I move the missed workout to Friday?

A: Yes, just be careful not to start "stacking" workouts on top of each other. Missing several workouts during the week cannot be made up in a couple of days on the weekend.

Q: I can only make it to the gym once a week. Is one strength training session really worth it?

A: Strength can be maintained by lifting once per week.

## HEALTH AND TRAINING

Q: What if I get sick; can I still train?

A: If your symptoms are above the neck and minimal (runny nose, headache, scratchy throat), go ahead and work out if you feel up to it. Cut your intensity to Zones 1 and 2. Reduce the total workout time or stop altogether if you feel bad once you begin the workout.

If your symptoms are below the neck or intense (cough, chills, vomiting, achy muscles, fever, sore throat), do not even start the workout. A virus likely causes these symptoms. Ignoring the symptoms and trying to train through the illness carries the risk of a more serious illness that can literally sideline you for months. Missing a few days of training to get well is your best investment of time.

Q: What happens if I miss some training days due to illness?

A: If you miss one to three days, resume your training as shown on the plan, skipping the workouts you missed. If you miss a week or more, consider adjusting your competition goals accordingly. Depending on how you recover, you may want to repeat a week or two of training to get you back on track. Whatever you do, take it easy coming back—you do not want another setback.

## INCORPORATING RACING IN TRAINING

**Q:** Can I race—do a triathlon—instead of doing a scheduled brick on a weekend when a brick is scheduled?

**A:** Yes, but try to keep overall time and the goal of the scheduled workout in mind. Too much racing while training for a half-Ironman or full Ironman can get in the way of long training sessions or cause excessive fatigue.

**Q:** Can I do a 10K running race instead of a fast running workout that falls in the middle of the week?

**A:** You can substitute a 5K or 10K running race for a fast running workout. Sometimes a fast midweek run has recovery workouts before and after in order to keep the run quality high. Depending on the particular training plan and your personal goals, you may need to rearrange other workouts as well. Look at the pattern of training within the week and decide what weekend pattern best suits your personal needs.

## SAFE TRAINING PLAN SHORTCUTS

**Q:** I don't have 13 weeks until race day. Can I jump in midplan and still be okay?

**A:** If your current weekly training volume is close to the time shown on the training plan, you can jump in midplan. Even if your training volume is close to that shown on the plan, take a look at the workout intensities. If the training volumes are similar but your training intensity has been lower, reduce the training intensity shown on the plan to a level that is close to what you've been accustomed to.

**Q:** I had a great summer of racing. Now I want to stay fit over the winter months, but the off-season training volumes for the yearlong Olympic plan are too much for me. What should I do to stay fit?

A: You can still use the format of the yearlong plan as your guide. Depending on your time constraints, you can either reduce the daily training volume by 20 to 30 minutes—or more—or you can eliminate some of the workouts altogether. For example, you may only have time for two workouts in each sport each week instead of three. In this case you would eliminate the E1 workouts in each sport.

Q: I love the 26-week Ironman plan, but I noticed that it is slightly different from the 13 Weeks to a Sub-13-Hour Ironman plan. Can I mix the two plans? In other words, I like the layout of the Sub-13-Hour plan, so can I just switch to that plan?

A: You are correct; the two training plans are slightly different in the last 13 weeks leading up to race day. Athletes have used both methods (i.e., the existing 26-week plan and the 26-week plan modified in the last 13 weeks to match the Sub-13-Hour performance plan) and both methods have produced successful results. Take a look at the last 13 weeks heading into race day and use the plan that best suits your body's response to stress and rest.

Q: I am stoked! I just successfully completed a 12-week plan and had a fantastic race. I entered another event four weeks out. What should I do now?

A: You can repeat the last four weeks of your original training plan—but be sure you take a few days, up to a week, after the event to recover. This means you might have to pull back some of the intensity, some of the workout time, or a bit of both.

## TRANSITIONS IN TRAINING

Q: How can I move from one training plan to another?

A: Depending on which training plans you are looking at, the answer varies. However, if you look closely, you will find that each training plan has a pattern of stress and rest. If you can find a training week within another plan that's close to your current training pattern, switching to a new plan should not be a problem.

Q: I tapered training for my race. If I'm going to start training again, do I need to begin training at the low volume of race week?

A: First, be sure to recover from your race. Race recovery is dependent on many factors, including race distance, athlete experience, race difficulty, and weather. In general, for shorter races, you should expect full recovery around one week. For Ironman races, full recovery may take three to four weeks. You can resume training after your recovery at a level that you would have considered a moderate training week in your original plan. You may need to reduce that volume slightly, and you may need to reduce workout intensity as well.

Q: Some plans show weekend workouts with the long run on Saturday and the long bike ride on Sunday, while other plans have the long bike first. Which is better?

A: If you are a person who can easily be injured from running, always do your long training runs before the long bike ride. If you are a very strong and healthy runner, but need help building cycling strength, put your long bike ride before your long run. If you want to alternate formats so one week the long run is first and the next week the long bike ride is first, that may help you benefit from the best of both formats.

Armed with the tools and information provided in this book, you should be well on the way to improved performance.

# 2

# LEVELS OF EXERCISE

*Individualization in training is one of the main requirements of contemporary training and it refers to the idea of each athlete, regardless of level of performance, being treated individually according to his or her abilities, potential, learning characteristics, and specificity of the sport.... Quite often coaches apply a completely unscientific approach in training by literally following training programs of successful athletes, completely disregarding his or her athlete's personality, experience, and abilities.*

—TUDOR BOMPA, *THEORY AND METHODOLOGY
OF TRAINING*

Perhaps you have been on a group ride or run, or in a particular lane at a group practice, where the speeds were sizzling from the start. For a few moments you were right there hanging with the pack. Then you dropped like a rock. Your heart was pounding, your legs were burning, and you gave it all you had. The group speed was obviously too fast for you to sustain. But other people were going that fast, so what were they doing that you weren't?

It seems to make sense that if you want to be fast in a race, you have to train that way. That is true to some extent, but you can't train at that rate all the time and make progress. Athletes who train at a consistently fast rate end up going one mediocre speed—not too fast, not too slow. They are too tired for their arms and legs to turn over a fast pace, yet they feel enough spunk to go at a decent pace. This chapter helps you avoid that rut by discussing training and racing intensities, as well as by giving you self-tests to estimate training zones. In Chapters 19 through 21, you will find tools to help you evaluate whether you are making progress.

Building and improving fitness is analogous to building a house. The first part, the foundation, must be constructed properly or the rest of the house will not hold up—at least not for very long. After the foundation is laid, a strong frame and roof can be built. The best results come from an orderly process in the initial stages of the construction. When it comes to the finishing details, the order of some tasks can be adjusted to accommodate the construction schedule. Then, once the house is constructed, it must be maintained. If the house is properly maintained, improvements can be made to suit the needs and wants of the owner. These improvements are typically done a few at a time.

So it goes with fitness. You need a solid base before you add long duration or long bouts of speed. If long duration is attempted prior to a gentle increase in training volume, there is a high risk of injury. If long bouts of speed are added before a good base of fitness is achieved, you can expect short-lived success and a high risk of injury. Once a certain level of fitness is achieved, it needs to be maintained. With each season, further improvements can be made, but it can often take many years to build a world-class multisport athlete.

## PERIODIZATION

You may or may not be striving to be world-class. Either way, periodization will help to guide your training for faster or longer races. Briefly, a periodized plan manipulates exercise volumes and intensities over the course of weeks, months, and years.

A periodization plan for an Olympic athlete will span the course of several years. This type of plan is designed to have the athlete at peak fitness and speed for the Olympic Games. No athlete, even an Olympic-caliber athlete, can maintain peak fitness year-round. True peak performances are planned and can occur only about two or three times per year.

Although the goal is to have the Olympic athlete at peak performance for the Olympic Games, that athlete must first qualify for the Olympic trials. At the writing of this text, the process to qualify for and compete in the Olympic Games for the sport of triathlon is a two-year, multiple-race process. Athletes must race well several times a year in order to make it to the Olympics. Top professionals can complete an Olympic-distance triathlon in around two hours, depending on course difficulty.

In sharp contrast to an Olympic-distance athlete, an Ironman-distance athlete will race less and plan for a peak performance once each year. Top professionals typically finish these races in eight to nine hours.

You may not be capable of achieving the time marks of top professionals, but your training process can utilize the training principles that elite athletes use. The deeper we look into a training plan for an individual sport, the more refinements of the training principles we'll find. For example, the details of the plan for an athlete preparing for his or her first sprint triathlon look different from the details of the plan for an athlete who is trying to get faster. The plan for a beginner triathlete is different if the athlete is fit than the plan needed for a currently hibernating athlete. Of course, the training plan for an Ironman-distance triathlon is different from the plan for an Olympic-distance event. Sometimes just completing the distance is enough of a challenge.

The old saying "The devil is in the details" holds true for training plans. When working with your training plan, keep in mind the following training principles:

*1.* Individual and progressive *overload* must be applied to achieve physiological improvement and bring about a training change. A widely accepted rule of thumb is to increase annual training hours or annual volume by 10 percent or less.

*2.* Training *volume* can be defined as the combination of frequency and duration. When looking at your training plan, annual training volume is one piece of the puzzle. Broken down, the monthly, weekly, and daily training volumes are as important as annual volume. Establishing your personal training volume based on what "the pros do" is faulty logic.

Your personal training volume, in order to bring about physiological improvement for you, should be based on your personal profile, past training volume, current lifestyle, goals, number of weeks you have to train before your key event, and your response to training.

3. The *duration* of your longest workout may or may not be the length of your goal race. Generally, the shorter the event and the more time you have to train before the event, the greater the likelihood that you will complete the event distance sometime within your training.

4. Depending on your current fitness, race goals, the sport you're competing in, and available training time, the *frequency* of your workouts will vary. Some athletes will work out only once a day, while others will work out two or more times a day. Frequency also encompasses the number of workouts per week. Not only is workout frequency important, but so is frequency of rest.

5. *Individual response* to training does vary. Given the same race goal and training plan, athletes can make improvements at different rates and can have varying gains in overall fitness.

6. The duration and frequency of workouts should vary with each particular training block, and within those workouts, the *intensity* varies depending on the goal of the workout. Intensity can be measured by heart rate, pace, miles per hour, power output, and rate of perceived exertion, to name a few methods. The appropriate intensity minimizes the risk of injury while stressing the body enough to achieve the goal on race day.

7. The *mode of training* becomes more important as race day approaches. For athletes utilizing a year-round approach to training, aerobic crosstraining in the early training blocks is appropriate. For example, northern latitude triathletes often use cross-country skiing workouts to bolster endurance for triathlon, running, and cycling. As the athletes approach their key event training, which is specific to the sport, generalized training will take a backseat. In other words, the *specificity* of training becomes more important.

8. Goal-oriented triathletes must consider *rest and recovery* as two critical training components. Performance gains are made when the body has a chance to repair and absorb the effects of the triathlete's training workload.

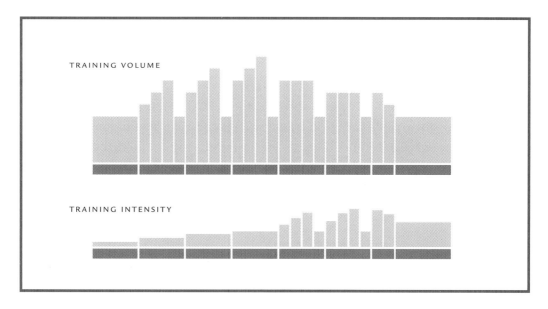

FIGURE 2.1  Typical Interrelationship of Volume and Intensity

In many textbook models, training volume increases during early training periods and training intensity increases at modest rates. As training volume decreases or remains constant, training intensity increases. These graphs display how training volume and intensity might interrelate on the same training plan for the same periods of training.

Figure 2.1 shows a textbook model displaying the interrelationship between training volume and training intensity. Training volume begins at a steady rate, then increases in three-week blocks. After each three-week build of training volume, one week of reduced volume is included to allow for recovery. After three blocks of increasing volume, training volume is reduced and intensity begins to increase. Near the end of the plan, volume and intensity decrease before a race or a block of races. This is one example of a training strategy covering over thirty weeks of training appropriate for sprint- and Olympic-distance racing.

Now take a look at Figure 2.2. Notice how training volume builds near the end of the training plan. This is a training strategy that might be used by an athlete looking to race long-distance events. He or she might keep volume

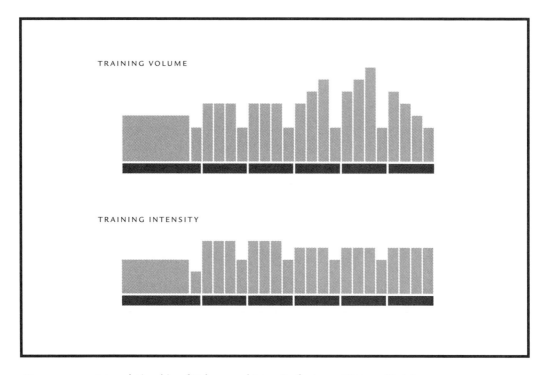

FIGURE 2.2   Interrelationship of Volume and Intensity for Long-Distance Training

For some training circumstances, such as training for long-distance racing, training volume may increase while training intensity decreases.

steady while including some higher-intensity training early in the plan. As the athlete gets closer to race day, volume builds to accommodate an event that will take ten-plus hours to accomplish. This particular athlete decreases intensity when volume starts to build and holds the intensity level steady.

These figures are just two examples of the endless training strategies that are available to accomplish a particular racing goal. The most important thing is that your training plan be appropriate for your fitness, lifestyle, and race goals.

There is a lot of terminology for training phases, and I've changed some of the terms used in the first edition in order to avoid confusion.

## RECOVERY

This phase is specifically intended to help you recover from the rigors of training and racing. There are no specific parameters, usually just basic guidelines to help maintain fitness. The most common guidelines I use are:

- *Take at least one to two days off from training each week.*
- *All training intensity is aerobic in nature.*
- *All training sessions are two hours or less.*

This phase is often one to four weeks in length for the competitive athlete.

## GENERAL PREPARATION

Many triathletes crosstrain during this phase of training, with the goal of building or maintaining cardiovascular fitness. There can be several blocks within this phase, such as General Preparation 1, 2, and 3. Intensity (discussed later in the chapter) tends to be mostly aerobic during this phase. Both General Preparation and Specific Preparation are often referred to as base training.

## SPECIFIC PREPARATION

The goal of this phase is to move toward sport-specific training, reducing or eliminating crosstraining. Race-paced training is introduced in this phase, but the race-paced work segments tend to be short with ample recovery at the beginning of the phase. The intention is to build neuromuscular movement patterns. As this phase continues, a greater percentage of the training resembles race pace. There can be several blocks within this phase, such as Specific Preparation 1, 2, and 3.

## PRE-COMPETITIVE PREPARATION

The goal of this phase is to prepare the athlete for his or her specific race requirements. These requirements—race time and intensity—are quite different for a sprint-distance triathlon than for an Ironman-distance triathlon, and vary with each individual athlete. An athlete who has minimal conditioning has different requirements from an athlete who is highly conditioned. There can be several blocks within this phase, such as Pre-competitive 1, 2, and 3. This phase can also include low-priority races, used as training events.

## COMPETITIVE

This phase may include a series of races over the course of six to eight weeks, such as a sprint-distance race series, or it may be a period of tapering volume in the lead-up to a single race, such as a half-Ironman or Ironman-distance event.

The outline of training phases shown in Figure 2.3 is perfect if you have several weeks to prepare for an event. If you have only six to twelve weeks to prepare for an event, you will obviously have a shallow level of fitness and your training phases will be quite truncated compared with someone who has maintained a training routine for several years.

All plans intentionally stress the body by increasing volume or intensity, and then allow it to rest, so your fitness level after the rest will be greater than before the stressful workout. This concept is called "overcompensation" or "supercompensation."

Supercompensation, however, is a fine line. Too much stress and the body will break down, resulting in illness or injury. Too little stress and no progress is made. Getting yourself into peak condition will require both science and art. Science provides data from laboratory studies. Art is knowing when to follow a plan exactly and when to deviate. Each training plan in this book will help you blend science and art and provide more tips on the art of training.

## INTENSITY

So how do you know how fast to swim, bike, or run? Table 2.1 lists seven heart-rate training zones and the training purpose of each zone. You can also reference the percentage of lactate threshold heart rate (LTHR) for each

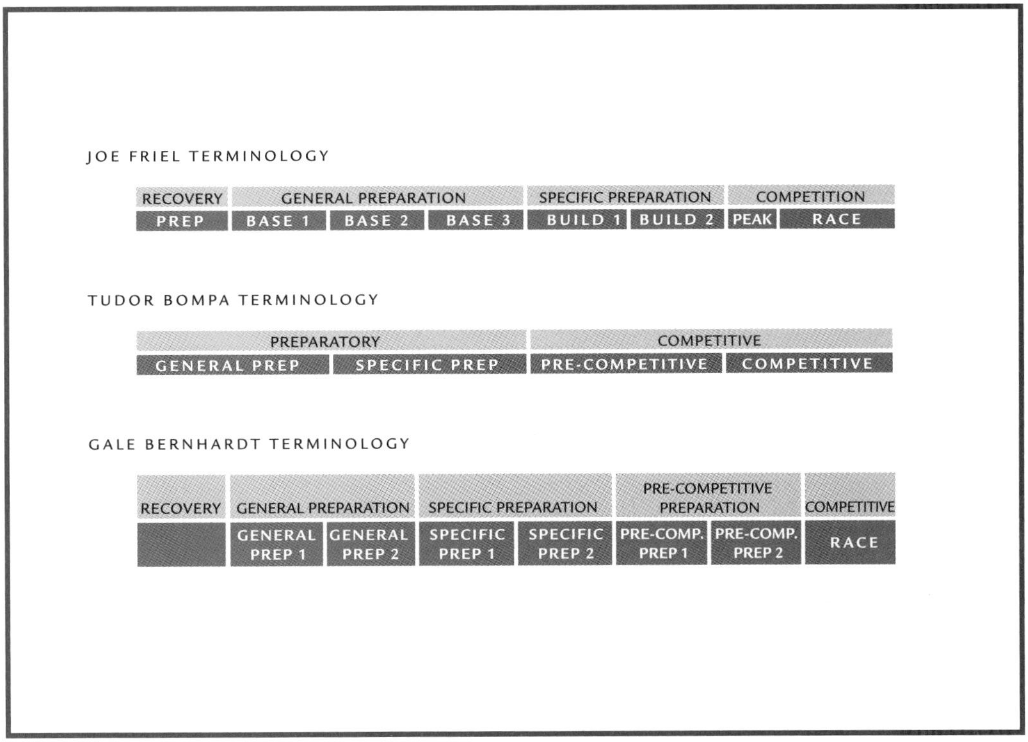

FIGURE 2.3   Training Terminology
The terminology used in this book most closely resembles Tudor Bompa's terminology and is utilized across multiple sports worldwide.

zone, or if you have yet to purchase a heart rate monitor, you can use the Borg scale of perceived exertion and the description of breathing and exertion. Because we will use the pace clock for swimming, lactate threshold heart rates are not given for the pool, but the Borg scale is applicable in the pool and should be correlated with the pool workouts in Chapter 19.

## ENERGY PRODUCTION

Before we discuss each training zone, it is important to understand more about energy production within the body. Our bodies need to have a continuous supply of energy—even to sleep. Energy is supplied by complex chemical reactions. The end result of these chemical reactions is a rich

### TABLE 2.1: REFERENCE SCALE FOR RATE OF PERCEIVED

| Zone | Swim Pace | % Lactate Threshold Heart Rate (Bike) | % Lactate Threshold Heart Rate (Run) | Rate of Perceived Exertion (RPE) |
|---|---|---|---|---|
| 1 | Work on form, no clock watching | ≤80 | ≤84 | 6–9 |
| 2 | T1 pace + 10 sec./100 | 81–88 | 85–91 | 10–12 |
| 3 | T1 pace + 5 sec./100 | 89–93 | 92–95 | 13–14 |
| 4 | T1 pace | 94–99 | 96–99 | 15–16 |
| 5a | T1 pace | 100–102 | 100–102 | 17 |
| 5b | T1 pace – 5 sec./100 | 103–105 | 103–106 | 18–19 |
| 5c | As fast as possible | 106+ | 107+ | 20 |

compound called adenosine triphosphate, or ATP. The potential energy within the ATP molecule is utilized for all processes requiring energy in the cells of your body.

There are two basic methods your body uses to produce ATP. One method is *aerobic* (meaning with the presence of oxygen) and the other is *anaerobic* (meaning without the presence of oxygen). The method of energy production your body uses depends on the rate of demand for energy (intensity) and the length of demand for energy (duration). Short bursts of high speed utilize the

## EXERTION AND TRAINING ZONES

| Breathing and Exertion (using running as the example) | Purpose and X-reference of Terms Commonly Used to Describe Each Zone |
|---|---|
| Gentle rhythmic breathing. Pace is easy and relaxed. For running, intensity is a jog or trot. | Easy, Aerobic, Recovery<br>*Typically used in building foundation fitness.* |
| Breathing rate and pace increase slightly. Many notice a change with slightly deeper breathing, although still comfortable. Running pace remains comfortable and conversations possible. | Aerobic, Extensive Endurance, Aerobic Threshold Endurance<br>*Athletes new to any triathlon distance will commonly stay in Zones 1 and 2.* |
| Aware of breathing a little harder, pace is moderate. It is more difficult to hold conversation. | Tempo, Intensive Endurance<br>*Ironman-distance race pace for experienced athletes is typically within Zones 1 to 3.* |
| Starting to breathe hard, pace is fast and beginning to get uncomfortable, approaching all-out, one-hour run pace. | Subthreshold, Muscular Endurance, Threshold Endurance, Anaerobic Threshold Endurance<br>*Olympic-distance race pace is typically at Zones 4 to 5a for experienced athletes.* |
| Breathing deep and forceful; many notice a second significant change in breathing pattern. Pace is all-out sustainable for one to 1 to 1.5 hours. Mental focus required, moderately uncomfortable and conversation undesirable. | Lactate Threshold Endurance, Anaerobic Threshold Endurance, Superthreshold, Muscular Endurance<br>*Olympic-distance race pace is typically at Zones 4 to 5a for experienced athletes.* |
| Heavy, labored breathing. Pace is noticeably challenging but sustainable for 15 to 30 minutes. Discomfort is high but manageable. | Aerobic Capacity, Speed Endurance<br>*Anaerobic Endurance sprint-distance race pace is typically at Zones 4 to 5b, with limited 5c for experienced athletes.* |
| Maximal exertion in breathing, pace is sprinting effort, high discomfort that is unsustainable for over one minute. | Anaerobic Capacity, Power<br>*Intervals done at this intensity are best gauged using pace or power rather than heart rate.* |

anaerobic system of energy production to fuel the muscles. For longer efforts, fat and glycogen are burned in the presence of oxygen to create ATP.

A small amount of energy is readily available to be utilized "on demand." For example, when you sprint to make it through an intersection before the light changes, a small amount of energy is needed instantly. The majority of the energy necessary for this sprint is created anaerobically. After you have made it through the intersection and a slower speed is resumed, energy is created mostly through aerobic means.

For short sprints, energy is primarily created anaerobically and uses ATP stored in the muscle cells in limited quantities to complete the work. It is readily available, but used up quickly. Aerobically produced ATP, on the other hand, takes more time for the body to produce, but is available in huge quantities. These large quantities of energy allow an athlete to exercise for several hours at easy to moderate speeds.

The energy production system within the body is quite complex. It is important to note that although an athlete may be swimming, riding, or running along at a moderate pace, some of the energy it takes to do so is produced anaerobically. In other words, both systems are working at the same time. As the intensity or speed increases, energy production and utilization need to happen more rapidly. Remember, the aerobic system needs time to produce energy; it is not as quick as the anaerobic system. So the body relies more on anaerobic energy production as the pace increases.

A by-product of the anaerobic energy production system is lactic acid. Lactic acid is often viewed negatively, but in fact it is a good energy source for the body. When given enough time, the body can process and use lactic acid to produce ATP. Lactate (a salt of lactic acid) is present in the blood at rest. Even while you're sitting and reading this book, there are low levels of lactate circulating in your bloodstream.

At low levels, lactic acid is not a problem. However, as you continue to increase your workout intensity, your body increases energy production, relying more heavily on anaerobic metabolism. More reliance on anaerobic metabolism means the lactate level in your blood begins to increase. When your body can no longer process lactic acid fast enough, lactate begins to accumulate at an increasing rate in the blood. This condition is called onset of blood lactate accumulation (OBLA) or lactate threshold. This accumulation has a close correlation with heart rate and ventilatory rate. Athletes can often tell when they have reached lactate threshold because their breathing becomes labored and they begin to feel a burning sensation in their muscles.

If athletes exceed lactate threshold pace, they can sustain the increased pace only for a few minutes before the discomfort forces them to slow down. The margin by which lactate threshold is exceeded is inversely proportional to the time the athlete is able to sustain that pace. In other words, if an athlete's lactate threshold heart rate is 162 and the heart rate is pushed to 172, he or she will be able to hold that pace for a shorter period of time than if working at a heart rate of 164.

Lactate threshold (LT) can be understood as the pace and correlating average heart rate that an athlete can sustain for approximately one hour while participating in a single sport. For example, the lactate threshold for a highly fit cyclist is approximately the pace and average heart rate that the athlete can hold for a 40K time trial on a bicycle. Research has found that lactate threshold heart rate varies depending on the particular sport. Generally speaking, running lactate threshold heart rates tend to be 5 to 10 beats higher than cycling lactate threshold heart rates.

Lactate threshold typically occurs at 55 to 65 percent of $VO_2max$ in healthy, untrained people. In highly trained endurance athletes, lactate threshold is often greater than 80 percent of $VO_2max$. Lactate threshold is trainable, and that's good news. In other words, you can train your body to process lactate at higher percentages of $VO_2max$, which means you can reach increased levels of speed before discomfort forces an end to the effort.

Studies have shown lactate threshold to be a reliable predictor for endurance race performance. $VO_2max$ is not nearly as reliable. So if you've been tested for $VO_2max$ and your numbers weren't stellar, don't panic.

It is important to know that the training zones are approximations. If you were to test blood lactate levels daily for a period of time, you would find that a heart rate of 162 would produce some variation in the levels of lactate. The more experience you gain as an athlete, the more tuned in you will become to your personal exercise intensity levels.

## TESTING

There are various ways to estimate your lactate threshold and the corresponding heart rate. One way is to go to a laboratory for a graded exercise test. In this test, the exercise workload is incrementally increased and blood samples are taken at specific intervals to measure the level of lactate in the blood. During a graded exercise test at a laboratory, the ratio of oxygen to carbon dioxide being expelled from your respiratory system can also be measured and used to estimate lactate threshold.

There are also ways to estimate lactate threshold heart rate in the field. For all of the tests, you'll need a wireless heart rate monitor. In order to get the best estimate, you need to be rested and highly motivated. If you do the test when you're tired, the results may be inaccurate. These tests, however, are not intended to find maximum heart rate because all the training and racing zones are based on a very trainable lactate threshold heart rate. To use this book and the training plans, determining your maximum heart rate is unnecessary. If you have any concerns about any of the tests, seek the advice of a physician first. It is not wise to conduct the tests during the first couple of workouts after a long period of inactivity.

Before beginning the tests to estimate lactate threshold heart rate, you can get a sense of the different racing and training zones by reviewing the rate of perceived exertion (RPE) and the corresponding description of breathing and exertion levels in Table 2.1. RPE uses the Borg scale, which was originally designed to correlate with heart rate for young athletes and derived by dividing the heart rate by 10. For example, easy exercise at a perceived exertion value of 6 was intended to correlate to a heart rate of 60. Although the numbers do not always correlate exactly to heart rate, the perceived exertion scale can be very valuable and is still widely used. For athletes training for their first triathlon (see Chapter 4 for a suitable plan), RPE can be used to estimate training zones until further interest in triathlon warrants the purchase of a heart rate monitor.

The heart rate monitor is one tool available to estimate exercise intensity. Monitors come in a variety of models and price ranges. The least expensive model simply reads heart rate. The more expensive models have the capability to store several hours of data, then download those data into a computer for analysis.

The heart rate monitor consists of a transmitter belt worn strapped around the chest, just below the breasts, and a receiver worn on the wrist or mounted on the handlebar of a bike. The transmitter belt picks up electrical impulses from the heart and relays the information to the receiver via an electromagnetic field. The receiver then displays the heart rate. It's like having a tachometer for the body, similar to the one on a sports car.

When trying to determine your own lactate threshold, record your RPE, breathing rate, and heart rate. When doing the test indoors, keep a copy of Table 2.1 handy, so you can refer to the Borg numbers and breathing rates. Specific field tests for estimating cycling lactate threshold heart rate are in Appendix A. Field tests for running can be found in Appendix B.

The methods outlined in Appendixes A and B are ways to estimate lactate threshold. There are other methods, but these work well. It is possible to use either the cycling or the running test to estimate LT heart rate (LTHR) for one sport and then use that value to estimate the LTHR for another sport. As mentioned previously, for multisport athletes, running LT is often 5 to 10 beats higher than cycling LT. Hence, if you did the cycling test and found your LT heart rate to be around 168, your running LTHR would probably be around 173 to 178.

Can an individual's lactate threshold heart rate change? Yes. Does the 5- to 10-beat rule hold true for all athletes when comparing LT heart rates for cycling and running? Most of the time, yes, but there are exceptions. So if the numbers seem off in your training, you can home in on a more precise number by doing a separate LT test in each sport and by being aware of your heart rate during training and racing.

In this book, heart rate is one tool used, in conjunction with rate of perceived exertion, to quantify training and racing intensities for cycling and running. Other tools for determining workloads on the bike are power meters such as an SRM, CompuTrainer, PowerTap, and Polar, to name a few. These tools are continually improving and growing in popularity among competitive athletes. Power meters provide intensity output in watts, and this measure is similar to having a pace clock when swimming or running. Instructions for using power meters are in Appendix C.

For swimming, use a time trial test to establish baseline fitness. Then use the results of this time trial, in conjunction with a pace clock, as a tool for gauging swimming intensity. Instructions for conducting the time trial, along with a few swimming workouts, are in Chapter 19.

# TRAINING ZONES

Once you've done the tests outlined in Appendixes A and B and in Chapter 19, you will have an estimate of your LTHR and seven training zones for each sport. Here's a bit about each zone:

### Zone 1
Zone 1 is used to build fitness in beginning athletes and for recovery purposes by more experienced athletes. The energy production is primarily aerobic. Zone 1 is also used in conjunction with Zone 2 to build exercise endurance for long-distance racing.

### Zone 2
Zone 2 is used to build fitness and maintain current levels of fitness. Lactate begins to increase, but the accumulation tends to be linear and manageable by the body for very long periods of time, such as Ironman-distance training and racing. Within this intensity zone is what many coaches call "aerobic threshold." Some scientists and coaches define the lactate measurement of 2 mmol/L and the associated heart rate as aerobic threshold. There is disagreement about this value. (See Zone 5a for further discussion.)

Often Zones 1 and 2 are used in conjunction with drills to improve athletic skills. Good form improves athletic economy, which translates to less oxygen needed for a given pace.

### Zone 3
Zone 3 intensity is used for early-season tempo work and to begin lactate threshold improvement. Zones 1 through 3 are used by experienced athletes training and racing in events lasting longer than about three hours.

### Zone 4
This zone is used in conjunction with intervals, hill work, and steady-state work to improve lactate threshold speed and muscular endurance. It is common for the intervals in this zone to have a work-to-rest ratio of 3:1 or 4:1 in cycling and running, respectively.

### Zone 5a

The lowest heart rate value in Zone 5a (100 percent of lactate threshold heart rate in Table 2.1) is called lactate threshold in this book. Some coaches and scientists call this value "anaerobic threshold." Laboratories often associate a blood lactate value of 4 mmol/L with lactate threshold. Be aware that the 4 mmol/L value is common for many athletes, but there are wide variations. Lactate threshold can be as low as 2 mmol/L or as high as 8 mmol/L for individual athletes. This is why the statement "Anaerobic threshold is 4 mmol/L" may be incorrect for some athletes. Quality laboratories typically provide lactate curves and interpret the data for you, eliminating a "one size fits all" value for both thresholds.

This zone is used in conjunction with intervals, hill riding, and tempo rides to improve lactate threshold speed and muscular endurance. It is often used in conjunction with Zone 4.

### Zone 5b

The major use for this zone is to improve anaerobic endurance. The cycling and running intervals in this zone often have a work-to-rest ratio of 1:1. This zone is also used in hill workouts.

### Zone 5c

Zone 5c is fast—really fast—or powerful swimming, cycling, or running. For example, sprinting to grab a competitor's wheel in a draft-legal race or climbing hills out of the saddle both elicit heart rates in Zone 5c. Exercise in Zone 5c cannot be maintained for extended periods of time. It is common for the intervals in this zone to have a work-to-rest ratio of 1:2 or more.

The preceding comments for each zone are not all-inclusive, but they do give an idea of the uses for each particular training zone. We will use the seven training zones to measure speed and help you avoid mediocre workouts. Remember that anyone can train and race hard, but not everyone is fast.

# 3

# BASIC NUTRITION FOR ENDURANCE TRAINING

*When I finally decided to start eating, at the age of 40, I went from a 98-pound weakling to a healthy female athlete. I felt strong for the first time ever. If you don't eat, you won't be able to endure. Don't wait until you are a master's athlete to learn the value of consuming enough food.*

—CATHY SLOAN, USA

Search for "diet" on one of the popular online bookstores and you'll find nearly seven thousand different books on the subject. If there were one golden diet that worked for everyone on earth, the person who discovered it would be rich and famous. But in all of the research I've done concerning nutrition for general health and nutrition for athletic performance, one thing I can say for certain is that there's not a single nutrition plan that works for everyone.

If we talk about diet in very general terms, perhaps there is one perfect diet—eat and drink enough of the right foods to build and maintain a healthy body. It's simple, but not easy. The difficult part comes when people want to know exactly what to eat. How many carbohydrates? How much fat and protein? How many calories? Precisely which foods should I eat each day to guarantee optimal health?

An appropriate diet for an individual depends on:

*Genetics:* Some people are born with faster metabolisms than others. Also, some people have inherited health issues that require medication. Some medications affect basal metabolism.

*Gender:* Men have a greater percentage of muscle mass than women, so they have a greater basal metabolic rate.

*Body Surface Area:* Given the same weight for two individuals, one tall and one short, the tall, thin person has a greater body surface area and therefore has a greater basal metabolism.

*Daily Routine Activity Level:* If your job has you sitting at a desk all day long with little movement, your caloric needs are different from someone in constant physical motion most of the day.

*Lifestyle and Personal Preferences:* Some people have a lifestyle of eating only home-prepared foods, while others are dependent on food prepared by others. Selecting foods that build healthy bodies—in both scenarios—is a challenge. All of us have foods we prefer and foods we simply do not enjoy.

*Exercise Activity Level:* Duration and intensity of exercise burn calories and can affect basal metabolism.

*Quality of Food Consumed:* Highly processed foods tend to have fewer nutrients than whole foods. Athletes who are concerned with health and performance should maximize the nutrient quality of food.

If you take one message from this chapter, remember that you are a study of one. Your unique genetics, history, and lifestyle all contribute to your nutritional status. You need to take responsibility for your health and track your health status with the help of your health-care professional. When your health status markers are out of line with what you expect for optimal health, you need to take action. Seek the advice of your family doctor and sports medicine specialists to help you improve your situation.

Let's take a look at one individual's story. Gale "Windy" Ann's story is one I share with many of the athletes I coach because it illustrates many of the nutrition rules that the rest of this chapter will cover in depth.

## Nutrition and Performance

Gale "Windy" Ann was a competitive racer, trying to get better. She wanted to lose some weight to help her edge toward faster race times and more podium spots. It seemed the women who were faster were thinner than she was. If she were lighter, could she race even faster? She was well read on diet and nutrition. Literature throughout the 1980s told her she could lose weight by following a low-fat diet of no fewer than 1,200 calories per day and exercising. So that is what she did.

Windy carefully monitored her calories and opted for high-value foods—those that were chock-full of vitamins and minerals, but also low in fat. Foods fitting this description were fruits and vegetables. She knew she needed protein, but she was well aware that statistics said the average American consumes entirely too much protein. She got most of her protein from nonfat dairy products and an occasional piece of fish or poultry.

After several years of competition and training, she was unable to change her body weight. How could that be, she wondered? She exercised between 6 and 10 hours each week, worked between 48 and 55 hours each week, and watched what she ate. Why didn't her body look like the body of a fit athlete? Why didn't she feel right? She had no energy and it seemed like she had one small, nagging injury each year that kept her from developing her full speed potential.

Frustrated with her situation, she sought the help of a registered dietitian in the early 1990s. The dietitian, Chris, asked her to keep food logs for a week and did an analysis. Keeping a food log was easy for Windy; she had meticulously counted calories for years. She could estimate portions without weighing them, though she occasionally checked her portions with a measuring cup or a scale. Chris found Windy's diet to be very high in vitamins and minerals, low in fat (only 10 percent of total caloric intake), low in protein (only 10 percent of total calories), and high in carbohydrates (80 percent of total calories). Her daily intake averaged around 1,300 calories per day, which she felt was perfect for losing weight (or perhaps 100 calories per day too high). It was also perfect, she believed, for an endurance athlete and for someone trying to keep her cholesterol, which ranged from 195 to 198, from getting any higher. Yet, if this diet was so perfect, why did her body not have that svelte, strong, athletic look promoted in magazines?

Chris told Windy that her caloric intake was too low. Based on Windy's work and exercise routine, Chris recommended that Windy increase her daily caloric

(CONTINUES)

(CONTINUED)

intake to around 2,300 calories. Not surprisingly, Windy wondered how she would ever lose weight this way.

Chris also thought Windy's fat and protein intake was too low. Windy suspected this as well. She had read about the work that Barry Sears did with the Stanford swim team. He helped them change their diet to 30 percent fat, 30 percent protein, and 40 percent carbohydrates. Windy wanted Chris's opinion about the 30-30-40 diet. Chris had also read about this new (at the time) diet and agreed Windy should give it a try. Windy would eat more food with higher proportions of fat and protein and lower levels of carbohydrate.

After one week, Windy returned to Chris's office to find she had lost three pounds. She felt better physically, although it felt like she was eating a ton of food. Now convinced she should make changes to her diet, Windy continued eating more calories and maintaining a macronutrient split that included more fat and more protein.

When Windy began her diet change, it was November. In the weeks and months following her diet change, she began to take notice of some big changes in parts of her life she had not known were affected by her diet. She had more energy and was sleeping through the night, not getting up three to five times, as she had before—sometimes for a snack. Her hair was growing faster and needed to be cut more often. She simply felt good.

Three years before starting the new diet, Windy had quit taking birth control pills. After this, her menstrual cycle was never regular. She just thought it was due to her being on the pill for so long. Within five months of changing her diet, Windy had regularly occurring menstrual cycles.

By the time the next racing season arrived, in May, Windy was feeling better than ever and had made it through a winter of training with no nagging injuries. The initial three pounds were all Windy lost, but the numbers on the scale now meant less to her. They meant less because she felt better and she was racing faster. Throughout the entire race season following her diet change, her racing times improved.

During the race season, she found she could consume a daily diet of approximately 30-30-40 proportions, but that she needed to change that regimen during races. She found she needed to consume a sports drink during longer races or she felt terrible. She also found she needed more carbohydrates in the hours following a hard workout or race to speed her recovery.

She was happy about her faster race times, regular menstrual cycle, lack of injuries, and how she felt better in general, but she was worried about her cholesterol level. She decided that if this new diet was good for her athletics but was putting her at risk for heart disease, she would head back to the old, low-fat diet. Fourteen months after her diet change, she had blood work done and was surprised to find her total cholesterol to be improved at 160.

Two years after changing her eating habits, Windy had lost an additional seven pounds. She was still getting faster race times, her menstrual cycle remained regular, she remained injury-free, and she felt great.

Although she no longer keeps food logs, Windy tries to balance her snacks and meals by eating some protein, fat, and carbohydrates. Her diet changes were based on her health and training needs. She no longer lives on nonfat yogurt, bagels, fruits, and vegetables. Fruits and vegetables are still a good part of her diet, but now she consumes lean meats and nuts as well. Fat is no longer an enemy. She minimizes her intake of highly processed foods and says she will never go back to her low-fat, low-calorie style of eating.

Windy's story shows how:

- *Extreme calorie restriction and chronic dieting slow metabolism.*
- *Very low-fat diets and/or very low-protein diets are correlated with amenorrhea in women. (Many studies correlate amenorrhea in female athletes to loss in bone density.)*
- *A body that receives inadequate nutrition will break down. This can mean more frequent colds and flu, or it can mean more serious physical injuries. The ill and injured cannot train or burn as many calories as they'd like, nor can they be competitive athletes who reach their full potential.*

On a positive note, Windy knew something was wrong and took action. She had too many things she wanted to do and had no time for injury or illness.

The beginning of Windy's story is a common one. Athletes, both female and male, want to lose weight to increase speed, so the first thing they do is cut calories from their diets. No one wants to diet for an extended time, so they cut a lot of calories over a short period of time to get it over with. When athletes cut significant calories from their diets in order to lose weight, the results are often counterproductive.

Looking at more athletes, in a specific study on triathletes, the dietary habits of four male and two female elite triathletes were examined. An analysis of a seven-day diet record showed their daily intake of calories and carbohydrates to be insufficient to support their estimated requirements. Their diets were also found to be low in zinc and chromium. The researchers recommended diet changes to increase food intake. Follow-up seven-day diet records found the athletes had increased average daily calories, increased carbohydrate consumption, and met their daily requirements for zinc, chromium, and all other nutrients. Their race results also displayed an improvement in performance.

In a separate study on trained cyclists, a high-fat diet was found to increase endurance. Five trained cyclists followed either a high-fat diet (70 percent fat, 7 percent carbohydrates, 23 percent protein) or a high-carbohydrate diet (74 percent carbohydrates, 12 percent fat, 14 percent protein) for two weeks. Endurance at 60 percent of $VO_2$max was measured before and after the dietary changes, and the high-fat diet was associated with significant increases in endurance.

If performance is not your only concern—perhaps you want to live to be a hundred years old—consider the people who live in Lerik, Azerbaijan, a small mountain town near the Iranian border. This village is famous for people living a hundred years or more. There are scores of old people living in the town; how do they do it?

The town is poorly served by medicine, most of the people are uneducated, and they eat very little and work like beasts of burden. Vegetables, fruits, and sour cheeses make up the majority of their diet. When Azerbaijan was part of the Soviet Union, doctors visited the town and took numerous blood samples, looking for some secret to their longevity. The tests were inconclusive. Researchers theorized the villagers' longevity was related to genetics and clean, stress-free living.

So how is it that these athletes, whether their discipline is triathlon, cycling, or merely surviving, can all follow completely different diets and all have improved or sustained high performance? Some of the athletes in the study ate a 30-30-40 diet, others simply increased calories, and still others ate a high-fat diet, and they all had performance increases. Then there are the Lerik "athletes," toiling each day and outliving most people, displaying sustained high performance. So how can we apply this to athletes? What *is* the perfect diet?

Most of us do not have the lifestyle of the people living in Lerik, so perhaps they are not a fair comparison. People living in modern cities deal with pollution, job-related toxins, job- and family-related stress, and water and foods that have been processed. Given the variables, how do we know what our own optimal diet is? The remainder of this chapter will provide information you can use to evaluate and improve your diet. A single chapter cannot cover all the information necessary to understand the topic of nutrition (and as technology develops, we will have new and more accurate information). But this chapter gives a good overview of macronutrients and micronutrients, some nutritional concerns common to athletes, and some tools to evaluate your diet.

## MACRONUTRIENTS

Depending on which book you read, there are either three or four macronutrients. The commonly agreed-upon macronutrients are carbohydrates, fat, and protein. Some sources consider water to be a fourth macronutrient, and we'll discuss it in this section.

### CARBOHYDRATES

Carbohydrates are almost exclusively found in plants and their processed by-products. Fruits, vegetables, beans, peas, and grains are sources of carbohydrates. The only animal sources that have significant carbohydrates are milk and yogurt.

Carbohydrates are made of sugar molecules and are divided into two major groups: complex carbohydrates and simple carbohydrates. Complex carbohydrates consist of many sugar molecules linked together. Foods in the complex group include vegetables, whole grains, beans, and peas. These

## Nutrition Rules

RULE NO. 1: Eat adequate calories.

RULE NO. 2: Do not try to lose weight with extreme calorie restrictions.

RULE NO. 3: Eat a balance of macronutrients.

RULE NO. 4: Drink plenty of water.

RULE NO. 5: There are no "bad" foods; however, some foods should be consumed with discretion.

RULE NO. 6: Fat is essential to optimal health.

RULE NO. 7: A healthy diet should contain a wide variety of minimally processed foods.

foods contain fiber and starches and are made of long, complex chains of sugar molecules. They are more difficult than simple carbohydrates for the body to break down into fuel.

Simple carbohydrates, sometimes referred to as simple sugars, include fructose (fruit sugar), lactose (milk sugar), sucrose, and glucose. Notice all of them end in the suffix "-ose," which identifies carbohydrates. A food product that has several "-ose" ingredients listed separately on its label actually contains that many simple sugars or combinations of sugars of different origin.

The body absorbs sugars and eventually converts them into glucose, the body's usable form of sugar. Sugar is absorbed into the blood, heart, skeletal muscle, and liver—in that order. When blood sugars reach homeostasis, or a state of balance in the blood, the heart and skeletal muscles accept glucose. The always-working heart uses glucose for energy and the skeletal muscles can also use it for energy. Skeletal muscles also have the capability to store glucose as glycogen, to use for work at a later time. The liver can also absorb glucose from the blood and convert it to glycogen. The glucose not immediately needed or stored by functioning body parts is converted to fat.

Insulin is a pancreatic hormone that regulates blood sugar, and its effects are most beneficial when it does so at a moderate pace. When insulin continuously spikes and dips or is produced in inadequate quantities, health problems arise, including hypoglycemia (low blood sugar), diabetes (high blood sugar), and some of the health issues related to coronary heart disease. It is preferable to maintain blood sugars and insulin response so that there are no large peaks or valleys.

The rate at which carbohydrates in a food are digested and their effect on the rise of blood glucose are described by the food's glycemic index. Foods that are easily digested and cause a pronounced rise in blood sugar have high glycemic index values. This pronounced rise of blood sugar initiates an insulin surge and stimulates body cells to store glucose as fat.

Foods that are more slowly digested have lower glycemic index values and do not cause the paired glucose and insulin spikes. The glycemic index values of some common carbohydrate foods are shown in Table 3.1. It is important to note that foods containing fats and proteins have lower glycemic index values because fat and protein take more time to digest.

High glycemic index foods are most valuable during exercise and post-exercise recovery. Otherwise, they should be used in moderation or in combination with fat and protein. When high glycemic index foods are combined with fat and protein, their absorption rate is slowed. As Nutritional Rule No. 5 states, there are no "bad" foods; however, some foods should be consumed with discretion.

## FAT

Normal body function requires a diet that includes fat. It also makes foods taste good, is enjoyable to eat, and makes us feel satisfied after its consumption. Fats are constructed of building blocks called fatty acids. The three major categories of fatty acids are saturated, polyunsaturated, and monounsaturated. The body can use all three kinds, but, as with carbohydrates, there are some fats that should be consumed in moderation.

Some of the fatty acids necessary for good health are called essential fatty acids (EFAs). EFAs contribute to a healthy body by improving hair and skin texture, reducing cholesterol and triglyceride levels, preventing arthritis, and contributing to healthy hormone levels. EFAs are found in large quantities in the brain, where they aid in the transmission of nerve

| TABLE 3.1: GLYCEMIC INDEX FOR COMMON CARBOHYDRATES | | | |
|---|---|---|---|
| **HIGH** (80 and higher) | **MODERATE** (50–79) | **LOW** (30–49) | **VERY LOW** (less than 30) |
| Apricots | Baked beans | Apples | Cherries |
| Bananas | Beets | Apple juice | Grapefruit |
| Carrots | Bran cereal | Barley | Peanuts |
| Corn | Energy bars | Black-eyed peas | Plums |
| Corn chips | Garbanzo beans | Figs | Soybeans |
| Corn flake cereal | Navy beans | Grapes | |
| Crackers | Oatmeal | Lentils | |
| French bread | Oranges | Lima beans | |
| Honey | Orange juice | Milk | |
| Mangos | Pasta | Peaches | |
| Molasses | Pinto beans | Pears | |
| Muesli | Potato chips | Rye bread | |
| Oat bran | Yams | Sweet potatoes | |
| Pastries | | Yogurt | |
| Potatoes | | | |
| Raisins | | | |
| Rice | | | |
| Rye crisps | | | |
| Shredded wheat | | | |
| Soda pop | | | |
| White bread | | | |
| Whole-grain cereal | | | |
| Whole-wheat bread | | | |

impulses and overall brain function. EFAs are also essential for rebuilding and producing new cells.

The body cannot manufacture EFAs—they must be obtained through the diet. Omega-3 and omega-6 fats are the two basic categories of EFAs. Omega-3 fats are found in wild, cold-water fish like salmon, mackerel, menhaden, herring, and sardines. They are also found in canola oil, flaxseed oil, and walnut oil. Omega-6 fats are found primarily in raw nuts, seeds, grapeseed oil, sesame oil, and soybean oil. To supply essential fatty acids, omega-6 fats must be consumed in raw or supplement form, or as pure liquid; they can't be subjected to heat in processing or cooking. Wild game, not subjected to chemical-laden, fatten-them-up, feedlot-style diets, is rich in both omega-3 and omega-6 fats.

The fats that should be consumed in moderation are the saturated variety. Excess consumption of saturated fats can raise cholesterol levels, particularly low-density lipoprotein (LDL) or "bad" cholesterol. Saturated fats are found in animal products and some tropical oils, like coconut and palm. Also, when some unsaturated oils are partially hydrogenated (a process that turns a liquid fat into a solid one), the new fat is more saturated. Hydrogenated fats contain trans-fatty acids, which are not well digested by the body and are thought to contribute to coronary artery disease. Hydrogenated and partially hydrogenated fats are prevalent in many processed foods like crackers, cookies, and some canned products. Read the label on your food products and look for the word "hydrogenated."

Polyunsaturated fats are found in corn, safflower, soybean, canola, and sunflower oils. Consumption of the polyunsaturated family may actually lower total cholesterol; however, it appears that large amounts of polyunsaturated fats also lower high-density lipoprotein (HDL) or "good" cholesterol. Some of the polyunsaturated oils do contain essential fatty acids, or EFAs.

Monounsaturated fats are also thought to positively influence health. They are found in nuts and some vegetables, and also in the oils of those foods, such as almond, avocado, olive, canola, and walnut oils.

Fat in the diet is essential to optimal health.

## PROTEIN

Protein in the diet is absolutely necessary for growth and development of the body. Next to water, protein makes up the greatest portion of our body weight. All our cells contain protein. Some food protein sources are considered complete proteins because they include all of the amino acids the body cannot manufacture on its own (the "essential" amino acids). Complete protein foods include meat, milk, eggs, poultry, fish, cheese, yogurt, and soybean products.

People who choose to be vegetarians need to be well educated on combining foods to achieve complete proteins. This is because most plant products—with the exception of soybeans—are incomplete proteins, meaning they are missing one or more of the essential amino acids. If a diet consistently omits one or more of the essential amino acids, a deficiency will develop, resulting in illness or injury.

## WATER

Between 40 and 60 percent of body weight is composed of water. Water is typically 65 to 75 percent of the weight of muscle and less than 25 percent of the weight of fat. This water is essential to a functioning body. A body can survive many days without food but only a few days without water.

Many people do not adequately hydrate. Most literature recommends drinking eight to ten glasses of water each day. If you are drinking eight to ten glasses each day and your urine is dark yellow in color and foul smelling, you are not drinking enough. Rather than aiming for a certain number of glasses of water per day, a better guideline is to drink enough water so that your urine is light in color and has minimal odor. Other signals of dehydration are constipation, fatigue, and headaches.

Caffeinated coffees, teas, and soft drinks can have a diuretic effect, which means they increase the normal urinary output, leaving less fluid in the body for normal functioning. It appears, however, that individual responses to caffeine vary. Routine caffeine consumption can cause tolerance and further influence caffeine's effect on individuals. In some studies, caffeine has been shown to increase calcium loss, so limiting its intake can help preserve precious bone. Depending on caffeine's effect on you, limiting daily intake of caffeine can keep the body hydrated.

A well-hydrated athlete performs better. Dehydration levels as low as 2 percent of body weight are thought to impair athletic performance—perhaps by as much as 20 percent.

## VITAMINS AND MINERALS

Vitamins and minerals are considered to be micronutrients because they are needed in smaller quantities than the macronutrients—carbohydrates, fat, protein, and water. Some vitamins and minerals are coenzymes, enabling the body to produce energy, grow, and heal.

Vitamins regulate metabolism and assist in the biochemical processes that release energy from digested food. Some vitamins are known for their antioxidant, cancer prevention, and cardiovascular disease protection properties. Vitamin E and vitamin C are two of the vitamins scientists believe we should supplement in our diet, because we probably do not get enough of these vitamins from our food. Some sources of vitamin E are nuts, seeds, whole grains, cold-pressed vegetable oils, and dark green, leafy vegetables. Vitamin C is found in green vegetables, citrus fruits, and berries, to name a few sources.

Minerals are necessary for the correct composition of body fluids, the formation of blood and bone, the regulation of muscle tone, and the maintenance of healthy nerve function. Calcium and iron are two of the minerals of most concern. Adequate calcium is necessary to ward off osteoporosis. Calcium can be found in dairy products, tofu, fortified orange juice, soymilk, and canned fish with bones (such as sardines and salmon). Iron is incorporated in hemoglobin and myoglobin and aids in the oxygenation of red blood cells and muscle. It is found in the largest quantities in the blood. Women lose blood and iron each month due to menstruation. Care must be taken to consume adequate iron so as not to become anemic. The best dietary sources of iron are red meat, eggs, and beans.

## ANTIOXIDANTS AND PHYTOCHEMICALS

Scientists have recognized for years that diets rich in fruits, vegetables, grains, and legumes appear to reduce the risk of a number of diseases, including cancer, heart disease, diabetes, and high blood pressure. Researchers have found these foods contain antioxidants, which protect cells against oxidation. Oxidation is damage to cells, similar to rust on metal.

Phytochemicals are another group of health-promoting nutrients thought to prevent a number of diseases and aid in the repair of cells when disease strikes. They give plants their rich color, flavor, and disease-protection properties. There are literally thousands of phytochemicals— tomatoes alone contain over ten thousand different varieties.

The recent discovery of phytochemicals illustrates how science continues to discover more and more about whole foods and their valuable properties. Dietary supplements cannot replace the value of whole foods, because supplements represent some of our current knowledge—and humankind's quantity of knowledge is still quite small. Therefore, a healthy diet should contain a wide variety of minimally processed foods.

## HOW MUCH OF WHAT?

Now things get sticky. We need carbohydrates, fat, and protein to sustain good health, but how much of each? How many calories are enough? How can you go about losing weight without compromising health? Should you take vitamin and mineral supplements? Long bouts of exercise need calorie supplementation, but how much and from what kind of foods? Long or exhausting exercise requires quick recovery—how is that best accomplished? The answer to all of these questions is, "Well, it depends."

If we first establish our dietary and fitness goals, prioritize those goals, and determine how to measure them, then the answers become clearer. Consider the following goals, listed here in order of importance to long-term wellness. Consume a diet that:

1. *Builds and maintains a healthy body in the short term and minimizes the risk of disease in the future;*
2. *Allows you to feel good physically and mentally;*
3. *Considers your genetic makeup;*
4. *Takes into account your lifestyle, fitness, and activity level; and*
5. *Enhances your athletic capabilities.*

If we eat with the main goal of building a healthy body, chances are good we will live a full and active life.

Before changing your diet, evaluate your current diet. If you consult a registered dietitian, he or she will ask you to keep a food diary. If you decide to evaluate your diet on your own, you will need to do the same thing. Use a reference book (such as *The NutriBase Nutrition Facts Desk Reference*) to measure the calories and macronutrients in your current diet. Log what foods you eat, how much, and when. Begin with tabulating just calories or log the grams of carbohydrate, fat, and protein as well. Record your information honestly and try not to change your eating behaviors just because you're keeping a food log. It may turn out you have been maintaining a healthy weight and eating 3,000 calories per day, and there's no reason for you to change anything. Or you may constantly feel weak and tired while eating 3,000 calories per day; in this case something needs to change. For now you're just recording, so suspend your judgment.

Next, answer the questions in the Health Questionnaire in Appendix D. After filling out the questionnaire, you will have information that will help you and your doctor determine how healthy you are. If you are not as healthy as you'd like to be, consider changing your diet or lifestyle or both, in consultation with a registered dietitian who specializes in sports medicine.

# BENCHMARK NUTRITION FORMULAS

So far, we have established a set of nutrition rules, prioritized the goals of a healthy diet, determined what you are currently eating, and recorded your current health status on the Health Questionnaire. You know where you are and, in general, where you want to go. Now how do you get there?

If you are satisfied with your current diet, if it meets both your needs and the goals of a healthy diet, celebrate! If you think your diet needs fine-tuning, or if you just want more information about measuring your intake of micronutrients and macronutrients, read on.

Some people prefer general dietary guidelines, while others want numbers. What follows is a bit of each.

## CALORIC INTAKE

One of the common formulas used to determine daily caloric intake needed to maintain body weight is 30 calories per kilogram of body weight. To find your weight in kilograms, take your weight in pounds and divide by 2.2. For example, if your weight is 140 pounds, your weight in kilograms is

$$140 \div 2.2 = 63.6 \; (or \; 64 \; kilograms)$$

Your daily caloric needs are

$$64 \times 30 = 1,920 \; calories$$

At 140 pounds, it takes roughly 80 calories per hour (1,920 calories per 24 hours) to fuel your body. Of course the exact value changes depending on if you are awake and active or sleeping, but 80 calories per hour is a good start. Modify this formula as appropriate:

> **Add** *more calories (about 100 to 300) to the daily total if you lead a highly active lifestyle. The following modifiers are gross values that include resting energy expenditure and exercise expenditure.*
> **Add** *about 0.13 to 0.16 calorie per minute, per kilogram of body weight, for swimming. (For example, 0.16 calorie per minute-kilogram × 60 minutes × 64 kilograms equals 614 calories needed for an hour of fast swimming.)*
> **Add** *about 0.15 to 0.17 calorie per minute, per kilogram of body weight, for cycling. (For example, 0.17 calorie per minute-kilogram × 60 minutes × 64 kilograms equals 653 calories needed for an hour of fast cycling.)*
> **Add** *about 0.14 to 0.29 calorie per minute (roughly the range from an 11-minute pace per mile to a 5-minute, 30-second pace per mile), per kilogram of body weight, for running. (For example, 0.2 calorie per minute-kilogram × 60 minutes × 64 kilograms equals 768 calories needed for an hour of fast running.)*
> **Add** *about 0.1 calorie per minute, per kilogram of body weight, for strength training. (For example, 0.1 calorie per minute-kilogram × 60 minutes × 64 kilograms equals 384 calories needed for an hour of strength training.)*
> **Subtract** *calories (about 100 to 300) from the daily total if your lifestyle or job is sedentary.*

So the 140-pound person in our example would need to consume some-where between 1,620 and 2,820 calories each day to maintain her weight, perhaps even more if she is training for an Ironman. She needs to consume more calories on active training days, then consume fewer calories when her body does not need them.

## WEIGHT LOSS

Before heading into a weight-loss program, it's important to recognize that severe caloric restrictions can decrease resting metabolic rate by 45 percent. Decreasing your metabolism is the last thing you want to do when you are trying to lose weight. One of the most commonly suggested ways to lose weight is to decrease your daily caloric intake by 200 to 300 calories, not dropping total caloric intake below 1,500. You can calculate how many calories it takes to maintain your current weight from your food log, assuming your weight has been constant. This slow approach to weight loss through reduced food intake reduces the risk of compromising health.

The strategy I recommend to athletes is to begin eating now the way you plan to eat at your new weight. This is a long-term strategy for success. Athletes who go on a diet to lose weight and then return to old eating habits will not keep the lower weight for long.

To illustrate how easy it is to eat for your new weight, let's look at an example. If you currently weigh 175 pounds and want to weigh 165 pounds, what is the difference in the daily caloric needs to maintain body weight, without looking at exercise? At 175 pounds (79.5 kilograms) your maintenance level is 2,385 calories per day (79.5 × 30). At your goal weight of 165 pounds (75 kilograms) you need 2,250 calories per day (75 × 30). Yes, that's right, a difference of only 136 calories per day, day in and day out.

## GOOD SOURCES FOR CALORIES

Current research shows a range for macronutrient consumption that will maintain or improve health and athletic training:

*Carbohydrates: 40 to 65 percent of total calories*
*Fat: 15 to 30 percent of total calories*
*Protein: 15 to 30 percent of total calories*

Exactly how much of each macronutrient each person should eat depends on the individual's health risks, dietary goals, and current mode of training. Health and athletic training needs are constantly changing, so diet must also change. Nutrition needs on a heavy training day are not the same as when an athlete is resting and exercising very little. Consider the following four suggested diet modifications:

1. *Carbohydrate consumption should be on the **higher end of the range** when you're training fast miles (Zones 4 and 5) or long miles (90 minutes or more).*
2. *Carbohydrate consumption should be in the **middle range** when you're training in Zones 1 to 3.*
3. *Carbohydrate consumption should be on the **lower end of the range** when you're trying to lose weight. (Do not try to lose weight and race at the same time. This can result in emotional instability or decreased performance.)*
4. *Protein consumption should be between **1.5 and 2.0 grams per kilogram of body weight**. Use values on the higher end when training hard, trying to build muscle mass, doing very long exercise (over three hours), or trying to maintain muscle mass when dieting.*

There are different ways to estimate calorie and nutrient needs. Some sources refer to macronutrient consumption as a percentage of calorie intake, while others talk about consuming a certain number of grams of each macronutrient. It can get confusing when the measuring systems are talked about interchangeably. It helps to know that not all food grams have equal energy values:

- *1 gram of carbohydrate contains about 4 calories*
- *1 gram of protein contains about 4 calories*
- *1 gram of fat contains about 9 calories*
- *1 gram of alcohol contains about 7 calories*

## FORMULAS FOR ENERGY NEEDS

For exercise longer than about an hour, consume—at minimum—30 to 60 grams of carbohydrates per hour of intense or long exercise. Some athletes need to consume more than 500 calories per hour, such as the ultra-endurance athlete profiled in the Nutrition Case Study sidebar. His experience is not isolated. Several athletes, male and female, can consume—need to consume—calories in excess of the suggested 30 to 60 grams of carbohydrates per hour. How much you need to consume depends on body size, pace, pre-event muscle glycogen storage, and individual metabolism. This energy can be taken in through fluid or solid sources. Be certain to consume adequate fluids as well: approximately 4 to 8 ounces of fluid every 15 to 20 minutes.

For exercise lasting less than three hours, many athletes find that consuming some 150 to 250 carbohydrate calories works just fine. For exercise over three hours, anecdotal evidence says many athletes need a minimum of 300 calories per hour and, on rare occasions, more than 500 calories per hour. Athletes who compete in events requiring between 6 and 17 hours to complete will tell you that nutrition can significantly influence the outcome of a race. Nutrition, in effect, becomes an event within the event.

Some of these ultra-endurance athletes prefer to include fat and protein in their exercise nutrition. The exact macronutrient proportions necessary for optimum performance are not clear.

Again, hydration needs to be maintained at some 4 to 8 ounces every 15 to 20 minutes. There are significant variations in individual sweat rates, with some individuals losing more fluid than they can replace or absorb. Fitness, environmental conditions, acclimation to heat, and genetic differences are some of the factors influencing individual fluid losses. One way to estimate your individual sweat rate is to weigh yourself, in the nude, before and after a one-hour running session. Repeat the test for a one-hour cycling session. You should also test different environmental conditions, such as cool winter training and hot summer training. For each test, note how much fluid you lost and your exercise intensity during the session. From these tests, you can estimate your sweat rate and therefore attempt to ingest fluids at a pace equal to your sweat rate to keep your body in balance.

It is important to note that excessive hydration with water can cause a condition called hyponatremia. This is a dangerous condition whereby athletes dilute the sodium content of their blood. High levels of hyperhydration and dehydration are both undesirable conditions; your body seeks balance.

For long exercise sessions or excessive sweat rates, there is a loss of electrolytes. The electrolytes lost in sweat causing the most concern are sodium and chloride (which combine to form salt). Once again, there are individual variations in the amount of sodium lost and how much sodium needs to be ingested to keep an athletic body in balance. For long exercise sessions, a rule of thumb is to include between 250 and 500 milligrams of sodium per hour, along with your fluid replacement strategy. Some ultra-endurance athletes may need to supplement sodium at rates higher than 500 milligrams per hour. It is best to begin on the low end of supplementation and make gradual adjustments as needed.

Other electrolytes of note are potassium, magnesium, and calcium. Many energy drinks include a combination of these electrolytes. You will need to experiment to determine the fluid and electrolyte replacement strategy that works best for you.

To speed recovery after long or exhausting workouts, consume liquid or solid fuel within 20 to 30 minutes after exercise. This fuel should contain 1.5 to 1.6 grams of carbohydrates per kilogram of body weight and 0.4 to 0.5 gram of protein per kilogram of body weight.

To further enhance recovery after long or exhausting workouts, consume liquid or solid fuel over the 24 hours after exercise that contains 6 to 8 grams of carbohydrates per kilogram of body weight.

Recovery foods include milkshakes, chocolate milk, bagels, cottage cheese, lean meat, fruit and protein powder smoothies, yogurt smoothies with fruit, and beef jerky combined with a sports drink. Some studies indicate that regular snacks of approximately 50 grams of carbohydrates, eaten every two hours, may optimize recovery. (Of course an evening meal containing adequate carbohydrates would be necessary to get you through a night's sleep. In other words, do not try to set an alarm to wake up every two hours to eat.)

## Nutrition Case Study

ATHLETE:     Jay Marschall, six-time Ironman finisher
AGE:         38 years old
HEIGHT:      5' 11"
WEIGHT:      165 lbs.
BEST TIME:   9:11:58
BEST FINISH: 46th overall, 9:27:06 (third male in the 35–39 age group)

*One of the most frequently asked questions I address is "What and how do you eat in the Ironman?" Well, over the years I have come up with my nutritional strategy through trial and error as well as research and pestering questions to other athletes.*

*I start by calculating the total number of calories I will burn in the race. I estimate this number to be 800 calories per hour on average (the swim is the least and the run is the most per hour). I then multiply this number by my projected finish time, in my case around nine hours, and come up with a total calorie expenditure of 7,200. I then subtract the amount of carbohydrate calories I estimate are stored in my body (approximately 2,000) and come up with around 5,200 calories that I will need to ingest to remain in energy balance. Now the question is, how do I get that many calories down, and through what type of food or drink?*

*In the early days I would stack a pile of PowerBars on my bike handlebar and watch them melt throughout the 112-mile ride. I never had the stomach to claw off even a mouthful. Then I decided to ask Mark Allen what he ate and he said, "Exceed Meal Replacement," which is the same thing as Ensure, a drink used primarily for the elderly. I thought this was a great idea. I only had to drink two large chocolate milkshakes during the bike to get 2,000 calories (one large bottle holds about 1,000 calories of Ensure). I decided to consume Ensure throughout the bike in small swallows and also sip water or a sports drink.*

*Some of my calories come from a sports drink mixed to a 6 percent solution, which I again consume in frequent small swallows on the bike and on the run. In addition to the fluid calories, I have found that a bit of solid food seems to help digestion and calm a queasy stomach. In the last couple of races I used peanut butter on a whole wheat roll as a good filler on the bike.*

*The remainder of my calories come from more sport drinks and/or carbohydrate gels, which I ingest every 20 to 30 minutes on the run. Oh yes: When I finish, I love to sit by the pool and have a grilled cheese sandwich, french fries, and a cold beer. Of course this is consumed within the 30-minute to one-hour optimal window for recovery!*

## PUTTING IT TOGETHER

Let's say our 64-kilogram athlete is doing a long ride of three hours. When we calculate the total calories she will need that day for her three-hour ride, we need to remember that the exercise rates include resting energy expenditure.

If we follow the calculations, her total calories today should be about 3,523:

$$1,920 - (3 \text{ hours} \times 80 \text{ calories per hour resting rate}) +$$
$$(0.16 \text{ calorie per minute-kilogram} \times 64 \text{ kilograms} \times$$
$$60 \text{ minutes per hour} \times 3 \text{ hours}) = 3,523$$

This moderately tough ride requires 1,843 calories of energy. If today's caloric needs are about 3,523 and we break down the macronutrients by percentages, due to the long ride, she'll place 60 percent of the calories as carbohydrates, or

$$3,523 \times 0.60 = 2,114 \text{ carbohydrate calories}$$

At 20 percent of the calories for fat

$$3,523 \times 0.20 = 705 \text{ fat calories}$$

And at 20 percent of the calories for protein

$$3,523 \times 0.20 = 705 \text{ protein calories}$$

On her long ride today, she will consume 350 carbohydrate calories per hour—or 1,050 calories total—and she will consume a post-ride recovery food containing 1.5 to 1.6 grams of carbohydrates per kilogram of body weight, totaling about 96 grams of carbohydrates (1.5 × 64). This will give her 384 more carbohydrate calories (or 96 × 4). The total ride calories and post-ride recovery calories consumed equal 1,434. This falls short of meeting her cycling energy requirements of 1,843. She will need to make up the calories in other snacks or meals if she expects to maintain her weight. This can be accomplished over the next few days.

Since her ride was a moderately fast group ride, she will need to consume between 6 and 8 grams of carbohydrates per kilogram of body weight over the next 24 hours to restore her glycogen levels. At 6 grams, she would need 384 grams of carbohydrates (including the post-ride recovery drink), and at 8 grams per kilogram of body weight, she would need 512 grams of carbohydrates. Choosing 512 grams, she needs to consume about 2,000 carbohydrate calories over 24 hours to restore her glycogen. She can consume some of those calories today and the remaining calories tomorrow.

Remember that she was aiming to consume 2,114 carbohydrate calories today. So, subtracting the 1,434 carbohydrate calories associated with riding and post-ride recovery, she would need to be sure to consume an additional 680 carbohydrate calories today.

Notice that the two sets of formulas provided for estimating macronutrient needs don't always mesh. If our sample athlete consumed 20 percent of her 3,523 calories as protein, those 705 calories ($0.20 \times 3{,}523$) translate to

*705 calories × 1 gram of protein per 4 protein calories ÷*
*64-kilogram athlete = 2.75 grams of protein per kilogram of body weight*

The perfect diet and nutrient breakdown depends on many factors. The best place to start is to simply log what you are doing now and use your Health Questionnaire in Appendix D to determine if your current diet is serving your needs. If your diet is not meeting your needs, then consider a change.

## NUMBERS, NUMBERS, NUMBERS

Now that you have formulas to estimate your caloric needs, macronutrient breakdowns, fueling during a long ride, and post-ride fueling strategies, here are some words of caution:

**The word "estimate" is critical.** Do not worry about getting the exact numbers when consuming calories. There is a margin of error on food product labels and there is a margin of error when estimating personal nutrition needs. Again, use the Health Questionnaire in Appendix D to determine if your nutrition program works for you. If you have determined you need 100 grams of carbohydrates and 33 grams of protein for post-ride recovery and a food source has 115 grams of carbohydrates and 25 grams of protein, it will work fine—don't worry.

I do not advise becoming a food log addict. **Use food logs to establish good eating behaviors** or as spot checks to see what is going on with your diet. It is possible to drive yourself nuts weighing and counting everything. Let food logs serve their purpose, but don't let them control you.

Just because you exercise, it does not mean you can eat unlimited quantities of food. **Every body has an energy balance system.** You need to learn to manage your own body and its special needs.

**Body weight is just a number.** Do not weigh yourself every day and look for changes. In fact, if you lose several pounds from one day to the next, it is probably due to dehydration. Try to remedy that situation by drinking more water. At most, weigh yourself weekly. Review the Health Questionnaire to gauge how you feel. Your overall health is a better measure of nutritional success than numbers on a scale.

## SUPPLEMENTS

The *American Heritage Dictionary* defines *supplement* as "something added to complete a thing or to make up for a deficiency." Notice it does not say, "a substitute for . . ." No amount of vitamin and mineral supplementation will make up for a crummy diet, something people do not seem to understand. As a case in point, I was talking with a young person sacking my groceries recently. He was inquiring about the volume and variety of vegetables I was purchasing. "Are you a vegetarian or something?" he asked.

"No, at our house we eat lots of different vegetables because they taste good and their vibrant colors make an exciting plate," I replied.

"Oh, I don't like vegetables, so I just eat meat and potatoes and take vitamins. Anyway, one vitamin pill has all the stuff I really need, so I don't have to worry about it. I'm training to be a boxer, so I need all the vitamins."

His thought process is all too common. While he continued sacking the groceries I explained about fiber, phytochemicals, and the unknown healthy substances probably also contained in real food. I explained how recent the discovery of phytochemicals was and that although we humans are pretty smart, we are a long way from knowing everything. The study of nutrition is still a young science. I further explained that supplements are meant to complement a diet high in whole foods but that no supplementation plan will make up for a diet high in processed foods, saturated fat, sugar, and salt and low in fiber and variety. The young man carried my groceries out to the car just so he could ask more questions. I am unsure if he will change his habits, but at least he was thinking about it.

Researchers are continually finding out more information about vitamin and mineral supplementation. A survey of top researchers asked what they take for vitamin and mineral supplementation, and the answers were not uniform. We will examine the supplements that continue to receive attention among scientists.

## MULTIVITAMINS AND MINERALS

Most experts recommend a multivitamin and mineral supplement. Some experts still hold a strong belief that we should be able to meet all of our vitamin and mineral needs from food, but more research is telling us that does not happen for most folks. U.S. Department of Agriculture data indicate that at least 40 percent of the people in the United States routinely consume a diet containing only 60 percent of the recommended daily allowances (RDA) of 10 selected nutrients. We would likely fare worse if more nutrients were evaluated.

There continues to be controversy as to whether or not athletes' requirements for vitamins and minerals exceed those of the average population. If athletes are consuming a balanced and varied diet and taking some supplements, perhaps that is enough.

## VITAMINS C AND E

The current recommendation is to supplement a multivitamin with 500 to 1,000 milligrams of vitamin C and 400 IU of vitamin E. Both of these are antioxidants, substances that block oxidative damage to the cells of our body. To maintain constant concentrations of vitamin C in the blood, it is best to take two doses, 8 to 12 hours apart.

## CALCIUM

The current recommendation is to consume somewhere between 1,000 and 1,500 milligrams of calcium daily. In order for calcium to be absorbed well, protein and vitamins C, D, E, and K all play a role. Several minerals also play important roles in calcium absorption. For example, too much magnesium, sodium, and/or phosphorus (found in many soft drinks and processed foods) can inhibit the absorption of calcium. Just supplementing the diet with calcium is not a cure-all.

Weight-bearing exercise plays an important role, though more is not necessarily better. Even men, who seem to be less prone to bone loss, can suffer when exercise levels are excessive. One study of University of Memphis male basketball players found they were losing about 3.8 percent of their bone mass from preseason to midseason of a single year. Bob Klesges, the head scientist, determined the ballplayers were losing substantial amounts of calcium through their sweat. He concluded this by collecting the sweaty T-shirts of the players and carefully wringing out their contents to be analyzed (yuck!).

He found the players gained back 1.1 percent of their bone mass during summer, but they lost an additional 3.3 percent when practices resumed, making their total losses now about 5.8 percent. With supplemental calcium, they were able to regain the losses.

So try to get 1,000 to 1,500 milligrams of calcium *from your diet* (an 8-ounce glass of milk contains 290 milligrams of calcium). If you are not getting enough through your diet, consider a supplement on the days when your food does not give you the recommended requirements. A superior supplement is calcium citrate malate, found in many calcium-enriched juices. On average, people absorb 35 percent of the calcium in calcium citrate malate, compared to 30 percent of the calcium in other supplements.

## IRON

Iron is an essential component of hemoglobin and myoglobin and functions in the oxygenation of red blood cells and muscle. Women especially can have problems with low levels of iron, developing anemia. One of the common causes of anemia is excessive menstrual flow. Aggravating the deficiency due to blood loss, some women consume inadequate dietary iron. Good food sources of iron are fish, meat, beans, whole grains, enriched breads, and enriched cereals. Iron supplements should not be self-prescribed but should be taken on the advice of a physician.

Constant fatigue is one of the common symptoms of anemia. Anemia can be easily identified through a simple blood test. In fact, blood tests can detect many problems associated with diet, health, and wellness. For athletes serious about wellness and competition, an annual blood test—preferably during recovery or in the off-season—is an excellent source of information. This baseline test can then be used to diagnose changes to blood chemistry when a competitive season seems to have gone awry.

# ERGOGENIC AIDS

The items I receive the most questions about are sport drinks, energy bars, and caffeine.

## SPORT DRINKS

The simple rule of thumb here is to drink the sport drink that tastes best to you and does not cause extra potty stops. If you select a drink that tastes good and use it for workouts over an hour long, it is generally beneficial. Be aware that some athletes have gastrointestinal problems with fructose-based sport drinks. If you are having difficulties, check to see if fructose is one of the main ingredients of the sport drink.

Some sport drinks now include protein. Common carbohydrat-to-protein ratios range from 4:1 to 7:1. In general, for short, fast events, I recommend sticking to a product that contains only carbohydrates. For events longer than about four hours, many athletes find that some protein seems to help. How much protein is in the mix is individual. Some athletes do fine with a 4:1 mix, while others experience gastrointestinal distress at this level. Test your sport drinks during training events.

## ENERGY BARS

Energy bars are useful for long rides, pre- and post-workout snacks, and pre-race snacks. They are not, however, one of the major food groups. Some athletes use them as a major source of calories, choosing them over fruits and vegetables because they are an easy food to acquire and prepare. Use them as supplements for sporting activities; they are not appropriate as meals. Eat minimally processed foods and, whenever possible, choose whole foods over highly refined foods such as energy bars.

## CAFFEINE

Caffeine may be the most widely used drug in the world. It stimulates the central nervous system, the adrenal system, the metabolic system, and the muscular system. While some studies have shown that caffeine influences the metabolic system by stimulating fat metabolism and sparing glycogen during aerobic exercise, the research on this theory is not conclusive. For example, some studies show that glycogen sparing is limited to the first 15 to 20 minutes of exercise. Additional studies, where the focus is on the measurement of free fatty-acid metabolism, which spares glycogen, show the response to fat-burning may not be optimal until three to four hours after ingestion.

Another theory is that caffeine lowers the level of perceived pain at a given pace, so athletes have the ability to produce more work or work for longer periods of time with the use of caffeine. When caffeine is used in conjunction with exercise, several studies support the notion that it appears not to have the diuretic effect that it has when consumed in a nonexercise situation.

Whether or not regular caffeine users need to abstain from caffeine use for some period of time prior to an important event in order to optimize the effects of caffeine is, again, uncertain. At least one study suggests that caffeine non-users and regular users respond similarly to caffeine when taken before exercise, so it may not be necessary for regular users to abstain from caffeine before important events. A second study shows that the ergogenic effect following a dose of 5 milligrams of caffeine per kilogram of body weight for regular caffeine users and non-users produced greater effects in non-users when compared to users in exercise times one and three hours after ingestion.

Some studies show that ingesting caffeine in the form of coffee is ineffective compared to ingesting pure caffeine. The reason for this is not clear.

A dose of 5 to 7 milligrams of caffeine per kilogram of body weight, given one hour prior to exercise, has been the typical protocol for most studies; however, doses as low as 3.3 to 4.4 milligrams of caffeine per kilogram of body weight have been shown to be effective.

| TABLE 3.2: CAFFEINE CONTENT OF COMMON FOODS | | |
|---|---|---|
| Product | Serving Size | Caffeine (mg) |
| Café latte | (8 oz.) | 35–60 |
| Cappuccino | (8 oz.) | 35–60 |
| Coffee | (8 oz.) | 100–250 |
| Cola | (8 oz.) | 38–46 |
| Espresso | (1 oz.) | 35–60 |
| Excedrin | (2 tablets) | 130 |
| Mountain Dew | (12 oz.) | 55 |
| No-Doz, regular | (1 tablet) | 100 |
| Pocket Rocket Chocolate | (1 packet) | 50 |

There can be negative side effects to caffeine consumption for some individuals. Some people do not tolerate caffeine well and become shaky, jittery, and unable to focus. It also is bothersome to some people's gastrointestinal system, producing stomach pain, abdominal cramps, and diarrhea. Caffeine was once banned by the U.S. Olympic Committee at levels measuring 12 mcg/ml of urine, but this restriction was removed in January of 2004. To reach this level would require the ingestion of nearly 1,200 mg of pure caffeine.

Although the exact mechanisms that cause caffeine to be an ergogenic aid (something that can increase muscular work capacity) are unclear, I did not find a single study that concluded that caffeine is ineffective.

If you decide to use caffeine, experiment with it during training sessions. It is best not to wait until a race or big event to test your tolerance and advantage levels. For racing, consume the caffeine approximately 30 minutes to one hour before race start.

Should you decide to utilize caffeine for training or racing, you can find it in products listed in Table 3.2.

# PART II

# Fast-Track Training

The plans in Part II are fast-track training plans to help you prepare for your event in a hurry. These plans take six weeks (for the "crash plan") to about three months of training to get to race day. The plans are for people who have minimal time—and in some cases minimal fitness—to devote to training. These athletes need an efficient plan to get them ready for race day.

# 4

## 12 WEEKS TO A SPRINT TRIATHLON FOR ATHLETES WITH LIMITED FITNESS

*I never thought it would be possible for me to become a triathlete, but after I read this chapter, I felt like someone was saying to me, "You can do it if you want to!"*
—HELENA MENDOZA, VENEZUELA

H ey, there's a sprint triathlon in about three months. Why don't you come along and do the race with me?"

"Are you kidding me? Triathlon is for maniacs who have nothing to do but train. I have a life. I don't have time for triathlon training."

"It doesn't take that much time. You can do it!"

"Naw, I've seen how much you train. I have to eat, sleep, and work. I don't want to give up _____." (Fill in the blank with one or more of the following: aerobics classes, kickboxing, softball, golf, waterskiing, spending time with family and friends, etc.)

"You don't need to train as much as I do."

"How much would I need to train?"

Good question.

## PROFILE

Okay, busy person, this chapter is designed to help a never-ever triathlete complete his or her first event. The training recommendations are for someone who has minimal time to devote to triathlon training.

Your athletic profile begins with swimming. You know how to swim, but it has been a long time since once-fit arms and legs have actually propelled your body through water. In other words, you lack swimming endurance.

As for cycling, you might ride a bicycle now and again, mostly around the neighborhood. On occasion you might ride a stationary bicycle at the health club while waiting for aerobics to begin or to warm up before weight lifting. As with swimming, you have no real endurance on the bike.

Finally, running. The running you do is mostly of short duration, like running bases in softball. Maybe you chase a ball while playing racquetball. You may have even run a 5K once.

So your multisport profile for endurance sports is not great, but you are not sitting around channel surfing either. This plan assumes you are currently active in sports three to six times a week. The specific sport is not as important as the fact that you are active doing something. If you are not currently active and decide to use this plan to get back into shape, be sure to consult a physician before beginning.

One of the most common mistakes made by people just beginning to train for a triathlon, or any other endurance event, is doing too much too soon. Early enthusiasm can lead to injury or overtraining. A 12-week plan to get you through your first triathlon is shown in Table 4.1. It gently builds aerobic endurance in all three sports.

## GOAL

This plan will take you from a current state of no swimming, minimal cycling, and no running to completing a 450- to 500-meter swim, 11- to 15-mile bike, and about a 3-mile run, consecutively—your first triathlon.

## THE PLAN

The plan assumes you are capable of swimming 50 meters without stopping. It may not be Olympic speed, but you can do it. This particular plan does not utilize the swim workout chapter (Chapter 19); rather, the workouts are listed on following pages in this chapter.

The first column of the plan has the week number (Sunday of Week 12 is when you will complete your race), the next seven columns are the days of the week, and the last column is the total training time for each week.

Where the row containing the week numbers intersects the columns with the day labels, you will see which sport you should be doing, a workout code or number, and the total time for the workout. For example, on Wednesday of Week 1, you will be doing a run, in training Zone 1, and the total time will be 5 minutes—yes, only 5 minutes. Do not panic and think it is not enough. Notice that by the end of Week 6, you will be running 30 minutes.

All you need for the swim is a comfortable swimming suit and goggles. For women, if you decide to go with a two-piece suit, be certain it is one designed for sports and not sunbathing. For the guys, if you are uncomfortable in a small Speedo-style suit or tight-fitting Lycra shorts, trunks will work fine.

As for goggles, everyone's face is different. Go to a sporting goods store where the salesperson is willing to let you try on several different styles and give tips on proper fit. The nosepiece should not dig into the bridge of your nose. The foam on goggle cups should cover your eye socket, forming a waterproof seal. It is not necessary to pull the strap over your head to get an idea of proper fit.

If you wear glasses, it is possible to get prescription goggles. Unless you are really optically impaired, it is possible to get by without special goggles until triathlon becomes an addiction. Most of the volunteers at a pool triathlon are willing to hold glasses, or you can position a person to hand you eyewear as you exit after an open-water swim.

An antidote for foggy goggles is shampoo. A mixture of half no-tears shampoo and half water will do the trick. A handy way to carry the mixture is in a clean, empty container for eyedrops. Pry the top off and pour the no-fog mixture in the bottle. Just before swimming, put a drop or two

## TABLE 4.1: 12 WEEKS TO A SPRINT TRIATHLON FOR ATHLETES

| Week | Mon. | Tues. | Wed. | Thurs. |
|------|------|-------|------|--------|
| 1 | Day off | Swim | Run | Bike |
|  |  | Workout #1 | E1 | E1 |
|  |  | 00:30 | 00:05 | 00:20 |
| 2 | Day off | Swim | Run | Bike |
|  |  | Workout #2 | E1 | E1 |
|  |  | 00:30 | 00:09 | 00:30 |
| 3 | Day off | Swim | Run | Bike |
|  |  | Workout #3 | E1 | accels. 4–6 × 30 sec. (1' 30") |
|  |  | 00:30 | 00:13 | 00:30 |
| 4 | Day off | Swim | Run | Bike |
|  |  | Workout #4 | E1 | accels. 4–6 × 30 sec. (1' 30") |
|  |  | 00:30 | 00:17 | 00:30 |
| 5 | Day off | Swim | Run | Bike |
|  |  | Workout #5 | E1 | E1 |
|  |  | 00:30 | 00:23 | 00:30 |
| 6 | Day off | Swim | Run | Bike or day off |
|  |  | Workout #6 | E1 | E1 |
|  |  | 00:30 | 00:10 | 00:30 |
| 7 | Day off | Swim | Run | Bike |
|  |  | Workout #7 | E1 | accels. 10–20–30–30–20–10 sec. (1' 30") |
|  |  | 00:30 | 00:30 | 00:30 |
| 8 | Day off | Swim | Run | Bike |
|  |  | Workout #8 | accels. 4–6 × 20 sec. (1' 30") | accels. 6 × 30 sec. (1' 30") |
|  |  | 00:30 | 00:30 | 00:30 |
| 9 | Day off | Swim | Run | Bike |
|  |  | Workout #9 | accels. 6–8 × 20 sec. (1' 30") | accels. 10–15–20–25–30–25–20–15–10 sec. (1' 30") |
|  |  | 00:30 | 00:30 | 00:45 |
| 10 | Day off | Swim | Run | Bike or day off |
|  |  | Workout #10 | E1 | E1 |
|  |  | 00:30 | 00:15 | 00:30 |
| 11 | Day off | Swim | Run | Bike |
|  |  | Workout #11 | E1 | accels. 6–8 × 10 sec. (1' 50") |
|  |  | 00:30 | 00:30 | 00:30 |
| 12 | Day off | Swim | Run | Bike |
|  |  | Workout #12 | E1 | accels. 3 × 10 sec. (1' 50") |
|  |  | 00:30 | 00:10 | 00:20 |

## WITH LIMITED FITNESS

| | Fri. | Sat. | Sun. | Weekly Total Workout Time |
|---|---|---|---|---|
| | Swim | Run | Bike | |
| | Workout #1 | E2 | E1 | |
| | | 00:07 | 00:30 | 02:02 |
| | Swim | Run | Bike | |
| | Workout #2 | E2 | E2 | |
| | | 00:11 | 00:45 | 02:35 |
| | Swim | Run | Bike | |
| | Workout #3 | E2 | E2 | |
| | | 00:15 | 01:00 | 02:58 |
| | Swim | Run | Bike | |
| | Workout #4 | E2 | E2 | |
| | | 00:20 | 01:15 | 03:22 |
| | Swim | Run | Bike | |
| | Workout #5 | E2 | E2 | |
| | | 00:26 | 01:30 | 03:49 |
| | Swim | Run | Bike | |
| | Workout #6 | E2 | E3 | |
| | | 00:30 | 00:45 | 02:55 |
| | Swim | Run | Bike | |
| | Workout #7 | E2 | E3 | |
| | | 00:35 | 01:30 | 04:05 |
| | Swim | Run | Bike | |
| | Workout #8 | E2 | E3 | |
| | | 00:40 | 01:45 | 04:25 |
| | Swim | Run | Brick | |
| | open-water swim | E2 | Bike—E3, 01:15 | |
| | or Workout #9 | | Run—E2, 00:15 | |
| | | 00:30 | 01:30 | 04:15 |
| | Swim | Day off | Brick | |
| | open-water swim | | Bike—E2, 01:30 | |
| | or Workout #10 | | Run—E3, 00:15 | |
| | | | 01:30 | 03:15 |
| | Swim | Bike | Brick | |
| | open-water swim | E1 | Bike 01:00, Run 00:30 | |
| | or Workout #1 | | Both fartlek | |
| | | 00:30 | 01:30 | 04:00 |
| | Bike or day off | Day off | Race! | |
| | E1 | | | |
| | 00:30 | | | 01:30 + Race |

in each lens of your goggles and rub it around. Be sure your fingers are clean and free of lotion. Rinse out the excess by giving the goggles a couple of dips in the pool or dousing them with some clean water from a water bottle. When you are swimming, if the water in the goggles irritates your eyes, you didn't rinse well enough. If the goggles fog, you rinsed too well. Definitely practice this prior to race day.

## SWIM

During Weeks 1 through 6, the swim workout on Friday is a repeat of Tuesday's workout. On Fridays, the goal is to put less effort into the swim than you did on Tuesday. Keep all swimming in Weeks 1 through 6 at an RPE in Zones 1 to 2. Try to relax when you swim, getting the most distance out of each stroke with the least amount of effort. Each swim workout is described below.

*Workout #1:* Swim 10 × 50 meters
*Rest:* 45 seconds between 50
*Tip:* This plan assumes you can swim down and back (50 meters) in a standard pool. You may have to rest a whole minute between 50s; that is okay. Until we add a warm-up and cool-down to swimming, make the first couple and last couple of 50s very easy. If the workout takes less than 30 minutes, just get out of the pool when you have completed the 500 meters of swimming.

*Workout #2:* Swim 10 × 50 meters
*Rest:* 30 to 45 seconds between 50s

*Workout #3:* Swim 10 × 50 meters
*Rest:* 20 to 30 seconds between 50s

*Workout #4:* Swim 8 × 75 meters
*Rest:* 30 seconds between 75s
*Tip:* We've bumped up the distance a bit and decreased the rest.

By now you are building some endurance in the pool. If you would like to swim a bit longer, do a few meters of warm-up before the 8 × 75 and/or do a few meters after the assigned set. In the weeks to come, you can add a warm-up, cool-down, and a few meters of kicking to any workout when you have the time and energy to do so. However, do not swim over the assigned time—usually 30 minutes.

*Workout #5:* Swim 8 × 75 meters
*Rest:* 20 seconds between 75s

*Workout #6:* Swim 8 × 75 meters
*Rest:* 10 seconds between 75s
*Tip:* You can do additional swimming, up to 30 minutes, if you have the time and energy.

For Weeks 7 through 12, we begin to speed up the Tuesday workouts. Your swim intensity (RPE) on Tuesdays should be in Zones 1 to 3 and the intensity on Fridays in Zones 1 to 2.

*Workout #7:* Swim 5 × 100 meters
*Rest:* 20 seconds between 100s
*Tip:* You can do additional swimming, up to 30 minutes, if you have the time and energy.

*Workout #8:* Swim 5 × 100 meters
*Rest:* 10 seconds between 100s
*Tip:* You can do additional swimming, up to 30 minutes, if you have the time and energy.

*Workout #9:* Swim 500 meters nonstop
*Tip:* Notice how much time it takes you to swim this 500. Your time will improve with training. Swim as much as 30 minutes, if you have the desire. If the race will be in open water, make an effort to

go to a swim beach with a lifeguard for the second workout this week. Inform the lifeguard you are practicing for your first triathlon, and ask him or her to keep an eye on you. Swim about the same amount of time in open water as you have been doing in each indoor workout. Make the workout feel easy. Try to relax your neck and shoulder muscles before entering the water. Swim to a buoy that is around 25 meters out (if possible), then swim back. Feel free to rest as much as you need between outings. If you will not be swimming in open water or do not have access to a safe open-water swimming situation, the swim workout on Friday should be a repeat of Tuesday's workout.

*Workout #10:* Swim 3 × 200 meters
*Rest:* 15 seconds between 200s
*Tip:* Swim up to 30 minutes. On Friday, swim about 15 to 30 minutes in open water or repeat Tuesday's workout.

*Workout #11:* Swim 500 meters nonstop
*Tip:* Make the odd-numbered 25-meter segments very easy and the even-numbered 25-meter segments a bit faster. For Friday, repeat Tuesday's workout or swim up to 30 minutes in open water.

*Workout #12:* Swim 500 meters nonstop
*Tip:* Make the first 100 very easy; try to relax your arms on the out-of-water portion (recovery) of the second 100; focus on a strong pull on the third 100 (feeling pressure on not only your hand, but your lower arm as well); relax your arms on the recovery of the fourth 100; and make each 25 a bit faster on the final 100. This is great practice for pacing, because it is how you will swim on race day.

# BIKE

Any style of bicycle will work. A road bike will be more efficient, but if your only velo is a mountain bike, it will do. To reduce injury, be certain the bike is correctly set up for you. Bike setup is not covered in this book, so you'll need to ask your local bike shop if any of the staff has specialty training for bike fitting, or consult *Triathlon Training Basics* or *The Female Cyclist: Gearing Up a Level,* published by VeloPress. If you purchase a bike from the local bike shop, a qualified salesperson should be willing to help you with proper fit. A final note on bike setup: A seat that is too high or too low can cause numbness in toes or genitals. Do not assume this pain is normal; you need to alleviate the problem.

A good pair of cycling shorts makes training much more enjoyable. The seam that typically creates the crotch on any pair of shorts or pants can be a point of discomfort when positioned between your body weight and a bicycle seat. For longer rides, apply a layer of petroleum jelly or a product such as Body Glide before putting on your cycling shorts to prevent saddle sores. Also, never wear dirty cycling shorts. After each cycling workout, change out of your shorts as quickly as possible and be sure to launder them after each use.

If you do not have a helmet, get one. Most races require the use of a helmet anyway. Any helmet that has the ANSI approval on the inside will work.

Unless you plan on walking the bike home at some point in training or racing, learn how to change a flat tire. Always carry a spare tube, a pump or a $CO_2$ cartridge tire-inflation device with you.

Most of the bike workouts in the first few weeks are in Zones 1 to 2. As the plan progresses, there is more Zone 3 work. There are a couple of workouts listed in Table 4.1 that say "accels 4–6 × 30 sec. (1' 30")." This is shorthand for four to six repetitions of 30-second efforts, with 1 minute, 30 seconds of easy spinning between accelerations. These are not all-out sprints, but rather a bit of speed play, allowing you to go fast without sending you into deep oxygen debt. Build speed throughout the acceleration. Be sure to warm up before and cool down after the accelerations.

The longest ride is in Week 8 and is 1 hour, 45 minutes long. For the bike rides that designate Zone 3 riding, you can ride a rolling course and allow your exertion to be as high as Zone 3 on the uphills and as low as Zone 1 on the way down. Do not feel compelled to make the entire ride in Zone 3.

## RUN

Invest in a good pair of running shoes designed specifically for your feet. Go to a running store and tell the salesperson about your exercise history and why you need new running shoes. The salesperson should have you try on several shoes. Do a bit of jogging in each pair before making the final choice. A good salesperson can help you decide which style is best for your foot anatomy and current training routine. If you are new to running, keep in mind that the style of shoe that is best for you may change over time.

Do not run in your aerobics, softball, weight-training, or lawn-mowing shoes. Once you purchase running shoes, use them for that purpose only.

The run workouts gently build over time to minimize the risk of injury. In general, the Wednesday runs are all Zone 1 throughout the first six weeks, and the Saturday runs can be in Zones 1 and 2. But when Zone 2 is designated, it means you can be anywhere in Zone 1 or 2.

When the runs begin to open into Zone 3 intensity, as with the bike, do not feel compelled to make the whole run in Zone 3. Some Wednesday runs begin to add accelerations, similar to the bike accelerations. These are not all-out sprints, but rather a gentle building of speed.

## BRICK

A "brick" workout is a bike ride immediately followed by a run. You will do three brick workouts prior to your race. Use these workouts to figure out how to make your bike-to-run clothes or shoe changes as fast as possible. Some athletes complete the entire event in the clothing that they used to start the swim. Other athletes prefer to slip on a pair of baggy shorts for the bike ride or the run. Just keep in mind that the time it takes you to change clothes is included in your overall race time.

## RACE DAY

Prior to race day, get a map of the course from the race director. If the event is near your home, do some of your training rides and runs on the course. At a minimum, drive the course before race day so you know what to expect.

On race morning, get to the transition area with time to spare. Get your transition area set up, being careful not to be a rack hog. Then take a few moments to orient yourself. Find a landmark near your bike so you can locate your personal transition space when exiting the swim area. Note the entrance and exit to the transition area.

On the swim leg of the race, pace yourself exactly as you did on the Tuesday prior to the race. On the bike leg of the race, ride no faster than you have in training—this goes for the run as well.

Most of all, relax, have fun, and enjoy the experience. If you trained right and race conservatively, this race should leave you with a desire to do more triathlons.

## MODIFYING THE PLAN

**Q:** I'm a swimmer. Can I just do my masters swim workouts instead of the swims shown in the plan? And can I swim three days instead of two?

**A:** Yes, swimming with masters works fine. Since you are adding two more sports to your training, be aware of your energy levels. You may have to back off some in the pool to put your energy into the new sports.

**Q:** I already ride my bike two or three times a week for 45 to 60 minutes. I don't want to give that up. Do I have to cut back?

**A:** You can keep your cycling at two days a week for 45 to 60 minutes. Be aware of your intensity and cut back on ride time or speed if you find yourself getting too tired. If you would like to keep a third cycling day in the mix, begin by making it shorter—around 30 minutes—until you see how your body handles the new sports.

**Q:** I currently run three days a week, running about three miles on two days and five or six miles on the third day. Can I maintain my running workouts with this plan?

**A:** Know that overall training volume in all sports contributes to running injuries. Monitor your body closely to see if you are experiencing any aches or pains. Deal with the issue early, before the ache becomes an injury. Cut back on running until you build up your fitness in the other sports, which is likely after your first sprint race.

# 5

## 6 WEEKS TO AN OLYMPIC TRIATHLON FOR ATHLETES WITH LIMITED TIME

*One of the toughest aspects of my training is knowing which races*
*I am ready for and which ones I should save for next year.*

—ADAM BOOK, USA

There is an Olympic-distance triathlon (swim 1,500 meters, bike 24.8 miles, run 6.2 miles) in a nearby city. The event is only six weeks away— is there enough time to make your triathlon debut? While I usually encourage first-timers to try a sprint-distance event before moving to Olympic status, a reasonably fit person can be ready to race in five to six weeks. Want to tri?

## PROFILE

The plan shown in Table 5.1 outlines the path to race day. This particular plan is designed for athletes who maintain their health and are fit year-round. Their fitness might include some combination of running, spin classes, or outdoor biking. They may currently swim a few laps or have swimming experience from past years, and they might be involved in other sports. Their current regimen gives them the capability to run for about 30 minutes twice a week. They can bike comfortably for about an hour. Since most Olympic-distance triathlons are held in open water, this athlete needs to be comfortable swimming with wildlife—and not just the fish.

## GOAL

Given the assumptions in the last paragraph, the goal is to complete an Olympic-distance triathlon in about six weeks, with a race finish time under four hours. The estimated finish time comes from assuming a 2- to 3-minute pace per 100 meters for the 1,500-meter swim. This puts the total swim time between 30 and 45 minutes. If you are capable of riding a bike for about 25 miles, averaging 15 to 18 miles per hour, the bike leg of the race will take around 1:22 to 1:40. Finally the run, averaging 10- to 12-minute miles, will take 1:02 to 1:15. Throw in a few minutes for transition time and the event will total three to four hours on a Sunday morning. If this sounds like something you would like to try, let's go.

## THE PLAN

The plan lists swim workouts by number. Specifics for each numbered workout are outlined in this chapter. More than likely, if you are using this plan you do not own a heart rate monitor nor do you have a good idea about what kind of pace to hold in training and in the race. Assuming these statements are true, use your breathing and the rate of perceived exertion chart in Table 2.1 to gauge training and racing intensity. To simplify, I will refer to training zones listed in the chart and we will use those zones for all three sports.

| TABLE 5.1: 6 WEEKS TO AN OLYMPIC TRIATHLON FOR ATHLETES WITH LIMITED TIME | | | | | | | | |
|---|---|---|---|---|---|---|---|---|
| **Week** | **Sport** | **Mon.** | **Tues.** | **Wed.** | **Thurs.** | **Fri.** | **Sat.** | **Sun.** |
| *1* | Brick | | | | | | Brick | |
| | Swim | Day off | Workout #1 | | | Workout #2 | | |
| | Bike | | | | 00:45 | | 00:15 | 01:00–01:30 |
| | Run | | | 00:30 | | | 00:15–00:30 | |
| *2* | Brick | | | | | | Brick | |
| | Swim | Day off | Workout #3 | | | Workout #4 | | |
| | Bike | | | | 00:45 | | 00:15 | 01:30–02:00 |
| | Run | | | 00:30 | | | 00:15–00:30 | |
| *3* | Brick | | | | | | Brick | |
| | Swim | Day off | Workout #5 | | | Workout #6 | | |
| | Bike | | | | 00:45 | | 00:30 | 02:00–02:30 |
| | Run | | | 00:30 | | | 00:30–00:45 | |
| *4* | Brick | | | | | | Brick | |
| | Swim | Day off | Workout #7 | | | Workout #8 | | |
| | Bike | | | | 00:45 | | 00:30 | 02:30–03:00 |
| | Run | | | 00:30 | | | 00:30–00:45 | |
| *5* | Brick | | | | | | Brick | |
| | Swim | Day off | Workout #9 | | | Workout #10 | | |
| | Bike | | | | 00:45 | | 00:30 | 02:30–03:00 |
| | Run | | | 00:30 | | | 00:45–01:00 | |
| *6* | Brick | | | | | | Brick | Race! |
| | Swim | Day off | Workout #11 | | | Day off | | |
| | Bike | | | | 00:45 | | 00:20 | |
| | Run | | | 00:20 | | | 00:10 | |

## SWIM

Back to swimming. The speed or intensity of the Tuesday swims should be Zone 1 or 2. The Friday swim can begin with moderate 100s in Zone 1 or 2, and progress to Zone 3 for the 50s. Meters and yards can be used interchangeably, depending on the pool where you train. Details for each workout follow.

*Workout #1:* Swim 10 × 50 meters
*Rest:* 15 to 30 seconds between 50s

*Workout #2:* Set 1, swim 4 × 100 meters; Set 2, swim 6 × 50 meters
*Rest:* 15 to 30 seconds between 100s; 1 to 2 minutes between sets; about 10 seconds between 50s

*Workout #3:* Swim 12 × 50 meters
*Rest:* 15 to 30 seconds between 50s

*Workout #4:* Set 1, swim 6 × 100 meters; Set 2, swim 6 × 50 meters
*Rest:* 15 to 30 seconds between 100s; 1 to 2 minutes between sets; about 10 seconds between 50s

*Workout #5:* Swim 14 × 50 meters
*Rest:* 15 to 20 seconds between 50s

*Workout #6:* Set 1, swim 8 × 100 meters; Set 2, swim 8 × 50 meters
*Rest:* 15 to 20 seconds between 100s; 1 to 2 minutes between sets; about 10 seconds between 50s

*Workout #7:* Swim 16 × 50 meters
*Rest:* 15 to 20 seconds between 50s

*Workout #8:* Set 1, swim 10 × 100 meters; Set 2, swim 8 × 50 meters
*Rest:* 15 to 20 seconds between 100s; 1 to 2 minutes between sets; and about 10 seconds between 50s

*Workout #9:* Swim 18 × 50 meters
*Rest:* 15 to 20 seconds between 50s

*Workout #10:* Set 1, swim 10 × 100 meters; Set 2, swim 10 × 50 meters
*Rest:* 15 seconds between 100s; 1 to 2 minutes between sets; 10 seconds between 50s

*Workout #11:* Swim 15 × 50 meters
*Rest:* 15 to 20 seconds between 50s

The Tuesday swims are intentionally shorter than the Friday sessions. The longer swim day builds endurance so you are eventually doing a 1,500-meter broken swim with minimal rest. This will be enough to get you through the event, without having to do long, boring, continuous swims in training. If it has been a while since you have swum in open water, it would be good to take a dip at a swim beach with a lifeguard on duty. An open-water swim can be substituted for one of the Tuesday or Friday workouts.

A practice open-water swim refreshes the memory that the water is probably dark, creepy-feeling, and colder than the pool. There might be mysterious floating objects that brush against your arms and legs; these are generally harmless, but can raise your heart rate to sonic speed. A practice swim can help calm your nerves, and unless you can swim a remarkably straight line, it is good to practice lifting your head every few strokes to sight landmarks to keep on course. There are no black lines to follow on the bottom of a lake or ocean.

## BIKE AND BRICK

The swim portion of training and racing will typically take the least amount of time; cycling will take the most. The plan is designed to build overall endurance on the bike during Sunday training sessions to minimize the risk of injury. This assumes you are riding a bicycle that fits you correctly. If there is any doubt, drop into a qualified bike shop and ask them to help you get set up.

The first ride of each week is on Thursday. It is intended to be an easy spin, mostly in Zone 1. To improve leg speed and coordination, throw in a few 30-second accelerations, building speed throughout the 30 seconds. Take 2 to 3 minutes of rest between accelerations. When ramping up the speed, try to relax your shoulders and toes. Go as fast as possible without allowing your butt to bounce off the bike seat. Although 45-minute sessions are shown on the plan, the ride can be as short as 30 minutes or as long as 60 minutes.

On Saturdays, you will do a brick, which means a bike ride immediately followed by a run. This combination workout helps build running endurance while minimizing injury risk—because the first part of the workout is cycling. The session also prepares legs for that strange feeling of running immediately after they have been spinning in circles. While you are at it, practice transitions in the garage (aka transition area) so it becomes easy to lay out all your gear in a small area and keep it organized.

The first three bricks, in Weeks 1, 2, and 3, are performed in Zones 1 to 2 for both sports. The bricks in Weeks 4 and 5 can be done anywhere in Zones 1 to 3. It is not necessary to maximize time in the upper zone. A range of running times is provided for the bricks to accommodate individual differences in fitness. If you decide to train on the low end, that will work fine.

A range of workout times is also shown for the Sunday bike rides. The first two long rides are in Zones 1 to 2 and the last three rides can be in Zones 1 to 3. Use the nutrition guidelines in Chapter 3 to stay well hydrated and fueled. Testing the routine on long rides will help you determine the appropriate macronutrient values. Start practicing this routine on the long Sunday rides in Week 1 and use the routine you have tested on race day.

## RUN

Since you have already been running, a good pair of running-only shoes should be in your wardrobe. Run twice a week. One of the run workouts was covered within the brick description; the other run workout is on Wednesday. Make Wednesday a form run that includes four to six repetitions of 20-second accelerations. Build speed throughout the acceleration to about a 5K race pace. Take easy, 2- to 3-minute jogs between accelerations. The remainder of that run is in Zones 1 to 2.

## TAPER AND RACE DAY

At the beginning of this chapter, I mentioned you could be race-ready in five to six weeks. If pressed for time, you could eliminate Week 5 and go right from Week 4 to Week 6. Eliminating Week 5 will mean eliminating a long swim practice that simulates race distance and builds overall endurance, but the race is still doable without it.

In either case, whether you choose five or six weeks of training, the last week on the schedule is a rest week. It is designed to have you feeling fresh for race day. Gather all the self-control you have to keep from doing more activity that week. Rest and visualize how much fun race day will be.

When race morning arrives, get to the transition area with plenty of time to spare. Keep your eating and drinking schedule the same as it has been for all Sunday long rides. Get your equipment set up and look for the perfect route into and out of the transition area. Know where your trusty velo is racked.

As you line up for the swim, unless you are very experienced in open-water swimming, position yourself on the outside and near the rear of the pack. Sometimes the swim can get rough with people thrashing about (remember that wildlife I mentioned?). So unless you are a very competent swimmer, place yourself away from the crowd. When swimming, recall good stroke form and the strong workouts you had in the pool. Try to relax and get into a rhythm.

After the swim and a fast transition, it is off on the bike course. On the bike as well as the run, try to control your pace so it is not beyond what you have practiced in workouts. Be certain to hydrate and fuel on both the bike and the run. After the ride, the second transition should be easy, because you have been practicing this one. After the second transition, start the run with a focus on relaxed shoulders and smooth, comfortable breathing. One strategy might be to walk through all the run aid stations to consume fluids and give yourself a break. A few seconds of walking will not extend your race time very much. At the end of the run, be sure to smile when crossing the finish line. You made it through the first of many triathlons.

# 6

# 13 WEEKS TO A HALF-IRONMAN FOR ATHLETES WITH LIMITED TIME

*I nearly went crazy in Week 5 with three days off! I was lost with nothing to do. Later in the plan I loved Mondays and Fridays, though. The last few weeks, fear, anxiety, and doubt began to creep into my psyche. After a long ride, it was difficult just to run one ten-minute mile— how could I do a half-marathon? The last couple of weeks I realized I had paid my dues, completed the miles and stayed with The Plan. Regrets? I think I could have pushed harder because I sprinted to the finish with "gas in the tank." Oh, I had some tough miles, but I tasted the fruits of my efforts . . . awesome!*

—MIKE POPLIN, USA

The scene: Your reading chair. Flip . . . flip . . . flip through the pages of a triathlon magazine. A thought-bubble floats up: "A half-Ironman . . . wow, that would be fun. Ah, one on the schedule, but it is less than three months away. Can I be ready for a race of this distance given only about 13 weeks to train and 6 to 11 training hours a week?"

Yes you can! The plan in this chapter prepares a seasoned triathlete to complete a half-Ironman event, while minimizing training. Speed is not an issue; rather, minimizing training hours and injury risk and increasing the odds of having fun are key.

## PROFILE

You are an experienced triathlete and have completed sprint- and Olympic-distance races. Either by choice or circumstance, you have only 13 weeks to train for a half-Ironman. Before beginning this plan, you are capable of swimming three times per week for around an hour. Holding a 1:45–2:00 pace per 100 meters for the 1.2-mile swim seems possible (total swim time of 38 to 43 minutes). You are currently able to bike comfortably for an hour and a half or so. You average from 15 to 18 mph for 56 miles (total bike time between 3:07 and 3:45). Your long run is currently around 1:15 and a half-marathon pace of 10- to 11-minute miles is not unreasonable for you (total run time between 2:07 and 2:30). Up to this point, you have been training around six to nine hours each week, which is very comfortable.

Your typical training week needs to be fairly light during the week, due to a long list of commitments; however, weekends are open for long training hours. At least one day each week must be a rest day with no training, as this keeps you healthy and in good spirits.

## GOAL

Complete a half-Ironman race in six to seven hours. If necessary, you are willing to walk to keep healthy and comfortable.

## THE PLAN

Table 6.1 is a 13-week plan to get you ready for the half-Ironman, while mini-mizing injury risk and training hours. When looking at the first week of the training plan, you should be thinking, "Wow, that is too easy." On the other hand, if you are thinking the first week will be a struggle, more training time is necessary before embarking on this journey. With that said, let's take a broad look at the plan.

Weekly training hours have a pattern of building for three weeks, then reducing for a week or two. This pattern allows the body to be stressed, to prepare for the event, and to rest, making physical repairs and gains. Don't be tempted to increase training hours during any rest week, no matter how good you feel. Notice the weekly volume pattern does not change much from Weeks 1 to 3 and Weeks 9 to 11. The change is a volume shift to the two weekend days. By Week 11, the Saturday and Sunday combined training hours equal seven—about the total estimated finish time for the event. Overall intensity begins in heart rate Zones 1 to 2 and builds to Zone 3 for all three sports.

Swimming time stays between 0:45 and 1:00. If you have the time and energy, Saturday swims can be up to 1:15. The weekend long bike ride builds from 1:30 to 4:00, and the long run builds to 2 hours.

For all three sports, training and racing will stay well below lactate threshold heart rate—the heart rate typically held for Olympic-distance races. It will be desirable to minimize the time spent in Zones 4 and higher during the half-Ironman race. (Tip: Try not to choose a hilly course for your first event.)

The coded workout descriptions for cycling and running are in Chapters 20 and 21. If the plan calls for a cycling or running "form" workout, use your choice of any of the form or speed drills. For swimming, a form workout includes several drills during the warm-up and a focus on good form throughout the session. Speed is less important than good technique.

Some of the workouts within Table 6.1 need a bit more instruction, specifically on swimming workouts and the bricks.

## SWIM

*Weeks 1 to 4: Include at least one 800- to 1,000-meter steady swim or a broken set with rest intervals no greater than 10 seconds. On Saturdays, make the main set of the swim workout 1,000 to 1,500 meters.*

*Weeks 5 to 8: Include at least one 800- to 1,000-meter steady swim (or a broken swim with rest intervals no greater than 10 seconds), rest two to three minutes, and immediately swim another 400 to 600 meters. On Saturdays, make the main set of the swim workout in the 1,500 to 2,000 meters.*

*Weeks 9 to 11: Include at least one steady swim set, with minimal rest of 60 seconds or less, totaling 30 to 40 minutes. On Saturdays, make the main set of the swim workout 2,000 meters.*

## TABLE 6.1: 13 WEEKS TO A HALF-IRONMAN FOR ATHLETES

| Week | Sport | Mon. Time | Tues. Time | Tues. Code | Wed. Time | Wed. Code | Thurs. Time | Thurs. Code |
|---|---|---|---|---|---|---|---|---|
| 1 | Swim | Day off | 00:45 | Form | | | 01:00 | E3 |
| | Bike | | | | 01:00 | Form | | |
| | Run | | 00:30 | E2 | | | 00:30 | Form |
| 2 | Swim | Day off | 00:45 | Form | | | 01:00 | E3 |
| | Bike | | | | 01:00 | Form | | |
| | Run | | 00:30 | E2 | | | 00:45 | Form |
| 3 | Swim | Day off | 00:45 | Form | | | 01:00 | E3 |
| | Bike | | | | 01:00 | Form | | |
| | Run | | 00:45 | E2 | | | 01:00 | Form |
| 4 | Brick | | | | | | | |
| | Swim | Day off | 00:45 | Form | | | 00:45 | E3 |
| | Bike | | | | | | 00:30 | Form |
| | Run | | 00:30 | E2 | 00:30 | Form | | |
| 5 | Swim | Day off | 00:45 | Form | Day off | | 00:30 | E1 |
| | Bike | | | | | | 01:00 | Form |
| | Run | | 00:30 | E2 | | | | |
| 6 | Swim | Day off | 00:45 | Form | | | 01:00 | E3 |
| | Bike | | | | 01:00 | Form | | |
| | Run | | | | | | 00:45 | Form |
| 7 | Swim | Day off | 00:45 | Form | | | 01:00 | E3 |
| | Bike | | | | 01:00 | Form | | |
| | Run | | 00:15 | E2 | | | 01:00 | Form |
| 8 | Brick | | | | | | | |
| | Swim | Day off | 00:45 | Form | | | 01:00 | E3 |
| | Bike | | | | | | | |
| | Run | | | | 01:00 | E2 | | |
| 9 | Brick | | | | | | 01:00 | |
| | Swim | Day off | 00:45 | Form | | | | |
| | Bike | | 00:30 | E1 | | | 00:30 | E2 |
| | Run | | | | 00:15 | E1 | 00:30 | E2 |
| 10 | Swim | Day off | 00:45 | Form | | | 01:00 | E2 |
| | Bike | | | | 01:00 | E2 | | |
| | Run | | | | | | 00:30 | E2 |
| 11 | Swim | Day off | 00:45 | E2 | | | 00:30 | E1 |
| | Bike | | | | 01:00 | Form | | |
| | Run | | 00:30 | E1 | | | 00:45 | Form |
| 12 | Brick | | | | | | | |
| | Swim | Day off | 00:45 | Form | | | 01:00 | E3 |
| | Bike | | | | 01:00 | Form | | |
| | Run | | | | | | | |
| 13 | Brick | | | | | | | |
| | Swim | Day off | | | | | 00:30 | Form |
| | Bike | | | | 00:45 | Form | | |
| | Run | | 00:30 | Form | | | | |

## WITH LIMITED TIME

| Fri. Time | Fri. Code | Sat. Time | Sat. Code | Sun. Time | Sun. Code | Weekly Training Hours | Weekly Hours by Sport | |
|---|---|---|---|---|---|---|---|---|
| 01:00 | E2 | | | | | | Swim | 02:45 |
| 00:45 | E1 | 01:30 | E2 | | | | Bike | 03:15 |
| | | | | 01:00 | E2 | 08:00 | Run | 02:00 |
| | | 01:00 | E2 | | | | Swim | 02:45 |
| 01:00 | E1 | 02:00 | E2 | | | | Bike | 04:00 |
| | | | | 01:15 | E2 | 09:15 | Run | 02:30 |
| | | 01:00 | E2 | | | | Swim | 02:45 |
| 01:00 | E1 | 02:15 | E2 | | | | Bike | 04:15 |
| | | | | 01:15 | E2 | 10:00 | Run | 03:00 |
| | | 02:00 | Text | | | | Swim | 01:30 |
| | | | | Day off | | | Bike | 03:00 |
| 01:00 | E1 | 01:30 | Text | | | | | |
| | | 00:30 | Text | | | 06:00 | Run | 01:30 |
| Day off | | 01:00 | E2 | | | | Swim | 02:15 |
| | | 02:30 | E2 | | | | Bike | 03:30 |
| | | | | 01:30 | E3 | 07:45 | Run | 02:00 |
| Day off | | 01:00 | E2 | | | | Swim | 02:45 |
| | | 03:00 | E3 | | | | Bike | 04:00 |
| | | | | 01:30 | E2 | 09:00 | Run | 02:15 |
| Day off | | 01:00 | E2 | | | | Swim | 02:45 |
| | | 03:15 | E2 | | | | Bike | 04:15 |
| | | | | 01:45 | E3 | 10:00 | Run | 03:00 |
| | | 02:15 | | | | | Swim | 01:45 |
| | | | | Day off | | | Bike | 02:30 |
| 01:00 | E1 | 01:30 | Form | | | | | |
| | | 00:45 | Form | | | 06:00 | Run | 01:45 |
| Day off | | 01:00 | E3 | | | | Swim | 01:45 |
| | | 03:15 | E2 | | | | Bike | 04:15 |
| | | | | 01:45 | E2 | 08:30 | Run | 02:30 |
| Day off | | 01:00 | E3 | | | | Swim | 02:45 |
| | | 03:30 | E3 | | | | Bike | 04:30 |
| | | | | 02:00 | E3 | 09:45 | Run | 02:30 |
| Day off | | 01:00 | Form | | | | Swim | 02:15 |
| | | 04:00 | E2 | | | | Bike | 05:00 |
| | | | | 02:00 | E2 | 10:30 | Run | 03:15 |
| | | 01:30 | Text | | | | Swim | 01:45 |
| | | 01:00 | Text | 00:45 | E1 | | Bike | 02:45 |
| 01:00 | E2 | 00:30 | Text | | | 06:00 | Run | 01:30 |
| | | 00:30 | | Race! | | | | |
| Day off | | | | 6–7 | | | Swim | 00:30 |
| | | 00:20 | E2 | hours | Race! | | Bike | 01:05 |
| | | 00:10 | E2 | | | 02:15 | Run | 00:40 |

## BRICKS

The total brick workout time is shown in the top row of any week containing a brick. The breakdown of the brick is shown in the bike and run row details.

*Week 4:* *Bike for 90 minutes, with the first 60 minutes in Zones 1 to 2 and the last 30 minutes all in Zone 3. Go right into the run, allowing heart rate to be anywhere in Zones 1 to 3. If you feel great, spend more time in Zone 3.*

*Week 12:* *Ride the bike for an hour, with the first 40 minutes in Zones 1 to 2 and the last 20 minutes all in Zone 3. Go right into the 30-minute run, with the first 15 minutes in Zones 1 to 2 and the last 15 minutes all in Zone 3.*

## MODIFYING THE PLAN

**Q:** There is a great group ride on Wednesday night. They typically ride 1:15 to 1:30, and blazing fast. Can this ride be included in the plan?

**A:** If you have the time and energy to complete the longer ride, it will work. My concern is "blazing fast." Allowing others to dictate your training usually leads to illness, injury, or failure to meet personal goals.

**Q:** I would like to ride a bit on Friday. Will that ruin the plan?

**A:** A ride of 30 to 60 minutes (E1, E2, or form) will be fine.

**Q:** I have more running fitness than the plan shows. Can I add more time?

**A:** Adding around 15 minutes to each week of Weeks 1 to 7 is fine. It is not necessary to run over 2 hours.

**Q:** What is the shortest that my long run can be?

**A:** A long run of about 1 hour, 30 minutes will be enough to get most people comfortably through the event.

**Q:** I'm currently strength training. Can I continue my lifting routine?

**A:** Yes, you can continue to strength train; however, make sure that the weight room doesn't leave your legs feeling sore and heavy. Also, see the strength training guidelines described in Chapter 22 for a good reference.

(Note that the Q and A section in Chapter 7 may be helpful as well.)

## RACE DAY

As you progress through the training plan, remember to refuel and keep hydrated as described in Chapter 3. Rest, recovery, and refueling go a long way to keeping you on track to reach the goal.

On race day, wear a heart rate monitor and stay mostly in Zones 1 to 3. One of the biggest mistakes triathletes make when they step up to a longer race distance is beginning the event at an Olympic-distance pace. Relax and control your speed during the swim and bike. Be willing to take walking bouts during long training runs, as well as during the race.

Practice using the rate of perceived exertion (RPE), in addition to the heart rate monitor, as a guide for pace during training. This will be helpful in the event of a heart rate monitor malfunction. Another trick is to imagine anything that might go amiss during the race and plan strategies to solve problems before race day. These mental tools will help you be cool, calm, and relaxed on race day. Enjoy!

# 7

# 13 WEEKS TO AN IRONMAN FOR ATHLETES WITH LIMITED TIME

*In an Ironman race I got a flat tire 15 miles into the bike after having a good swim and feeling great to boot. I was all thumbs trying to change the tire and ran into problems. I lost almost an hour. My race goals out the window, I started feeling sorry for myself. Then, I had a thought—find Norton Davey, the 81-year-old Ironman, and keep him company on his run. I found Norton and had one of the best experiences of my life, keeping him company during his marathon. I was thrilled to be able to run, walk, and talk with this legend.*

—TOM MANZI, USA

The training plan in this chapter garnered more reader response than any other training plan I've written. After reading stories in magazines about weeks with 20-plus hours of training to compete in an Ironman-distance event, athletes would give up on the idea because 20 hours of training is like a second job. Athletes like Brian Dowling followed the training plan in this chapter and had great success. Their success stories spread, and the myth that you can't do an Ironman on less than 20 hours of training each week died. If you want to cross the finish line of an Ironman without giving up your life, read on.

So, been racing a while, have you? Doing the same races year after year? Looking for a new challenge? You would like to do an Ironman, but jeeeeeez, there is just too much training involved. Or is there?

If you are contemplating an Ironman-distance race, do not have much time, and simply want to complete the event without illness or injury (your world-record performance comes next year), this chapter is for you. It is certainly not for beginner athletes, but it is for newcomers to the Ironman distance. The plan is a 13-week training plan that culminates in completing your first Ironman race in about 12 to 14 hours. Since you do not have much time to train, the largest training week will be about 13 hours; other weeks are less.

## PROFILE

You are an experienced triathlete. You have completed sprint- and Olympic-distance races. Life, however, has your schedule in a stranglehold and training time is at a premium. Before beginning this plan, you are capable of swimming three times a week for around an hour. You estimate you could hold a 1:45–2:00 pace per 100 meters for the 2.4-mile swim (total swim time of 1:14 to 1:25). You are currently able to cycle comfortably for an hour and a half or so. It is possible you average from 15 to 18 mph for 112 miles (total bike time between 6:15 and 7:30). Your long run is currently in the 1:15 to 1:30 range. You think a marathon pace of 10- to 11-minute miles is possible (total run time between 4:15 and 5:00). Up to this point, you have been training around 8 to 10 hours each week, which is very comfortable.

Your typical training week is fairly light during the week, due to a long list of commitments; however, weekends are open for long training hours. You need at least one day totally off from training each week, because it keeps you healthy and in good spirits.

## GOAL

Your goal is to complete an Ironman-distance race in 12 to 14 hours. If necessary, you are willing to walk to comfortably complete the race. What this means is that even if you are on the top end, estimating your finish time at 14 hours, there is still a 3-hour buffer in order to complete the race under the 17-hour cutoff imposed by many races.

## THE PLAN

Table 7.1 is a 13-week plan to get you ready for your first Ironman while minimizing injury and training hours. When looking at the first week of the training plan, you should be thinking, "Wow, that's too easy." On the other hand, if you are thinking the first week will be a struggle, more training time is necessary before embarking on this journey.

With that said, let's look at the plan in general. Notice that the Saturday and Sunday training hours build throughout the 13 weeks. Weekend cycling begins at 1:30 and builds to 5:00 two weeks prior to the race. The long run begins at 1:30 and builds to 3:00 in Week 11. Swimming begins at 1:00 and builds to 1:30—not as much growth as cycling and running.

In the first four weeks of the plan, midweek workouts and weekend workouts increase to build overall endurance. Intensity stays fairly low. In the second four weeks of the plan, the weekend volume continues to grow, not missing a beat after the rest week, Week 4. Because weekend workouts will be the main focus, there are more days of rest during Weeks 5, 6, and 7 to allow for recovery. By the end of Week 7, you'll train a total of 8 hours over the two weekend days.

The weekend training continues to build to about 9.5 hours by the end of Week 11. The long run on Sunday of Week 11 will be your last long workout before reducing training volume and resting. Weeks 12 and 13 are designed to allow you to recover and fill your muscles full of glycogen. Short workouts with short accelerations are designed to keep arms and legs feeling fresh. Do not be tempted to increase training volume during Weeks 12 and 13.

For all three sports, you should stay well below lactate threshold heart rate—the heart rate you have held for Olympic-distance races. Being an experienced Olympic-distance racer, you know you've produced heart rates in Zones 4 and low 5 during training and races. You will want to avoid those zones during your Ironman race. (Tip: Try not to choose a hilly course for your first event.)

## TABLE 7.1: 13 WEEKS TO AN IRONMAN FOR ATHLETES

| Week | Sport | Mon. Time | Tues. Time | Tues. Code | Wed. Time | Wed. Code | Thurs. Time | Thurs. Code |
|---|---|---|---|---|---|---|---|---|
| 1 | Swim | Day off | 01:00 | Form | | | 01:00 | E3 |
| | Bike | | | | 01:00 | Form | | |
| | Run | | 00:30 | E2 | | | 00:30 | Form |
| 2 | Swim | Day off | 01:00 | Form | | | 01:15 | E3 |
| | Bike | | | | 01:15 | Form | | |
| | Run | | 00:30 | E2 | | | 00:45 | Form |
| 3 | Swim | Day off | 01:15 | Form | | | 01:15 | E3 |
| | Bike | | | | 01:30 | Form | | |
| | Run | | 00:45 | E2 | | | 01:00 | Form |
| 4 | Brick | | | | | | | |
| | Swim | Day off | 00:45 | Form | | | 01:00 | E3 |
| | Bike | | | | | | 00:30 | Form |
| | Run | | 00:30 | E2 | 00:30 | Form | | |
| 5 | Swim | Day off | 01:00 | Form | Day off | | 00:30 | E1 |
| | Bike | | | | | | 01:00 | Form |
| | Run | | 00:30 | E2 | | | | |
| 6 | Swim | Day off | 01:00 | Form | | | 01:00 | E3 |
| | Bike | | | | 01:15 | Form | | |
| | Run | | | | | | 00:45 | Form |
| 7 | Swim | Day off | 01:00 | Form | | | 01:00 | E3 |
| | Bike | | | | 01:15 | Form | | |
| | Run | | 00:15 | E2 | | | 01:00 | Form |
| 8 | Brick | | | | | | | |
| | Swim | Day off | 01:00 | Form | | | 01:00 | E3 |
| | Bike | | | | | | | |
| | Run | | | | 01:00 | E2 | | |
| 9 | Brick | | | | | | 01:00 | |
| | Swim | Day off | 01:00 | Form | | | | |
| | Bike | | 00:30 | E1 | | | 00:30 | E2 |
| | Run | | | | 00:15 | E1 | 00:30 | E2 |
| 10 | Swim | Day off | 01:00 | Form | | | 01:00 | E2 |
| | Bike | | | | 01:00 | E2 | | |
| | Run | | | | | | 00:30 | E2 |
| 11 | Swim | Day off | 01:00 | E2 | | | 00:30 | E1 |
| | Bike | | | | 01:00 | Form | | |
| | Run | | 00:30 | E1 | | | 00:45 | Form |
| 12 | Brick | | | | | | | |
| | Swim | Day off | 01:00 | Form | | | 01:00 | E3 |
| | Bike | | | | 01:00 | Form | | |
| | Run | | | | | | | |
| 13 | Brick | | | | | | | |
| | Swim | Day off | | | | | 00:30 | Form |
| | Bike | | | | 00:45 | Form | | |
| | Run | | 00:30 | Form | | | | |

## WITH LIMITED TIME

| Fri. Time | Fri. Code | Sat. Time | Sat. Code | Sun. Time | Sun. Code | Weekly Training Hours | Weekly Hours by Sport | |
|---|---|---|---|---|---|---|---|---|
| | | 01:00 | E2 | | | | Swim | 03:00 |
| 00:45 | E1 | 01:30 | E2 | | | | Bike | 03:15 |
| | | | | 01:30 | E2 | 08:45 | Run | 02:30 |
| | | 01:15 | E2 | | | | Swim | 03:30 |
| 01:00 | E1 | 02:00 | E2 | | | | Bike | 04:15 |
| | | | | 01:45 | E2 | 10:45 | Run | 03:00 |
| | | 01:15 | E2 | | | | Swim | 03:45 |
| 00:30 | E1 | 02:30 | E2 | | | | Bike | 04:30 |
| | | | | 02:00 | E2 | 12:00 | Run | 03:45 |
| | | 02:00 | Text | | | | | |
| | | | | Day off | | | Swim | 01:30 |
| 01:00 | E1 | 01:30 | Text | | | | Bike | 03:00 |
| | | 00:30 | Text | | | 06:00 | Run | 01:30 |
| Day off | | 01:15 | E2 | | | | Swim | 02:45 |
| | | 03:00 | E2 | | | | Bike | 04:00 |
| | | | | 02:15 | E3 | 09:30 | Run | 02:45 |
| Day off | | 01:15 | E2 | | | | Swim | 03:15 |
| | | 03:30 | E3 | | | | Bike | 04:45 |
| | | | | 02:30 | E2 | 11:15 | Run | 03:15 |
| Day off | | 01:15 | E2 | | | | Swim | 03:00 |
| | | 04:00 | E2 | | | | Bike | 05:15 |
| | | | | 02:45 | E3 | 12:15 | Run | 04:00 |
| | | 02:15 | | | | | | |
| | | | | Day off | | | Swim | 02:00 |
| 01:00 | E1 | 01:30 | Form | | | | Bike | 02:30 |
| | | 00:45 | Form | | | 06:15 | Run | 01:45 |
| Day off | | 01:00 | E3 | | | | Swim | 02:00 |
| | | 04:00 | E2 | | | | Bike | 05:00 |
| | | | | 02:15 | E2 | 10:00 | Run | 03:00 |
| Day off | | 01:30 | E3 | | | | Swim | 03:30 |
| | | 04:30 | E3 | | | | Bike | 05:30 |
| | | | | 02:30 | E3 | 12:00 | Run | 03:00 |
| Day off | | 01:30 | Form | | | | Swim | 03:00 |
| | | 05:00 | E2 | | | | Bike | 06:00 |
| | | | | 03:00 | E2 | 13:15 | Run | 04:15 |
| | | 01:30 | Text | | | | | |
| | | | | | | | Swim | 02:00 |
| | | 01:00 | Text | 00:45 | E1 | | Bike | 02:45 |
| 01:00 | E2 | 00:30 | Text | | | 06:15 | Run | 01:30 |
| | | 00:30 | | Race! | | | | |
| Day off | | | | 12–14 | | | Swim | 00:30 |
| | | 00:20 | E2 | hours | Race! | | Bike | 01:05 |
| | | 00:10 | E2 | | | 02:15 | Run | 00:40 |

You'll find the coded workout descriptions in Chapters 19, 20, and 21. Some of the workouts within Table 7.1 need more detailed instructions, specifically the swimming and the bricks. Those descriptions follow.

## SWIM

Use Chapter 19 to plan your daily workouts according to the codes provided. The guidelines are specific to Ironman training. If you need or would like more options for swim workouts, consider using the waterproof workouts *Workouts in a Binder®: Swim Workouts for Triathletes* (VeloPress). You can use this handy waterproof booklet right on the pool deck.

*Weeks 1 to 4: Include at least one 1,000-meter steady swim or a 1,000-meter broken set with rest intervals no greater than 10 seconds. On Saturdays, make the main set of the swim workout in the 1,000- to 1,500-meter range.*

*Weeks 5 to 8: Include at least one 1,650-meter steady swim (or a 1,000-meter broken set with rest intervals no greater than 10 seconds), rest 2 to 3 minutes, and immediately swim another 500 to 800 meters. On Saturdays, make the main set of the swim workout in the 1,500- to 2,500-meter range.*

*Weeks 9 to 11: Include at least one steady swim set, with minimal rest of 60 seconds or less, totaling 45 to 60 minutes. On Saturdays, make the main set of the swim workout in the 2,000- to 3,000-meter range.*

## BRICKS

The total brick workout time is shown in the top row of any week containing a brick. The breakdown of the brick is shown in the bike and run row details.

*Week 4: Ride your bike for 1:30, with the first 60 minutes in Zones 1 to 2 and the last 30 minutes all in Zone 3. Go right to the run, allowing heart rate to be anywhere in Zones 1 to 3. If you feel great, spend more time in Zone 3.*

*Week 12: Ride the bike for 1 hour, with the first 40 minutes in Zones 1 to 2 and the last 20 minutes all in Zone 3. Go right into the 30-minute run, with the first 15 minutes in Zones 1 to 2 and the last 15 minutes all in Zone 3.*

## MODIFYING THE PLAN

Q: If I find I'm getting tired, what can I do to make some modifications without killing the plan?

A: It is okay to:

- *Totally skip an E1 workout and rest instead.*
- *Reduce the Saturday bike ride by up to 30 minutes or reduce the Sunday run by 15 minutes.*
- *Do an entire E2 workout with your heart rate in Zone 1.*

Q: What is the absolute minimum number of hours I can do and still complete the Ironman race?

A: There is no standard answer for this. The plan shown here, along with the modifiers already suggested, is along the lines of a minimal plan already. The answer really depends on each individual athlete. The more you cut training hours, the longer and more torturous the race will be and the greater the risk of injury.

Q: Can I do some Zone 3 intervals [M2 (3Z)] on an E3 day?

A: Yes, try to keep the work-to-rest ratio at 3:1 or 4:1 and slowly build up the Zone 3 work time, beginning at about 20 minutes total.

Q: What will happen to me if I get into a Zone 4 heart rate during training and racing? Will I flame out and die?

A: The plan is intended to keep you burning fuel at a mostly aerobic rate. During training, you are trying to teach the body to be an efficient fat-burning machine. When getting into the heart-rate zones near lactate threshold, the body shifts to using more glycogen as a fuel—as opposed to a greater percentage of fat and oxygen. At the same time, short bouts into Zone 4 will not send you into flame-out status. Although a heart rate monitor is a good tool, it is not an absolutely precise measure of the percentage of aerobic metabolism and anaerobic metabolism that is fueling your body. A few beats either side of the zones should not be a problem.

**Q:** I have more bike fitness than the plan shows. Can I increase the bike time?

**A:** Yes, you can modify all weeks and build the longest ride to about 6 hours if you have the time.

## RACE DAY

As you progress through the training plan, remember to refuel and keep hydrated as described in Chapter 3. Rest, recovery, and refueling will go a long way toward keeping you on track to reach your goal.

On race day, wear your heart rate monitor and stay in Zones 1 to 3. One of the biggest mistakes beginning Ironman racers make is starting the event at an Olympic-distance pace. Relax, control your speed, and be willing to take walking bouts during long training runs and the race. If your heart rate monitor malfunctions, use RPE as your guide for pacing. Most of all, look around, have fun, and enjoy your incredible fitness!

# PART III

# Duathlon, XTERRA, and General Multisport Training

The plans in Part III are designed for duathlon, XTERRA, or other off-road events and general multisport fitness. The duathlon plans help single-sport athletes make the move from one to two sports. Both the cyclist to duathlete and runner to duathlete plans are 10 weeks long.

The mountain bike triathlon plan is 12 weeks long and includes workouts to specifically address the demands of racing off-road for approximately two hours. If your race takes longer, there are recommendations for modifying the plan.

Finally, there is a multisport fitness plan in this part of the book. This plan is longer than the other plans in this part, coming in at 24 weeks. The plan helps an athlete who enjoys participation in sports other than swimming, cycling, and running to blend triathlon sport fitness with other sports. "Other" sport examples are basketball, softball, soccer, racquetball, and tennis, to name a few.

# 8

# CYCLIST TO DUATHLETE

*My training consisted of hard training almost all the time. I can re-member riding with another racer and commenting about a "good hard ride"—that was the norm for me. Whenever I rode, I was al-ways in Zones 3, 4, or 5—never in Zones 1 or 2. Now training in the lower zones makes all the sense in the world. It's a building-block ap-proach to training and racing. To train smart, it's the relative quality that counts, not how hard you are always riding.*

—JEFF FRYER, USA

Many athletes arrive at multisport from a single-sport background. Without planning, a first duathlon—run, bike, run—can be frustrat-ing. Typically, the move to duathlon for a cyclist is more difficult than for a runner. I know a cyclist (not Jeff Fryer) who showed up on race day with no previous run training. "After all," he said, "everyone knows how to run and I have loads of fitness from cycling. How hard can this possibly be?"

He began the first run in his domestic-chore shoes and felt pretty cocky. Not a great finish, but he didn't clock a snail's pace either. He jumped on his noble steed and passed countless people on the bike—time trialing was his strength. "Man, this multisport stuff is great and easy! I am going to place for sure; I'm hot today," he said.

In the second transition, his trusty grass-stained shoes awaited that sec-ond run. Oh, that second run. The Tin Man from Oz could have moved faster out of the transition area and would likely have had better form as well.

"What the heck happened?" he wondered. His legs seemed filled with cement and his shins were killing him. "It seemed like such an easy transition to make—from cyclist to duathlete."

Making the transition from training for one sport to training for two can be easier with a little planning. The plan in this chapter is for a cyclist preparing for a first duathlon. Tips on transitioning are in the sidebar "Key Points—Cyclist to Duathlete."

## PROFILE

This plan is for a person who is primarily a cyclist who wants to try something new this season—a duathlon. This athlete has a good base in cycling and currently trains around six hours per week.

## GOAL

At the end of 10 weeks, complete a duathlon consisting of a 5K run, a 30K bike, and a second 5K run.

## THE PLAN

Table 8.1 is a 10-week plan that transforms a cyclist into a duathlete. The plan minimizes risk by slowly building total weekly run time from 30 minutes to a maximum of 1 hour, 20 minutes. Daily run time builds from 5 minutes (yes, run only 5 minutes on the first day) to between 45 and 60 minutes. In general, the run training contains less intensity than the bike training does.

The coded workout descriptions in the plan (such as E1, M5, and so on) are fully explaained in Chapters 20 and 21. Some more specific instruction for various workouts follows in the remaining paragraphs of this chapter.

On Tuesday of the first week of the plan, run for 5 minutes and immediately jump on the bike for an hour ride. Wednesday of that week is

> ## Key Points—Cyclist to Duathlete
>
> - Invest in a good pair of running shoes to decrease injury risk.
> - The early weeks of short runs immediately followed by a bike (combination or "combo" workouts) help in transition training.
> - The long run is slowly built to around one hour.
> - There is room in the plan for three bricks (a bike ride immediately followed by a run). Use these workouts to practice smooth and speedy transitions.
> - Race simulation days allow you to work the bugs out of the transitions and get the feel of the event.

a form workout, cycling only. All Wednesday bike rides can last from 45 to 60 minutes.

Thursday of the first week is a 10-minute run, immediately followed by a 1-hour bike. This particular ride has a short tempo section. Friday is a day off and Saturday is again a run immediately followed by a bike ride. The run-to-bike workouts, combination or "combo" workouts, have you run when your legs are fresh, allowing overall training endurance to be maintained, and they are early practice for the first transition.

The Sunday bike ride assumes you have been comfortably riding a hilly course in previous weeks. If this is not the case, reduce the intensity of these rides.

Week 2 is very similar to Week 1, only the run time builds and a Friday workout is added. The Friday ride can be 45 to 60 minutes, although 60 minutes is typically shown on the plan. On Thursday's combo workout, the 15-minute tempo segment should be in the last 25 minutes of the ride.

Up to Week 4, all combination workouts are run-to-bike workouts. On Thursday of Week 4, you will do your first "brick"—a workout in which the bike ride is immediately followed by the run. All combo workouts remain

| Week | Sport | Mon. Time | Tues. Time | Tues. Code | Wed. Time | Wed. Code | Thurs. Time | Thurs. Code |
|---|---|---|---|---|---|---|---|---|
| **TABLE 8.1: CYCLIST TO DUATHLETE PLAN** | | | | | | | | |
| 1 | | Day off | | | | | | |
| | Run | | 00:05 | E1 | | | 00:10 | E1 |
| | Bike | | 01:00 | E2 | 00:45 | S3 (4–6) | 01:00 | M1 (15) |
| 2 | | Day off | | | | | | |
| | Run | | 00:10 | E1 | | | 00:15 | E1 |
| | Bike | | 00:45 | E2 | 00:45 | S3 (4–6) | 00:40 | M1 (15) |
| 3 | | Day off | | | | | | |
| | Run | | 00:15 | E1 | | | 00:20 | E1 |
| | Bike | | 00:40 | E2 | 00:45 | S3 (4–6) | 00:35 | M1 (20) |
| 4 | | Day off | | | Day off | | Brick | |
| | Run | | 00:10 | E1 | | | 00:10 | E1 |
| | Bike | | 00:45 | E2 | | | 00:45 | E2 |
| 5 | | Day off | | | | | | |
| | Run | | 00:15 | E1 | | | 00:15 | E2 |
| | Bike | | 00:30 | E2 | 01:00 | S3 (4–6) | 00:45 | M5 (15) |
| 6 | | Day off | | | | | Brick | |
| | Run | | 00:20 | E1 | | | 00:20 | E2 |
| | Bike | | 00:30 | E2 | 01:00 | S3 (4–6) | 00:45 | M5 (20) |
| 7 | | Day off | | | | | | |
| | Run | | 00:15 | E1 | | | 00:30 | S2 |
| | Bike | | 00:30 | E2 | 01:00 | S3 (4–6) | 00:45 | M5 (20) |
| 8 | | Day off | | | Day off | | | |
| | Run | | 00:15 | E1 | | | 00:15 | E1 |
| | Bike | | 00:45 | E2 | | | 00:45 | S4 |
| 9 | | Day off | | | | | | |
| | Run | | 00:20 | E1 | | | 00:20 | S2 |
| | Bike | | 00:30 | E2 | 01:00 | E2 | 00:30 | S4 |
| 10 | | Day off | | | Day off | | | |
| | Run | | 00:10 | E1 | | | 00:10 | E1 |
| | Bike | | 00:50 | E2 | | | 00:50 | S4 |

run-to-bike sequences, unless "brick" is specifically shown for that day, such as in Week 6 and Week 8. The last workout in Week 4 is a time trial. After a good warm-up, ride as fast as possible and record the time for a distance between 5 and 8 miles. This time can be used later in training to benchmark improvements.

| Fri. Time | Fri. Code | Sat. Time | Sat. Code | Sun. Time | Sun. Code | Weekly Training Hours | Weekly Hours by Sport | |
|-----------|-----------|-----------|-----------|-----------|-----------|----------------------|-----|-----|
| Day off | | | | | | | | |
| | | 00:15 | E1 | | | | Run | 00:30 |
| | | 01:00 | E2 | 02:00 | E3 | 06:15 | Bike | 05:45 |
| | | | | | | | | |
| | | 00:20 | E1 | | | | Run | 00:45 |
| 01:00 | E2 | 00:35 | E2 | 02:00 | E3 | 06:30 | Bike | 05:45 |
| | | | | | | | | |
| | | 00:25 | E2 | | | | Run | 01:00 |
| 01:00 | E2 | 00:30 | E2 | 02:00 | E3 | 06:30 | Bike | 05:30 |
| | | | | | | | | |
| | | 00:30 | E2 | | | | Run | 00:50 |
| 00:45 | S3 (4–6) | | | 01:00 | T2 | 04:05 | Bike | 03:15 |
| | | | | | | | | |
| | | 00:35 | E2 | | | | Run | 01:05 |
| 01:00 | E2 | | | 02:00 | E4 | 06:20 | Bike | 05:15 |
| | | | | | | | | |
| | | 00:45 | E3 | | | | Run | 01:25 |
| 01:00 | E2 | | | 02:00 | E4 | 06:40 | Bike | 05:15 |
| | | | | | | | | |
| | | 00:45 | E2 | | | | Run | 01:30 |
| 01:00 | E2 | | | 02:00 | E4 | 06:45 | Bike | 05:15 |
| | | Day off | | | Brick | | | |
| | | | | 00:20 | E3 | | Run | 00:50 |
| 01:00 | E2 | | | 01:00 | M5 (20) | 04:20 | Bike | 03:30 |
| Day off | | | | | Race sim. | | | |
| | | | | 00:40 | Split | | Run | 01:20 |
| | | 01:30 | E2 | 00:40 | M5 (15) | 05:30 | Bike | 04:10 |
| Day off | | | | Race! | | | | |
| | | | | | | | Run | 00:20 |
| | | 00:30 | S4 | | | 02:30 | Bike | 02:10 |

Training continues along a similar pattern described for Weeks 1 to 4, up to Week 9. There is a race simulation at the end of Week 9 when your total run time is split, half before the ride and half after the ride. Begin the workout with a 20-minute E2 run. Dash into your garage (aka transition area) and hop on the bike for a 40-minute ride, including a 15-minute tempo section near the end of the ride. After the bike ride, go back into the garage to transform once again into a runner for a 20-minute E3 run. Completing this workout does a lot for your fitness and self-confidence.

Week 10 is a rest week of reduced volume to prepare you for the event. You can go into the race rested, confident, strong, and ready to compete. Good job—you are ready to go!

# 9

# RUNNER TO DUATHLETE

*You've got to let go of the idea of being only a thoroughbred runner. If you are going to be a good or great duathlete, or triathlete for that matter, you've got to ride your bike to gain strength cycling. It seems simple, but to be a good rider, you have to ride your bike. Giving up on seeing myself as that thoroughbred runner I described was a hard thing for me to do.*

—PAUL THOMAS,
WHO AT AGE 10 RAN A 10K IN 33:52
AND A MILE IN 4:55;
GOING ON TO BECOME THE U.S. NATIONAL PRO
DUATHLON CHAMPION IN 1994 AND 1999

t's like riding a bike; once you learn, you never forget." Ever heard that old saw? It is true that once you've learned how to ride, it is easy to get back on a bike, pedal, and keep the rubber side down. Riding a bike is something nearly everyone knows how to do, even runners. Runners, like their cyclist counterparts in Chapter 8, assume that participation in a duathlon will be easy. After all, they have been running for quite a while, are in good shape, and have decent endurance. Just pop a little bike ride in the middle and *voilà!*—duathlete.

Although it is frequently easier for a runner to become a duathlete than it is for a cyclist, a runner should not underestimate the transition. Rene commented on her first duathlon, "You should have seen me on that first 5K. I killed 'em. My first transition was fast and I headed out on Fred's bike." Race day was the second time she had ever ridden this bike she borrowed from someone else. She continued, "I felt pretty good on the bike, really hauling—even passed a few people! Then on the second run, my shoulders cramped, my knees were killing me, and my legs were all rubbery. It felt like I didn't know how to run. I was reduced to a pathetic walk for the second 5K and my knees were sore for a week."

Rene failed to realize that riding a bike for fun around the neighborhood and racing a bike are two different things. She underestimated the importance of proper bike fit—not only to make her a more economical rider, but to prevent injury as well. She also underestimated the need to train on the bike so her muscles would adapt to the motion necessary for cycling. The 10-week plan shown in Table 9.1 would have helped Rene prepare for her first duathlon. Is this the plan for you?

## PROFILE

Table 9.1 is a game plan for a runner to participate in a first duathlon. This athlete is currently actively training as a runner, logging some six hours of training each week and running four to five days per week. This athlete is currently doing some speed work into at least Zone 3, perhaps including an occasional 5K or 10K race in training.

## GOAL

At the end of 10 weeks, complete a duathlon consisting of a 5K run, a 30K bike, and a second 5K run.

## THE PLAN

For a runner, it would not be unusual for half of the duathlon race time

> ## Key Points—Runner to Duathlete
>
> - Train on the bike you will use in the race. This seems obvious, but many people have made last-minute switches because someone was willing to loan them a "trick" bike. All gains that might have been made by technology were lost because legs cramped from riding in a new position.
> - Have the local bike shop help you get your position correct. Many studies have shown reduced oxygen consumption at a given workload when cycling positioning was optimized. Keep in mind you need to be comfortable in any optimal aerodynamic position.
> - "Spin" in smaller gears. When riding, try to spin between 85 and 120 rpm on the flats and 65 and 80 rpm on the hills.
> - Ride a straight line. This also seems obvious, but many athletes put their head down and just hammer on the cranks. Meanwhile, they weave dangerously, wasting energy.

to be spent on the bike. One strategy is to build overall race endurance using long bike rides. This strategy is used in the model in Table 9.1, which builds endurance on the bike so that a long ride of about 1:45 is possible in Week 7. Overall weekly cycling time also builds from about 1:15 in the first week to 3:20 in Week 9. This gentle build reduces risk of injury and helps a runner be more economical on the bike. For additional tips, see the sidebar "Key Points—Runner to Duathlete." The codes used in Table 9.1 (such as E2, S4, and so on) are fully explained in Chapters 20 and 21.

Let's look at Week 1 in more detail. Monday is a day off, as are all Mondays on this plan. If it works better for you to have a different day off, go ahead and shift the schedule to accommodate your personal needs. Tuesday of Week 1 is a 30-minute E2 run. Wednesday is a 45-minute run, including 15 minutes in Zone 3. Thursday is the first combination workout, beginning with a 30-minute easy E1 run, immediately followed by a 30-minute

| Week | Sport | Mon. Time | Tues. Time | Tues. Code | Wed. Time | Wed. Code | Thurs. Time | Thurs. Code |
|---|---|---|---|---|---|---|---|---|
| **TABLE 9.1: RUNNER-TO-DUATHLETE PLAN** | | | | | | | | |
| 1 | Brick | Day off | | | | | 01:00 | |
| | Run | | 00:30 | E2 | 00:45 | M1 (15) | 00:30 | E1 |
| | Bike | | | | | | 00:30 | E1 |
| 2 | Brick | Day off | | Brick | | | 01:00 | |
| | Run | | 00:30 | E2 | 00:45 | M1 (20) | 00:30 | E1 |
| | Bike | | 00:30 | E1 | | | 00:30 | E2 |
| 3 | Brick | Day off | | Brick | | | 01:00 | |
| | Run | | 00:30 | E2 | 00:45 | M1 (20) | 00:30 | E1 |
| | Bike | | 00:30 | E1 | | | 00:30 | E2 |
| 4 | Brick | Day off | | | Day off | | 01:00 | |
| | Run | | 00:30 | E2 | | | 00:30 | E1 |
| | Bike | | | | | | 00:30 | E2 |
| 5 | Brick | Day off | | Brick | | | 01:00 | |
| | Run | | 00:30 | E2 | 00:45 | M5 (15) | 00:15 | E1 |
| | Bike | | 00:30 | E2 | | | 00:45 | S3 (4–6) |
| 6 | Brick | Day off | | Brick | | | 01:00 | |
| | Run | | 00:30 | E2 | 00:45 | M5 (20) | 00:15 | E1 |
| | Bike | | 00:45 | E2 | | | 00:45 | S3 (4–6) |
| 7 | Brick | Day off | | Brick | | | 01:00 | |
| | Run | | 00:30 | E2 | 00:45 | M5 (20) | 00:15 | E1 |
| | Bike | | 00:45 | E2 | | | 00:45 | S3 (4–6) |
| 8 | Brick | Day off | | Brick | Day off | | 01:00 | |
| | Run | | | | | | 00:30 | E1 |
| | Bike | | 00:30 | E1 | | | 00:30 | E2 |
| 9 | Brick | Day off | | Brick | | | 01:00 | |
| | Run | | 00:30 | E2 | 00:45 | M5 (20) | 00:15 | E1 |
| | Bike | | 00:45 | E2 | | | 00:45 | S3 (4–6) |
| 10 | Brick | Day off | | Brick | | | 01:00 | |
| | Run | | 00:30 | E2 | 00:30 | S2 | 00:15 | E1 |
| | Bike | | 00:30 | E1 | | | 00:30 | S4 |

easy E1 bike ride. A run immediately followed by a bike is called a "brick."

In Week 1, the Friday workout is optional and all Friday workouts will remain optional throughout the 10-week plan. If you do decide to work out, make it a 30- to 45-minute run. Saturday of Week 1 is a 45-minute E2 bike. An E3 run on Sunday finishes out Week 1. Although 1:15 is shown for the Sunday run, this long run can go up to 1:30 depending on your personal fitness.

| Fri. Time | Fri. Code | Sat. Time | Sat. Code | Sun. Time | Sun. Code | Weekly Training Hours | Weekly Hours by Sport |
|---|---|---|---|---|---|---|---|
| Day off or | | | | | | | |
| 00:30 | E2 | | | 01:15 | E3 | | Run 03:30 |
| | | 00:45 | E2 | | | 04:45 | Bike 01:15 |
| Day off or | | | | | | | |
| 00:30 | E2 | | | 01:15 | E3 | | Run 03:30 |
| | | 00:45 | E2 | | | 05:15 | Bike 01:45 |
| Day off or | | | | | | | |
| 00:30 | E2 | | | 01:15 | E3 | | Run 03:30 |
| | | 01:00 | E2 | | | 05:30 | Bike 02:00 |
| Day off | | | | | | | |
| | | | | 01:00 | TT | | Run 02:00 |
| | | 01:00 | S3 (4–6) | | | 03:30 | Bike 01:30 |
| Day off or | | | | | | | |
| 00:30 | E2 | | | 01:15 | S2 | | Run 03:15 |
| | | 01:15 | E3 | | | 05:45 | Bike 02:30 |
| Day off or | | | | | | | |
| 00:30 | E2 | | | 01:15 | S2 | | Run 03:15 |
| | | 01:30 | E3 | | | 06:15 | Bike 03:00 |
| Day off or | | | | | | | |
| 00:30 | E2 | | | 01:15 | S2 | | Run 03:15 |
| | | 01:45 | E3 | | | 06:30 | Bike 03:15 |
| Day off | | | | | | | |
| | | | | 01:20 | | | |
| | | 01:00 | S4 | 00:20 | S4 | | Run 01:50 |
| | | | | 01:00 | E3 | 03:50 | Bike 02:00 |
| | | | | Race sim. | | | |
| 00:30 | E2 | | | 00:40 | Split | | Run 02:40 |
| | | 01:10 | E2 | 00:40 | M5 (15) | 06:00 | Bike 03:20 |
| Day off | | | | | | | |
| | | | | Race! | | | |
| | | 00:10 | E2 | | | | Run 01:25 |
| | | 00:20 | E2 | | | 02:45 | Bike 01:20 |

The pattern described for Week 1 is very similar for the remaining 10-week schedule, with two exceptions described in the next paragraphs. In this particular plan, any time a bike and a run workout are shown on the same day, bike first, then run immediately after—do a brick. If you would like to practice the first transition in a duathlon, make some of the Tuesday workouts combinations of running first, then cycling ("combo" workouts).

One of the workouts needing a bit more description is the time trial at the end of Week 4. This can be a self-administered time trial at the track or a 5K race. If you decide to run at the track, run as fast as possible for 3 miles. At the track or in a race, record in a journal your splits (the time for each mile), heart rate, weather conditions, and how you felt. This time trial can serve as a benchmark for future improvements.

The only other workout that deserves special mention is the race simulation at the end of Week 9. Begin the workout with a 20-minute E2 run. Dash into your garage (aka transition area) and get your bike for a 40-minute ride, including a 15-minute tempo section near the end of the ride. After the bike ride, it's back into the garage to immediately transform to a runner for a 20-minute E3 run. A good strategy is to make this run a negative-split effort. This means you run the second half of the run faster than the first half of the run. This strategy helps to keep you from going out too fast and fading at the end of the event. This race simulation is the end of the major portion of your preparation. The few days leading up to the race are for rest. Enjoy your race day!

# 10

# XTERRA AND OTHER MOUNTAIN BIKE TRIATHLONS

*My favorite quote must be said with bloodshot, bleary eyes and dried, sleeve-smeared snot across your face. As Dave French frequently said, "I look bad, but I feel good."*

—ROB FORISTER (AKA ROCKET ROB),
TRIATHLETE AND ULTRA DISTANCE RUNNER, USA

XTERRA is the most popular off-road triathlon. It and other mountain bike multisport events continue to grow in popularity. There are many shorter events that take one to two hours to complete and the mid-distance events commonly take between two and four hours. There are also multiday stage races offering a short-stage and a long-stage option. There is nothing like a little dirt to make you feel like a 10-year-old again.

This chapter includes a 12-week plan to prepare for a single-day mountain event. Many multisport athletes heading into an off-road event don't have great mountain bike skills. If your mountain bike skills are marginal, avoid beginning with a technical course. If nontechnical is not an option, you have other choices. For example, I coached an athlete who could ride a flat 40K bike leg in a triathlon in just over an hour. He decided to do a mountain bike event. After the first course preride, he called to report the bad news: "This course is only 14 miles and it is just awful. It is rocky, technical, there are water crossings, and it took me 2.5 hours to preride it. I will be out here forever!"

After talking awhile, I discovered a couple of things. First, he considered getting off the bike a major failure. His goal on the preride was to stay on his bike over the entire course. Second, when he did get off the bike to clear a difficult obstacle, he might remount the bike only to ride a few meters and have to dismount again.

I suggested he consider viewing the bike portion of the event like a puzzle. There is nothing wrong with getting off the bike and running with it—in fact, depending on the particular obstacle, that might be the best strategy. Also, he should look ahead and decide if it is best to run 15 meters or more. The real question is, "What is the fastest way to get through the course in one piece?"

After this discussion, he had a chance to preride the course two more times prior to race day. Each time he rode the course, he reduced the amount of time and energy it took him to complete the course originally. On race day, he completed the course in less than two hours and won his age group.

## PROFILE

This plan is for an athlete who can train about an hour each weekday and a couple of hours on one day of the weekend. The second weekend day allows about an hour of training. Total training hours available each week is about seven. You are already training some in all three sports and prefer not to have a day without some type of activity. You are capable of swimming at least 20 to 30 minutes. A bike ride of two hours is not a challenge; however, you may not have expert mountain bike handling skills. An hour run is no problem.

After looking at the training zone charts in Chapter 2, you have determined that most of your training has been in Zones 1 and 2. You might have had a bit more intensity than that, but not much. Also, you would like to add some strength training to your routine but are not sure where to start—especially with only 12 weeks until race day.

## GOAL

Complete an off-road triathlon after 12 weeks of preparation. Estimated race completion time is in the neighborhood of 2 hours. The swim will take between 15 and 30 minutes, depending on your swim ability and the particular race distance. The bike portion of the race is anticipated to take around 1 hour and the run will likely take 30 to 45 minutes.

## THE PLAN

Table 10.1 shows a simplified overview of the 12-week plan. The first column lists the week number, the second column shows the month each week falls in (if you start on the first Monday in May). The exact months are not important; they are simply used as examples and could start in April for a race in June, for instance. The third column is the particular training period, from Chapter 2, for each week. Weekly training hours are in the last column and vary between 4:15 and 7:15.

The detailed plan is in Table 10.2. Monday and Wednesday are typically swim days. Bike rides are on Wednesday, Friday, and Sunday. Run days are Tuesday, Thursday, and Saturday. On the days that a run and strength training are both scheduled, run first then strength train. It is most time-efficient if the two activities can be done one after the other, but they can be split.

## SPECIFIC PREPARATION

On the first Monday of the plan, the first swim is a time trial to establish baseline fitness. In general, all Mondays not in a rest week will include fast swimming. Most of the Wednesday swims will be easy form workouts.

Saturday runs in Specific Preparation should be on a trail if possible; this is indicated with the "Trail" note on the plan. If you have not been trail running, take it easy on the first few trail runs to allow tendons and ligaments to gain strength. It also takes time for body-awareness adjustments—judging obstacles that can be jumped over or stepped on and working on overall balance.

| Week | Month | Period | Weekly Planned Hours |
|------|-------|--------|----------------------|
| 1 | May | Specific Preparation | 07:15 |
| 2 | May | Specific Preparation | 07:15 |
| 3 | May | Specific Preparation | 07:15 |
| 4 | May | Specific Preparation | 04:15 |
| 5 | May/June | Pre-competitive | 07:15 |
| 6 | June | Pre-competitive | 07:15 |
| 7 | June | Pre-competitive | 07:15 |
| 8 | June | Pre-competitive | 04:15 |
| 9 | June/July | Competitive | 07:15 |
| 10 | July | Competitive | 06:45 |
| 11 | July | Competitive | 05:45 |
| 12 | July | Competitive | 02:55 + Race |

TABLE 10.1: PLAN OVERVIEW

Sunday bike rides are also to be done off-road when indicated by "MTB" on the plan. The Friday M2 rides are best completed on the road and should include four to six sets of 4-minute intervals in Zone 3 followed by 1 minute rest intervals (or, 4–6 × 4 min., 1 min. RI). Because of the intensity of the Friday M2 ride, the Sunday ride that week will be easy and preferably on the road so you can control intensity.

The fourth week is a rest week, when volume is reduced. The running time trial scheduled for that week should be done at the track. The cycling time trial is 5 miles long and is also best done on the road, unless you would like to track technical skill improvement as well as fitness improvement. In that case, find an off-road loop approximately 3 miles long to conduct the time trial. Record all time trial results in a journal.

Instead of doing the run and bike time trials on the weekend of Week 4, another option is to do an off-road brick on Saturday and take Sunday as a day off. Make the off-road brick an hour on the mountain bike and transition right to 30 minutes of trail running. Make the first half of the time in each sport at Zone 1 to 2 intensity. Ride the second half of the time as you feel (at any intensity) and make the second half of the run in Zones 1 to 3.

Do the time trial option if you need to establish training zones or if you want indicators of your level of fitness. Consider the brick option if you have established training zones and you have fitness measurements.

# PRE-COMPETITIVE PREPARATION

Notice that the strength maintenance (SM) phase begins in Week 5. Although this plan does not follow the customary strength training progression, strength gains can be made with this modified format if you are cautious.

Go ahead and follow the instructions for SM in Chapter 22, just be conservative when increasing weight on the last set. Legs need to be fresh for running and cycling. However, some athletes are able to slowly increase the weight of that last set over the course of several weeks, making strength gains.

The first week of this period, Week 5, includes a swim time trial. Repeat the same distance covered in the first time trial. The Monday swims in Weeks 6 and 7 are faster, muscular endurance swims.

Friday of Week 5 is a road bike session, similar to the session in Week 2. This session reaches for higher speeds: 4–6 × 4 min. into Zones 4 and 5a (1 min. RI).

The Sunday ride in Week 5 should be an easy ride on the road. The Sunday rides in Weeks 6 and 7 are both off-road. Off-road running is scheduled on Saturday in Weeks 5 and 7, allowing for higher speed than in the Specific Preparation period. One interval session is scheduled for running, in Week 6. For the M2 (4 to 5aZ) run, do the following: 4–6 × 4 min. (1 min. RI). This is best done on a flat or slightly uphill course.

To complete the Pre-competitive period, rest week (Week 8) duplicates the rest in Week 4 with running and cycling time trials.

As with Week 4, you have the option to do an off-road brick on Saturday and take Sunday as a recovery day. Make the off-road brick an hour on the mountain bike and transition right to 30 minutes of trail running. For this brick, make the first half of the time in each sport at Zone 1 to 2 intensity. Ride and run the second half of the time simulating your race-pace intensities.

| Week | Sport | Mon. Time | Mon. Code | Tues. Time | Tues. Code | Wed. Time | Wed. Code | Thurs. Time |
|------|-------|-----------|-----------|------------|------------|-----------|-----------|-------------|
| | | | | | **TABLE 10.2: MOUNTAIN BIKE TRIATHLON PLAN** | | | |
| 1 | Strength | | | 00:45 | AA | | | |
| | Swim | 00:30 | T1a | | | 00:30 | E (Speed) | |
| | Bike | | | | | 00:30 | S3 (4–5) | |
| | Run | | | 00:30 | E2 | | | 00:30 |
| 2 | Strength | | | 00:45 | AA | | | |
| | Swim | 00:30 | E3 | | | 00:30 | E (Form) | |
| | Bike | | | | | 00:30 | S2 | |
| | Run | | | 00:30 | E2 | | | 00:30 |
| 3 | Strength | | | 00:45 | AA | | | |
| | Swim | 00:30 | E3 | | | 00:30 | E (Speed) | |
| | Bike | | | | | 00:30 | S3 (4–5) | |
| | Run | | | 00:30 | E2 | | | 00:30 |
| 4 | Strength | | | 00:45 | AA | | | |
| | Swim | 00:30 | E2 | | | | | |
| | Bike | | | | | 00:30 | S2 | |
| | Run | | | 00:30 | E2 | | | 00:30 |
| 5 | Strength | | | 00:30 | SM | | | |
| | Swim | 00:30 | E (Form) | | | 00:30 | T1a | |
| | Bike | | | | | 00:30 | S3 (4–5) | |
| | Run | | | 00:30 | E2 | | | 00:45 |
| 6 | Strength | | | 00:30 | SM | | | |
| | Swim | 00:30 | M | | | 00:30 | E (Speed) | |
| | Bike | | | | | 00:30 | S2 | |
| | Run | | | 00:30 | E2 | | | 00:45 |

Do the time trial option if you want an update on your fitness indicators. Consider the brick option if you do not need or want the data from the time trials.

## COMPETITIVE PREPARATION

The final four weeks heading into race day include workouts with higher speeds and decreasing volume. The pattern is similar to previous training blocks. Needing special instruction are the Thursday runs:

| Thurs. Code | Fri. Time | Fri. Code | Sat. Time | Sat. Code | Sun. Time | Sun. Code | Weekly Training Hours | Weekly Hours by Sport | |
|---|---|---|---|---|---|---|---|---|---|
| | | | | | | | | Strength | 00:45 |
| | | | | | | | | Swim | 01:00 |
| | 01:00 | E2 | | | 02:00 | MTB (E3) | | Bike | 03:30 |
| S2 | | | 01:00 | Trail (E3) | | | 07:15 | Run | 02:00 |
| | | | | | | | | Strength | 00:45 |
| | | | | | | | | Swim | 01:00 |
| | 01:00 | M2 (3Z) | | | 02:00 | R (E2) | | Bike | 03:30 |
| S2 | | | 01:00 | Trail (E3) | | | 07:15 | Run | 02:00 |
| | | | | | | | | Strength | 00:45 |
| | | | | | | | | Swim | 01:00 |
| | 01:00 | S5 | | | 02:00 | MTB (E3) | | Bike | 03:30 |
| S2 | | | 01:00 | Trail (E3) | | | 07:15 | Run | 02:00 |
| | Day off | | | | | | | Strength | 00:45 |
| | | | | | | | | Swim | 00:30 |
| | | | | | 01:00 | T2 (5) | | Bike | 01:30 |
| S2 | | | 00:30 | T1 | | | 04:15 | Run | 01:30 |
| | | | | | | | | Strength | 00:30 |
| | | | | | | | | Swim | 01:00 |
| | 01:00 | M2 (4–5aZ) | | | 02:00 | R (E2) | | Bike | 03:30 |
| S2 | | | 01:00 | Trail (E4) | | | 07:15 | Run | 02:15 |
| | | | | | | | | Strength | 00:30 |
| | | | | | | | | Swim | 01:00 |
| | 01:00 | E2 | | | 02:00 | MTB (E4) | | Bike | 03:30 |
| M2 (4–5aZ) | | | 01:00 | E2 | | | 07:15 | Run | 02:15 |

*Week 9: 4–6 × 20 sec. on a flat course (1 min., 40 sec. RI)*

*Week 10: 4–6 × 20 sec. on slight downhill (1 min., 40 sec. RI)*

*Week 11: 4–6 × 30 sec. on slight downhill. (1 min., 30 sec. RI)*

## BRICKS

The brick in Week 10 is on the road, with the last 30 minutes of the bike and the last 15 minutes of the run in Zones 4 to 5a. If you want to do the Week 10 brick off-road, then make the first half of the time in each sport

| Week | Sport | Mon. Time | Mon. Code | Tues. Time | Tues. Code | Wed. Time | Wed. Code | Thurs. Time |
|------|-------|-----------|-----------|------------|------------|-----------|-----------|-------------|
| | | | | | | | **TABLE 10.2: MOUNTAIN BIKE TRIATHLON PLAN (CONTINUED)** | |
| 7 | Strength | | | 00:30 | SM | | | |
| | Swim | 00:30 | M | | | 00:30 | E (Form) | |
| | Bike | | | | | 00:30 | S3 (4–5) | |
| | Run | | | 00:30 | E2 | | | 00:45 |
| 8 | Strength | | | 00:30 | SM | | | |
| | Swim | 00:30 | E2 | | | | | |
| | Bike | | | | | 00:30 | S2 | |
| | Run | | | 00:30 | E2 | | | 00:30 |
| 9 | Strength | | | 00:30 | SM | | | |
| | Swim | 00:30 | E2 (Speed) | | | 00:30 | T1a | |
| | Bike | | | | | 00:30 | S3 (4–5) | |
| | Run | | | 00:30 | E2 | | | 00:45 |
| 10 | Strength | | | 00:30 | SM | | | |
| | Swim | 00:30 | A | | | 00:30 | E (Form) | |
| | Bike | | | | | 00:30 | S2 | |
| | Run | | | 00:30 | E2 | | | 00:45 |
| 11 | Strength | | | 00:30 | SM | | | |
| | Swim | 00:30 | A | | | 00:30 | E (Form) | |
| | Bike | | | | | 00:30 | E2 | |
| | Run | | | 00:30 | E2 | | | 00:45 |
| 12 | Strength | | | | | | | |
| | Swim | 00:30 | E (Speed) | | | | | |
| | Bike | | | 00:45 | A7 | | | 00:30 |
| | Run | | | | | 00:30 | A7 | |

at mostly Zone 1 to 2 intensity. Ride and run the second half of the time simulating your race-pace intensities.

The brick in Week 11 can be done off-road with the last half of the time scheduled for each sport done at race pace.

## RACE WEEK

Finally, in Week 12, incorporate intervals into the A7 bike with four sets of 90-second intervals (3 min. RI), and the A7 run with three sets of 90-second intervals (3 min. RI). The short brick on Saturday is an equipment check mostly. It is just enough exercise to loosen the legs without exerting too much energy. On race day, have fun and get dirty.

| Thurs. Code | Fri. Time | Fri. Code | Sat. Time | Sat. Code | Sun. Time | Sun. Code | Weekly Training Hours | Weekly Hours by Sport | |
|---|---|---|---|---|---|---|---|---|---|
| | | | | | | | | Strength | 00:30 |
| | | | | | | | | Swim | 01:00 |
| | 01:00 | S5 | | | 02:00 | MTB (E4) | | Bike | 03:30 |
| S2 | | | 01:00 | Trail (E4) | | | 07:15 | Run | 02:15 |
| | Day off | | | | | | | Strength | 00:30 |
| | | | | | | | | Swim | 00:30 |
| | | | | | 01:00 | T2 (5) | | Bike | 01:30 |
| S2 | | | 00:30 | T1 | | | 04:00 | Run | 01:30 |
| | | | | | | | | Strength | 00:30 |
| | | | | | | | | Swim | 01:00 |
| | 01:00 | E2 | | | 02:00 | MTB (E4) | | Bike | 03:30 |
| S1 | | | 01:00 | Trail (E4) | | | 07:15 | Run | 02:15 |
| | | | | Brick | | | | Strength | 00:30 |
| | | | | | | | | Swim | 01:00 |
| | 01:00 | E1 | | | 01:30 | Text | | Bike | 03:00 |
| S1 | | | 00:30 | E2 | 00:30 | Text | 06:45 | Run | 02:15 |
| | | | Day off | | Brick | | | Strength | 00:30 |
| | | | | | | | | Swim | 01:00 |
| | 01:00 | S3 (6–8) | | | 01:00 | Text | | Bike | 02:30 |
| S1 | | | | | 00:30 | Text | 05:45 | Run | 01:45 |
| | Day off | | Brick | | Race! | | | Strength | 00:00 |
| | | | | | | | | Swim | 00:30 |
| S5 | | | 00:30 | E2 | | | | Bike | 01:45 |
| | | | 00:10 | E2 | | | 02:55 | Run | 00:40 |

# MODIFYING THE PLAN

Q: What if my event will take longer, say around three hours. How do I modify this schedule?

A: Depending on the anticipated length of your swim, swim time may not need to be increased at all. Increase swim time if:

*a)* you simply enjoy swimming,

*b)* you think the swim will take longer than 30 minutes, or

*c)* you are a competitive swimmer. If the swim is increased, increase the Monday workouts to about 45 minutes.

The Sunday long ride can be built in 15- to 30-minute increments to about 3 hours. If you are pressed for time, 2.5 hours will do the job. All other rides will be fine as shown on the schedule. If the run will take around an hour, the schedule shown will work. Increasing the run time beyond what is shown on the schedule may help build fitness, but I would not recommend going over 1.5 hours.

Q: If my event will only take 1 hour, how do I modify the schedule?

A: The swim days can be as short as 20 minutes. Friday bike rides can be reduced to as little as 30 minutes and Sunday rides can be reduced to around 1:15 or 1:30. Weekday runs can remain at 30 minutes, not building to 45 minutes as specified in the plan. Saturday runs can remain at 1 hour or be reduced to 30 to 45 minutes. All interval segments will need to be reduced proportionally to the running or cycling time reduction.

# 11

# MULTISPORT FITNESS PLAN

*Walking the wire in the circus we call triathlon.*
—MICHAEL SMEDLEY, USA TRIATHLON NATIONAL
RESIDENT TEAM MEMBER AND 1999 RUNNER-UP AT
ITU NORTH AMERICAN CHAMPIONSHIPS

So how about a plan for an all-around athlete? One that allows for participation in other sports like racquetball, handball, tennis, softball, or soccer? At the same time, being able to incorporate a 5K or 10K race or maybe a sprint triathlon. You don't plan on winning the race, but you want to have enough fitness to enjoy yourself. Maybe you'd like to lift weights, too. How do you blend everything together with limited training time and without doing the same boring routine for weeks on end? And one more thing: You'd like to feel fast and strong for some of the workouts, races, or sporting events.

If the paragraph above sounds like something you might be thinking, this chapter is specially designed to fit your needs. It has allowances for other sports and gives guidelines for change. It is designed for a lifestyle of fitness. That means being fit enough to participate in a shorter running race, a sprint-distance triathlon, or a team sport. There is even room for a week-long summer vacation!

## PROFILE

This plan is designed for a person with a fitness lifestyle. You like to be active almost every day, but no more than an hour on weekdays. Saturday or Sunday workouts can be up to two hours, but not more. You participate in other sports two days per week, sports other than swimming, cycling, running, or weight training. The sport may change with the season, but the team counts on your participation.

## GOAL

Your major goal is to stay fit and healthy. Subgoals include a couple of running races and one or two sprint-distance triathlons. Perhaps you downplay competitiveness; but secretly or not, you think kicking butt now and again is really fun.

## THE PLAN

Table 11.1 lists 24 training weeks, a column for the month, and columns designating the training period and the weekly training hours. The final column is a list of possible activities. If there is no race or you decide not to race, other workout options are given for that day. The months are there only as examples—the first week can begin on the Monday of any month. At the beginning of each week of the plan, you need to decide which workouts will be fast, intense, or long. These are considered breakthrough (BT) workouts. One of the dangers of being a fitness buff with a hint of a competitive edge is the desire for all workouts to be fast or long or hard. You need to decide each week where to put your maximum energy or effort. Notice the "Code" column next to Tuesday and Thursday on Table 11.2 is left blank. This is so you can pencil in "BT," "Easy" or "Form." As the plan progresses, if you decide to keep both sport days as BT workouts, another workout in swimming, cycling, or running may have to change. The change can be a shorter distance or lower speed; the choice depends on your overall goals.

In general, most non-elite athletes can handle between two and four BT workouts per week. You may find that the number of BT workouts possible for you in a week depends on how much stress there is in your everyday life. Learning how to manage your workouts to accommodate how you feel, either by changing the intensity or shortening the distance, is an invaluable skill for an athlete at any level.

# GENERAL PREPARATION 1

General Preparation 1 training entails getting a routine established both in the weight room and in other sport activities. Table 11.2 shows sport participation on Tuesday and Thursday throughout the entire plan. If your sport days happen to be Wednesday and Friday, move the workouts around so strength training days are separated by 48 hours. You may also want to shift workouts so runs are separated by 48 hours as well.

As an example, an athlete using this plan might play basketball, racquetball, handball, or squash on Tuesday and Thursday. One assumption the plan makes is that you are running around, using your legs on the sport days. Be sure to warm up with 10 to 20 minutes of jogging in Zones 1 and 2 before starting the game. A few short accelerations may also help sport readiness. Sport days are some mix of aerobic and anaerobic activity.

Strength training during this training block can be either the anatomical adaptation (AA) phase listed in Chapter 22 or your own program. Another option is to strength train AA on Monday and participate in a body pump or circuit training class on Wednesday. In any case, planned strength training will enhance overall sport performance.

Another feature of the overall plan is the rest week scheduled every fourth week. This allows the body a chance to recover and grow stronger. Rest is essential to improved performance in all sports.

Notice the swimming time trial in the first week. This time trial will provide a benchmark from which to gauge fitness progress. The average time for 100 meters should improve in subsequent time trials.

| Week | Month | Period | Weekly Planned Hours | Activities |
|------|-------|--------|----------------------|------------|
| | | **TABLE 11.1: PLAN OVERVIEW** | | |
| 1 | March | General Preparation 1 | 06:00 | |
| 2 | March | General Preparation 1 | 06:00 | |
| 3 | April | General Preparation 1 | 06:00 | |
| 4 | April | General Preparation 1 | 05:00 | |
| 5 | April | General Preparation 2 | 06:20 | |
| 6 | April/May | General Preparation 2 | 06:40 | |
| 7 | May | General Preparation 2 | 06:45 | |
| 8 | May | General Preparation 2 | 05:00 | |
| 9 | May | Specific Preparation | 06:45 | |
| 10 | May | Specific Preparation | 07:10 | |
| 11 | May/June | Specific Preparation | 07:30 | |
| 12 | June | Specific Preparation | 05:00 | |
| 13 | June | Pre-competitive 1 | 07:30 | 10K |
| 14 | June | Pre-competitive 1 | 07:30 | |
| 15 | June/July | Pre-competitive 1 | 07:30 | |
| 16 | July | Recovery | TBD | Vacation |
| 17 | July | Pre-competitive 2 | 07:30 | |
| 18 | July | Pre-competitive 2 | 08:00 | |
| 19 | July | Pre-competitive 2 | 07:00 | Triathlon |
| 20 | July/August | Pre-competitive 2 | 04:45 | 5K |
| 21 | August | Competitive | 07:30 | |
| 22 | August | Competitive | 07:30 | |
| 23 | August | Competitive | 07:30 | |
| 24 | August | Competitive | 03:00+ | Triathlon |

# GENERAL PREPARATION 2

In General Preparation 2, the strength training routine changes to maximum strength (MS). In this block of training, consider one of the MS days a BT workout. The second MS day can be a bit lighter, or you can participate in body pump or circuit training. Select one sport day to be a BT workout; the second one should be easy or form work. The third BT workout is the Sunday bike ride. Not only is there slightly more intensity allowed in the Sunday ride, but the ride also grows in length as the weeks progress.

The Saturday run also increases in length, but the increments are very small, only five minutes. The rest week in this block includes a run with a short tempo segment, which should be fun.

## SPECIFIC PREPARATION

Strength training in Specific Preparation period moves to one day per week of strength maintenance (SM). Strength training remains in the SM phase for the remainder of the training plan. Power endurance training is not used in this training plan because it's assumed that explosive work is already included within your sport workouts. A short bike and a short swim—or a day of golf—replace the second strength training day. No, a swim and bike workout does not equal a golf day, but depending on your personal goals, a day of golf might be more appropriate than swimming or cycling. One swim day per week is enough to get you through the triathlon later in the summer. One bike day, Sunday, builds overall endurance and will also get you through a race. Those who decide to swim and bike instead of golf on Wednesday will likely be stronger on race day than the golfers. It is, however, possible to be an active participant in each sport.

Again, select one of the sport days as a BT workout. By this time, the sport day may have changed to something like soccer, softball, or inline hockey. The other BT workouts for each week are both a swim and a run, or a swim and a bike ride. In Week 11, the two sport days can be BTs or you can choose to make the Sunday bike ride an E3; this is left up to the individual athlete.

## PRE-COMPETITIVE PREPARATION 1

Wednesday remains a swimming and cycling day throughout the rest of the schedule—or, as mentioned in the Specific Preparation description, this could be a golf day.

On Saturday of Week 13, there is an optional 10K race or a fast group run. The race would be most comfortably run in Zones 1 to 3. However, a breakthrough strategy would be to begin the first quarter of the event in Zones 1 to 2, the middle half of the event in Zones 2 to 3, and the last quarter of the race in Zones 3 to 5a. A 5K could be included as well; simply add more warm-up and cool-down time to the event. Notice how the workout intensity moves toward race pace in this phase of training.

| | | TABLE 11.2: MULTISPORT PERFORMANCE PLAN | | | | | | |
|---|---|---|---|---|---|---|---|---|
| Week | Sport | Mon. Time | Mon. Code | Tues. Time | Tues. Code | Wed. Time | Wed. Code | Thurs. Time |
| 1 | Strength | 01:00 | AA | | | 01:00 | AA | |
| | Sport | | | 01:00 | | | | 01:00 |
| | Swim | | | | | | | |
| | Bike | | | | | | | |
| | Run | | | | | | | |
| 2 | Strength | 01:00 | AA | | | 01:00 | AA | |
| | Sport | | | 01:00 | | | | 01:00 |
| | Swim | | | | | | | |
| | Bike | | | | | | | |
| | Run | | | | | | | |
| 3 | Strength | 01:00 | AA | | | 01:00 | AA | |
| | Sport | | | 01:00 | | | | 01:00 |
| | Swim | | | | | | | |
| | Bike | | | | | | | |
| | Run | | | | | | | |
| 4 | Strength | 01:00 | AA | | | Day off | | |
| | Sport | | | 01:00 | | | | 01:00 |
| | Swim | | | | | | | |
| | Bike | | | | | | | |
| | Run | | | | | | | |
| 5 | Strength | 01:00 | MS | | | 01:00 | MS | |
| | Sport | | | 01:00 | | | | 01:00 |
| | Swim | | | | | | | |
| | Bike | | | | | | | |
| | Run | | | | | | | |
| 6 | Strength | 01:00 | MS | | | 01:00 | MS | |
| | Sport | | | 01:00 | | | | 01:00 |
| | Swim | | | | | | | |
| | Bike | | | | | | | |
| | Run | | | | | | | |
| 7 | Strength | 01:00 | MS | | | 01:00 | MS | |
| | Sport | | | 01:00 | | | | 01:00 |
| | Swim | | | | | | | |
| | Bike | | | | | | | |
| | Run | | | | | | | |
| 8 | Strength | 01:00 | MS | | | Day off | | |
| | Sport | | | 01:00 | | | | 01:00 |
| | Swim | | | | | | | |
| | Bike | | | | | | | |
| | Run | | | | | | | |
| 9 | Strength | 01:00 | SM | | | | | |
| | Sport | | | 01:00 | | | | 01:00 |
| | Swim | | | | | 00:30 | E (Form) | |
| | Bike | | | | | 00:30 | E1 | |
| | Run | | | | | | | |

| Thurs. Code | Fri. Time | Fri. Code | Sat. Time | Sat. Code | Sun. Time | Sun. Code | Weekly Training Hours | Weekly Hours by Sport | |
|---|---|---|---|---|---|---|---|---|---|
| | | | | | | | | Strength | 02:00 |
| | | | | | | | | Sport | 02:00 |
| | 00:30 | T1a | | | | | | Swim | 00:30 |
| | | | | | 01:00 | E2 | | Bike | 01:00 |
| | | | 00:30 | E1 | | | 06:00 | Run | 00:30 |
| | | | | | | | | Strength | 02:00 |
| | | | | | | | | Sport | 02:00 |
| | 00:30 | E2 | | | | | | Swim | 00:30 |
| | | | | | 01:00 | E2 | | Bike | 01:00 |
| | | | 00:30 | E1 | | | 06:00 | Run | 00:30 |
| | | | | | | | | Strength | 02:00 |
| | | | | | | | | Sport | 02:00 |
| | 00:30 | E2 | | | | | | Swim | 00:30 |
| | | | | | 01:00 | E2 | | Bike | 01:00 |
| | | | 00:30 | E2 | | | 06:00 | Run | 00:30 |
| | Day off | | | | | | | Strength | 01:00 |
| | | | | | | | | Sport | 02:00 |
| | | | 00:30 | E3 | | | | Swim | 00:30 |
| | | | | | 01:00 | E2 | | Bike | 01:00 |
| | | | 00:30 | E2 | | | 05:00 | Run | 00:30 |
| | | | | | | | | Strength | 02:00 |
| | | | | | | | | Sport | 02:00 |
| | 00:30 | E2 | | | | | | Swim | 00:30 |
| | | | | | 01:15 | E3 | | Bike | 01:15 |
| | | | 00:35 | E2 | | | 06:20 | Run | 00:35 |
| | | | | | | | | Strength | 02:00 |
| | | | | | | | | Sport | 02:00 |
| | 00:30 | E2 | | | | | | Swim | 00:30 |
| | | | | | 01:30 | E3 | | Bike | 01:30 |
| | | | 00:40 | S2 | | | 06:40 | Run | 00:40 |
| | | | | | | | | Strength | 02:00 |
| | | | | | | | | Sport | 02:00 |
| | 00:30 | E2 | | | | | | Swim | 00:30 |
| | | | | | 01:30 | E3 | | Bike | 01:30 |
| | | | 00:45 | E2 | | | 06:45 | Run | 00:45 |
| | Day off | | | | | | | Strength | 01:00 |
| | | | | | | | | Sport | 02:00 |
| | | | 00:30 | E2 | | | | Swim | 00:30 |
| | | | | | 01:00 | S3 | | Bike | 01:00 |
| | | | 00:30 | M1 (15) | | | 05:00 | Run | 00:30 |
| | | | | | | | | Strength | 01:00 |
| | | | | | | | | Sport | 02:00 |
| | 00:30 | T1a | | | | | | Swim | 01:00 |
| | | | | | 01:30 | E2 | | Bike | 02:00 |
| | | | 00:45 | E3 | | | 06:45 | Run | 00:45 |

## TABLE 11.2: MULTISPORT PERFORMANCE PLAN (CONTINUED)

| Week | Sport | Mon. Time | Mon. Code | Tues. Time | Tues. Code | Wed. Time | Wed. Code | Thurs. Time |
|------|-------|-----------|-----------|------------|------------|-----------|-----------|-------------|
| 10 | Strength | 01:00 | SM | | | | | |
| | Sport | | | 01:00 | | | | 01:00 |
| | Swim | | | | | 00:30 | E (Speed) | |
| | Bike | | | | | 00:45 | E2 | |
| | Run | | | | | | | |
| 11 | Strength | 01:00 | SM | | | 01:00 | AA | |
| | Sport | | | 01:00 | | | | 01:00 |
| | Swim | | | | | 00:30 | E (Form) | |
| | Bike | | | | | 01:00 | E2 | |
| | Run | | | | | | | |
| 12 | Strength | 01:00 | SM | | | Day off | | |
| | Sport | | | 01:00 | | | | 01:00 |
| | Swim | | | | | | | |
| | Bike | | | | | | | |
| | Run | | | | | | | |
| 13 | Strength | 01:00 | SM | | | | | |
| | Sport | | | 01:00 | | | | 01:00 |
| | Swim | | | | | 00:30 | E (Form) | |
| | Bike | | | | | 01:00 | S5 | |
| | Run | | | | | | | |
| 14 | Strength | 01:00 | SM | | | 01:00 | MS | |
| | Sport | | | 01:00 | | | | 01:00 |
| | Swim | | | | | 00:30 | E (Form) | |
| | Bike | | | | | 01:00 | S4 | |
| | Run | | | | | | | |
| 15 | Strength | 01:00 | SM | | | 01:00 | MS | |
| | Sport | | | 01:00 | | | | 01:00 |
| | Swim | | | | | 00:30 | E (Form) | |
| | Bike | | | | | 01:00 | S5 | |
| | Run | | | | | | | |
| 16 | Strength | | | | | | | |
| | Sport | Vacation | | Vacation | | Vacation | | |
| | Swim | | | | | | | |
| | Bike | | | | | | | |
| | Run | | | | | | | |
| 17 | Strength | 01:00 | SM | | | | | |
| | Sport | | | 01:00 | | | | 01:00 |
| | Swim | | | | | 00:30 | E (Form) | |
| | Bike | | | | | 01:00 | S4 | |
| | Run | | | | | | | |
| 18 | Strength | 01:00 | SM | | | | | |
| | Sport | | | 01:00 | | | | 01:00 |
| | Swim | | | | | 00:30 | E (Form) | |
| | Bike | | | | | 01:00 | S5 | |
| | Run | | | | | | | |

| Thurs. Code | Fri. Time | Fri. Code | Sat. Time | Sat. Code | Sun. Time | Sun. Code | Weekly Training Hours | Weekly Hours by Sport | |
|---|---|---|---|---|---|---|---|---|---|
| | | | | | | | | Strength | 01:00 |
| | | | | | | | | Sport | 02:00 |
| | | | 00:30 | M | | | | Swim | 01:00 |
| | | | 01:30 | E3 | | | | Bike | 02:15 |
| | | | 00:55 | E2 | | | 07:10 | Run | 00:55 |
| | | | | | | | | Strength | 02:00 |
| | | | | | | | | Sport | 02:00 |
| | 00:30 | E2 | | | | | | Swim | 01:00 |
| | | | 01:30 | E2 | | | | Bike | 02:30 |
| | | | 01:00 | E3 | | | 08:30 | Run | 01:00 |
| | | Day off | | | | | | Strength | 01:00 |
| | | | | | | | | Sport | 02:00 |
| | | | 00:30 | M | | | | Swim | 00:30 |
| | | | 01:00 | S3 | | | | Bike | 01:00 |
| | | | 00:30 | E2 | | | 05:00 | Run | 00:30 |
| | | | | | | | | Strength | 02:00 |
| | | | | | | | | Sport | 02:00 |
| | 00:30 | E1 | | | | | | Swim | 01:00 |
| | | | 01:30 | E1 | | | | Bike | 02:30 |
| | | | 01:00 | A1c | | | 08:30 | Run | 01:00 |
| | | | | | | | | Strength | 02:00 |
| | | | Brick | | | | | Sport | 02:00 |
| | 00:30 | E2 | | | | | | Swim | 01:00 |
| | | | 01:00 | E2 | 01:00 | E1 | | Bike | 03:00 |
| | | | 00:30 | Text | | | 08:30 | Run | 00:30 |
| | | | | | | | | Strength | 01:00 |
| | | | | | | | | Sport | 02:00 |
| | 00:30 | E2 | | | | | | Swim | 01:00 |
| | | | 01:30 | E4 | | | | Bike | 02:30 |
| | | | 01:00 | E2 | | | 07:30 | Run | 01:00 |
| | | | | | | | | Strength | 00:00 |
| | Vacation | | Vacation | | | | | Sport | 00:00 |
| | | | | | | | | Swim | 00:00 |
| | | | | | | | | Bike | 00:00 |
| | | | | | | | | Run | 00:00 |
| | | | | | | | | Strength | 01:00 |
| | | | | | | | | Sport | 02:00 |
| | 00:30 | T1a | | | | | | Swim | 01:00 |
| | | | 01:30 | E2 | | | | Bike | 02:30 |
| | | | 01:00 | M5 (20) | | | 07:30 | Run | 01:00 |
| | | | | | | | | Strength | 01:00 |
| | | | | | | | | Sport | 02:00 |
| | 00:30 | E2 | | | | | | Swim | 01:00 |
| | | | 02:00 | E4 | | | | Bike | 03:00 |
| | | | 01:00 | E2 | | | 08:00 | Run | 01:00 |

| Week | Sport | Mon. Time | Mon. Code | Tues. Time | Tues. Code | Wed. Time | Wed. Code | Thurs. Time |
|------|-------|-----------|-----------|------------|------------|-----------|-----------|-------------|
| | | | | | | | **TABLE 11.2: MULTISPORT PERFORMANCE PLAN (CONTINUED)** | | |
| 19 | Strength | 01:00 | SM | | | | | |
| | Sport | | | 01:00 | | | | 01:00 |
| | Swim | | | | | 00:30 | E (Form) | |
| | Bike | | | | | 01:00 | S4 | |
| | Run | | | | | | | |
| 20 | Strength | Day off | | | | Day off | | |
| | Sport | | | 01:00 | | | | 01:00 |
| | Swim | | | | | | | |
| | Bike | | | | | | | |
| | Run | | | | | | | |
| 21 | Strength | 01:00 | SM | | | | | |
| | Sport | | | 01:00 | | | | 01:00 |
| | Swim | | | | | 00:30 | E (Form) | |
| | Bike | | | | | 01:00 | S5 | |
| | Run | | | | | | | |
| 22 | Strength | 01:00 | SM | | | | | |
| | Sport | | | 01:00 | | | | 01:00 |
| | Swim | | | | | 00:30 | E (Form) | |
| | Bike | | | | | 01:00 | S4 | |
| | Run | | | | | | | |
| 23 | Strength | 01:00 | SM | | | | | |
| | Sport | | | 01:00 | | | | 01:00 |
| | Swim | | | | | 00:30 | E (Form) | |
| | Bike | | | | | 01:00 | S5 | |
| | Run | | | | | | | |
| 24 | Strength | 01:00 | SM | | | Day off | | |
| | Sport | | | 01:00 | | | | 01:00 |
| | Swim | | | | | | | |
| | Bike | | | | | | | |
| | Run | | | | | | | |

Week 14 has a brick scheduled: a bike immediately followed by a run. The bike effort is mostly Zone 1 to 2, while the run is Zone 1 to 2 for the first 15 minutes and Zones 3 to 4 for the last 15 minutes. Be sure to cool down with walking and stretching after.

The final week of this block is a vacation. Structured workouts are an option. A suggestion would be three days of running at 20 to 30 minutes per session. Workout specifics are up to you. If vacation is an active holiday with

| Thurs. Code | Fri. Time | Fri. Code | Sat. Time | Sat. Code | Sun. Time | Sun. Code | Weekly Training Hours | Weekly Hours by Sport | |
|---|---|---|---|---|---|---|---|---|---|
| | | | Day off | | Brick/Race | | | Strength | 01:00 |
| | | | | | | | | Sport | 02:00 |
| | 00:30 | E1 | | | | | | Swim | 01:00 |
| | | | | | 01:00 | Text | | Bike | 02:00 |
| | | | | | 01:00 | Text | 07:00 | Run | 01:00 |
| | | | | | | | | Strength | 00:00 |
| | | | | | | | | Sport | 02:00 |
| | 00:30 | E2 | | | | | | Swim | 00:30 |
| | | | | | 01:30 | E1 | | Bike | 01:30 |
| | | | 00:45 | A1c | | | 04:45 | Run | 00:45 |
| | | | | | | | | Strength | 01:00 |
| | | | | | | | | Sport | 02:00 |
| | 00:30 | A | | | | | | Swim | 01:00 |
| | | | | | 01:30 | E2 | | Bike | 02:30 |
| | | | 01:00 | M5 (25) | | | 07:30 | Run | 01:00 |
| | | | | | | | | Strength | 01:00 |
| | | | | | | | | Sport | 02:00 |
| | 00:30 | E2 | | | | | | Swim | 01:00 |
| | | | | | 01:30 | T2 (5–8) | | Bike | 02:30 |
| | | | 01:00 | E2 | | | 07:30 | Run | 01:00 |
| | | | | | | | | Strength | 01:00 |
| | | | | | | | | Sport | 02:00 |
| | 00:30 | S3 | | | | | | Swim | 01:00 |
| | | | | | 01:30 | E2 | | Bike | 02:30 |
| | | | 01:00 | M2 (4–5aZ) | | | 07:30 | Run | 01:00 |
| | | | Day off | | | | | Strength | 01:00 |
| | | | | | | | | Sport | 02:00 |
| | | | | | | | | Swim | 00:00 |
| | | | | | Race/ | Text | | Bike | 00:00 |
| | | | | | Brick | | 03:00 | Run | 00:00 |

swimming, hiking, walking, and other physical activities, no structured workouts are necessary. If you come back totally exhausted from vacation, it would be best to insert a rest week similar to Week 12 in place of Week 17.

The vacation week is a "Recovery" phase. Although recovery is usually associated with the end of a season, I will often schedule one or two recovery weeks within a long training plan. A mid-season recovery is very rejuvenating, both physically and mentally for the athlete. A small break can mean the difference between a mediocre and stellar second half of the season.

## PRE-COMPETITIVE PREPARATION 2

Special workouts of note during this block include a 2-hour bike ride at the end of Week 18, which could easily be one of the many fundraising activities held all summer long—a ride for a cause. The second item of note is the brick at the end of Week 19. It includes an hour bike and an hour run. The first half of each sport is at Zone 1 to 2 effort and the last half is Zone 3 to 4. This brick could easily be replaced by a sprint-distance triathlon.

The last item of note in this block is the fast run or race on Saturday of Week 20. A 5K event would be the recommended distance. Be sure to warm up before and cool down after the race.

## COMPETITIVE PREPARATION

The last block of this plan includes a 25-minute tempo run on Saturday of Week 21 and a bicycle time trial on Sunday of Week 22. The bike time trial distance can be anywhere between 5 and 8 miles. This time trial is a fun way to see how fast you can go. It can also be used to chart future training progress.

Week 23 should include running intervals on Saturday of four to six sets of 3 to 4 minutes, increasing heart rate into Zones 4 to 5a. Take 1 minute of easy jogging between run intervals.

The final week of this block includes a sprint triathlon. If a competition is not in your area, create your own event. Make your car the transition area. Complete a swim between 400 and 500 meters, ride 13 to 15 miles on the bike, and run around 3 miles. Plan to finish your personal event with a smile on your face and perhaps a small victory dance at the car—hey, you only live once.

# MODIFYING THE PLAN

**Q:** My race days do not line up with the ones on the plan. What should I do?

**A:** You can move entire weeks around or use the "three BT rule" to change the workout intensity of one or more sessions during your race week.

**Q:** My vacation is not in Week 16, now what?

**A:** It would be a miracle if anyone's schedule perfectly matched the one on Table 11.2. You may need to eliminate or shift some of the weeks. Be careful, though, not to eliminate a rest week when you are creating a plan that spans 8 or 12 weeks.

**Q:** In a rest week, it works better for me to take Thursday off and miss a sport day. What should I do on Wednesday?

**A:** Depending on the training period, either strength train or swim and bike on that day, as you have done in the previous four weeks.

**Q:** A 10K is not in my dreams—perhaps only a 5K. Do I need to run an hour for my longest run?

**A:** If a 5K is your goal event, a 45-minute run will do the trick. The minimum I would suggest is 30 minutes.

# PART IV

# Training for Improved Performance

The training plans in Part IV span six months to one year in length. There is a six-month plan for half-Ironman-distance and another for Ironman-distance racing. The third plan in this part is a yearlong Olympic-distance training plan.

Although it is highly unlikely you can use any of the plans exactly as they appear in the book, you can use the format and general design to make the plan fit your personal needs. You may need to reduce the hours of one or more of the workouts. It may be necessary to reduce the intensity of one workout per week. You may need to put hill repeats in cycling instead of running due to your personal race goals and performance limiters. Do not be afraid to make those design modifications, because the optimal design is the one that meets your needs best. Refer back to Chapter 1 for some suggestions to modify training plans, including the ones in this part of the book, and you'll find information to guide you there.

# 12

# FASTER SPRINT-DISTANCE PERFORMANCE

*I love sprint racing because the end is always close enough in my mind's eye to deal with whatever suffering is required to push harder from each second to the next. After a few races, you need to accept that there is no pain you face on the course that haunts you like knowing you left something in reserve at the finish line.*

—DONAVON GUYOT, USA TRIATHLETE,
1990 JUNIOR NATIONAL CHAMPION AGES 15–17

I find that many athletes think that long-distance racing is the ultimate form of difficulty in triathlon. Personally, I would rather race a long-distance event than suffer the lactate hell of a sprint-distance race (I'm talking about *really* racing, all out, as fast as possible).

If you are like Donavon and you think racing fast is really fun, and you don't mind suffering the leg-searing effort of racing fast, perhaps this plan is for you. This chapter helps time-crunched athletes prepare to race faster. Weekly training hours range from 1:45 to 5:00, so training remains manageable even with a hectic lifestyle.

## PROFILE

This plan is built for the summer triathlete. Triathlon training is seasonal for you, but you are physically active all year. You may or may not be an experienced triathlete. Either way, you are looking to do a sprint-distance triathlon at the end of the summer, after about 15 weeks of training. You know how to swim and can comfortably get through 30 minutes in the pool; a 30-minute bike ride or run is comfortable.

## GOAL

Your goal is to complete a sprint-distance event or a slightly longer event at a fast pace, perhaps faster than last summer.

## THE PLAN

Table 12.1 lists 15 training weeks, a column for months, a column designating the training period, and the weekly training hours leading up to the race. The months are there for example only—the first week can begin on Monday in any month. Athletes in the Southern Hemisphere will certainly have different training months from those in the Northern Hemisphere.

In this plan, faster racing is accomplished by structuring a progression of faster, or more intense, workouts. Training hours need not be extravagant. In general, the first few weeks build overall training volume and increase endurance. Once weekly training volume is built to 5 hours, more intensity, or longer-interval speed work, is added. Every third week is a rest week to allow for recovery. Some athletes find that a three-week rotation of training is a good way to rest and manage stress.

Table 12.2 displays the plan in detail. Every Monday is a day of rest. Tuesday and Thursday are swimming days. Wednesday and Saturday are cycling days, with Saturday being the day to build overall cycling endurance. Friday and Sunday are running days; longer runs are completed on Sunday. The schedule can be rearranged to meet personal needs; however, try to

| | | | Weekly Planned |
|---|---|---|---|
| **TABLE 12.1: PLAN OVERVIEW** | | | |
| Week | Month | Period | Hours |
| 1 | May | Specific Preparation 1 | 02:50 |
| 2 | May | Specific Preparation 1 | 03:30 |
| 3 | May | Specific Preparation 1 | 01:45 |
| 4 | May | Specific Preparation 2 | 03:45 |
| 5 | May/June | Specific Preparation 2 | 04:00 |
| 6 | June | Specific Preparation 2 | 02:30 |
| 7 | June | Pre-competitive 1 | 04:30 |
| 8 | June | Pre-competitive 1 | 05:00 |
| 9 | June/July | Pre-competitive 1 | 02:45 |
| 10 | July | Pre-competitive 2 | 05:00 |
| 11 | July | Pre-competitive 2 | 05:00 |
| 12 | July | Pre-competitive 2 | 02:45 |
| 13 | July | Pre-competitive 3 | 04:30 |
| 14 | July/August | Pre-competitive 3 | 04:00 |
| 15 | August | Competitive | 01:35 + Race |

alternate sports and not train two days in a row for the same sport. Workout codes are explained in Chapters 19, 20, and 21. There's also a cheat sheet at the beginning of the book, "Workout Codes Quick Reference."

# SPECIFIC PREPARATION 1

The training during this block is mostly low-intensity aerobic activity and form work. General swim descriptions are in Chapter 19, and more ideas for short swim workouts can be found in Chapters 5 and 15. Additional workouts can be found in the waterproof workout booklet *Workouts in a Binder®: Swim Workouts for Triathletes*. Some of the workouts in the reference chapters are longer than necessary for this plan. Those workouts can be reduced in volume, but you should keep the major theme of the workout the same. In other words, if you are using a workout designed for improving 1,500-meter swimming and your race distance is 800 meters, the main set can be cut down by 25 to 50 percent.

Week 13, the first rest week, begins with a swimming time trial. After a day of rest, you'll do an easy brick on Thursday and a second brick on Saturday. One swim and two bricks are the pattern for all subsequent rest weeks.

| | | | | | | | | | |
|---|---|---|---|---|---|---|---|---|---|
| | | **TABLE 12.2: FASTER SPRINT-DISTANCE PERFORMANCE PLAN** | | | | | | | |
| Week | Sport | Mon. Code | Tues. Time | Tues. Code | Wed. Time | Wed. Code | Thurs. Time | Thurs. Code | |
| 1 | Brick | Day off | | | | | | | |
| | Swim | | 00:30 | E2 | | | 00:30 | E (Form) | |
| | Bike | | | | 00:30 | S2 | | | |
| | Run | | | | | | | | |
| 2 | Brick | Day off | | | | | | | |
| | Swim | | 00:30 | E2 | | | 00:30 | E (Speed) | |
| | Bike | | | | 00:30 | S2 | | | |
| | Run | | | | | | | | |
| 3 | Brick | Day off | | | Day off | | 00:30 | | |
| | Swim | | 00:30 | T1a | | | | | |
| | Bike | | | | | | 00:15 | E1 | |
| | Run | | | | | | 00:15 | E1 | |
| 4 | Brick | Day off | | | | | | | |
| | Swim | | 00:30 | E3 | | | 00:30 | E (Form) | |
| | Bike | | | | 00:30 | S1 | | | |
| | Run | | | | | | | | |
| 5 | Brick | Day off | | | | | | | |
| | Swim | | 00:30 | E3 | | | 00:30 | E (Speed) | |
| | Bike | | | | 00:30 | S1 | | | |
| | Run | | | | | | | | |
| 6 | Brick | Day off | | | Day off | | 00:45 | | |
| | Swim | | 00:30 | E3 | | | | | |
| | Bike | | | | | | 00:30 | S4 | |
| | Run | | | | | | 00:15 | S2 | |
| 7 | Brick | Day off | | | | | | | |
| | Swim | | 00:30 | M | | | 00:30 | E (Form) | |
| | Bike | | | | 00:45 | E2 | | | |
| | Run | | | | | | | | |
| 8 | Brick | Day off | | | | | | | |
| | Swim | | 00:30 | M | | | 00:30 | E (Speed) | |
| | Bike | | | | 01:00 | E4 | | | |
| | Run | | | | | | | | |
| 9 | Brick | Day off | | | Day off | | 00:45 | | |
| | Swim | | 00:30 | T1a | | | | | |
| | Bike | | | | | | 00:30 | S4 | |
| | Run | | | | | | 00:15 | S2 | |
| 10 | Brick | Day off | | | | | | | |
| | Swim | | 00:30 | M | | | 00:30 | E (Form) | |
| | Bike | | | | 01:00 | M2 (4–5aZ) | | | |
| | Run | | | | | | | | |
| 11 | Brick | Day off | | | | | | | |
| | Swim | | 00:30 | A | | | 00:30 | E (Speed) | |
| | Bike | | | | 01:00 | M2 (4–5aZ) | | | |
| | Run | | | | | | | | |

| Fri. Time | Fri. Code | Sat. Time | Sat. Code | Sun. Time | Sun. Code | Weekly Training Hours | Weekly Hours by Sport | |
|---|---|---|---|---|---|---|---|---|
| | | | | | | | Brick | 00:00 |
| | | | | | | | Swim | 01:00 |
| | | 00:30 | E2 | | | | Bike | 01:00 |
| 00:20 | E1 | | | 00:30 | E2 | 02:50 | Run | 00:50 |
| | | | | | | | Brick | 00:00 |
| | | | | | | | Swim | 01:00 |
| | | 00:45 | E2 | | | | Bike | 01:15 |
| 00:30 | E1 | | | 00:45 | E2 | 03:30 | Run | 01:15 |
| Day off | | 00:45 | | Day off | | | Brick | 01:15 |
| | | | | | | | Swim | 00:30 |
| | | 00:30 | E2 | | | | Bike | 00:45 |
| | | 00:15 | E2 | | | 01:45 | Run | 00:30 |
| | | | | | | | Brick | 00:00 |
| | | | | | | | Swim | 01:00 |
| | | 01:00 | E3 | | | | Bike | 01:30 |
| 00:30 | S2 | | | 00:45 | E3 | 03:45 | Run | 01:15 |
| | | | | | | | Brick | 00:00 |
| | | | | | | | Swim | 01:00 |
| | | 01:15 | E3 | | | | Bike | 01:45 |
| 00:30 | S2 | | | 00:45 | E3 | 04:00 | Run | 01:15 |
| Day off | | 01:15 | | Day off | | | Brick | 02:00 |
| | | | | | | | Swim | 00:30 |
| | | 00:45 | Text | | | | Bike | 01:15 |
| | | 00:30 | Text | | | 02:30 | Run | 00:45 |
| | | | | | | | Brick | 00:00 |
| | | | | | | | Swim | 01:00 |
| | | 01:15 | E4 | | | | Bike | 02:00 |
| 00:30 | M5 (15) | | | 01:00 | E2 | 04:30 | Run | 01:30 |
| | | | | | | | Brick | 00:00 |
| | | | | | | | Swim | 01:00 |
| | | 01:30 | E2 | | | | Bike | 02:30 |
| 00:30 | S2 | | | 01:00 | M2 (4–5aZ) | 05:00 | Run | 01:30 |
| Day off | | 01:30 | | Day off | | | Brick | 02:15 |
| | | | | | | | Swim | 00:30 |
| | | 01:00 | M5 (15–20) | | | | Bike | 01:30 |
| | | 00:30 | M5 (15–20) | | | 02:45 | Run | 00:45 |
| | | | | | | | Brick | 00:00 |
| | | | | | | | Swim | 01:00 |
| | | 01:30 | E2 | | | | Bike | 02:30 |
| 00:30 | S2 | | | 01:00 | A2* (5bZ) | 05:00 | Run | 01:30 |
| | | | | | | | Brick | 00:00 |
| | | | | | | | Swim | 01:00 |
| | | 01:30 | E2 | | | | Bike | 02:30 |
| 00:30 | S2 | | | 01:00 | A2* (5bZ) | 05:00 | Run | 01:30 |

| Week | Sport | Mon. Code | Tues. Time | Tues. Code | Wed. Time | Wed. Code | Thurs. Time | Thurs. Code |
|------|-------|-----------|------------|------------|-----------|-----------|-------------|-------------|
| 12 | Brick | Day off | | | Day off | | 00:45 | |
| | Swim | | 00:30 | M (Speed) | | | | |
| | Bike | | | | | | 00:30 | S4 |
| | Run | | | | | | 00:15 | S2 |
| 13 | Brick | Day off | | | | | | |
| | Swim | | 00:30 | A | | | 00:30 | E (OW) |
| | Bike | | | | 01:00 | S4 | | |
| | Run | | | | | | | |
| 14 | Brick | Day off | | | | | | |
| | Swim | | 00:30 | A | | | 00:30 | E (OW ) |
| | Bike | | | | 01:00 | A7 | | |
| | Run | | | | | | | |
| 15 | Brick | Day off | | | 00:30 | | Day off | |
| | Swim | | 00:20 | E (Speed) | | | | |
| | Bike | | | | 00:20 | E2 | | |
| | Run | | | | 00:10 | E2 | | |

TABLE 12.2: FASTER SPRINT-DISTANCE PERFORMANCE PLAN (CONTINUED)

# SPECIFIC PREPARATION 2

Tuesday swim workouts become a bit faster during this block. Endurance is still important, but speed is slightly increased. The distance of long weekend workouts continues to build, and speed is increased here as well. The speed increases are subtle; high speeds are reserved for later training blocks.

The brick on Saturday of Week 6 totals 1:15. It begins with a 45-minute bike and ends with a 30-minute run. Both bike and run segments begin in Zones 1 to 2 for the first half of the time. The second half of each one ends in Zones 2 to 3. Athletes with more fitness can aim to complete the second half of each workout all in Zone 3. The goal is to go faster in the second portion of time in each sport. Finishing the second half of each workout faster than the first is called a "negative split."

FASTER SPRINT-DISTANCE PERFORMANCE

| Fri. Time | Fri. Code | Sat. Time | Sat. Code | Sun. Time | Sun. Code | Training Hours | Weekly Hours by Sport | |
|---|---|---|---|---|---|---|---|---|
| Day off | | 01:30 | | Day off | | | Brick | 02:15 |
| | | | | | | | Swim | 00:30 |
| | | 01:00 | Text | | | | Bike | 01:30 |
| | | 00:30 | Text | | | 02:45 | Run | 00:45 |
| | | | | | | | Brick | 00:00 |
| | | | | | | | Swim | 01:00 |
| | | 01:15 | Text | | | | Bike | 02:15 |
| 00:30 | S2 | | | 00:45 | Text | 04:30 | Run | 01:15 |
| | | | | 01:00 | | | Brick | 01:00 |
| | | | | | | | Swim | 01:00 |
| | | 00:30 | E1 | 00:45 | Text | | Bike | 02:15 |
| 00:30 | S2 | | | 00:15 | Text | 04:00 | Run | 00:45 |
| | | | | Race! | | | Brick | 00:30 |
| | | | | | | | Swim | 00:20 |
| 00:30 | S4 | | | | | | Bike | 00:50 |
| | | 00:15 | S2 | | | 01:35 | Run | 00:25 |

# PRE-COMPETITIVE PREPARATION 1

This training block adds hill work on the bike to increase strength. Allow the hills to drive heart rate into higher training zones, but no higher than 5a for now. These combination workouts not only improve strength, they improve lactate threshold speed as well.

For running, Friday of Week 7 includes a short tempo run of 15 minutes. Sunday of Week 8 includes cruise intervals—specifically, M2 cruise intervals in Zones 4 to 5a: Do 4 to 5 intervals lasting 4 minutes. Take 1 minute of easy jogging between run intervals.

The rest week (Week 9) begins with a retest of the swimming time trial. The brick on Saturday of the rest week is 1:30, beginning with a 60-minute bike and ending with a 30-minute run. Both bike and run segments begin in Zones 1 to 2 and both finish with 15 to 20 minutes in Zones 4 to 5a. This is called a tempo finish.

## PRE-COMPETITIVE PREPARATION 2

In this block, swimming workouts include a mix of muscular endurance work and anaerobic endurance work. Cycling moves to cruise intervals, midweek: In Week 10, ride four to six sets of 3-minute intervals, increasing heart rate into Zones 4 to 5a, followed by a 1-minute rest interval (RI), or, 4–6 × 3 min. (1 min. RI); and on Wednesday of Week 11, 4–6 × 4 min. (1 min. RI), still increasing heart rate into Zones 4 to 5a. The Sunday run in both Weeks 10 and 11 includes anaerobic intervals. For both days, do A2 speed endurance workouts, increasing heart rate into Zone 5b in each 3-minute interval: 4–5 × 3 min. (3 min. RI).

This block ends with a 1:30 brick on Saturday of Week 12. The bike is an hour and the run is 30 minutes. Both workouts are negative split, using an out-and-back course. Go out at intensities in Zones 1 to 2; bring it home in Zones 4 to 5a. The second half of each workout should be faster. How fast can you go while keeping your heart rate as low as possible?

## PRE-COMPETITIVE PREPARATION 3

In this block, training is very fast or easy. Tuesday main-set swims are anaerobic. Thursday swims are in open water (OW)—in a safe situation only—or in the pool at an easy pace.

The bike on Saturday of Week 13 includes a good 40-minute warm-up, followed by 30 minutes at race pace, or speeds eliciting heart rates in Zones 4 to 5b. Spin an easy 5 minutes (or more) at the end. Be sure to stretch well.

The run on Sunday of Week 13 is 20 minutes in the lower zones and 20 minutes at race pace, or heart rates in Zones 4 to 5b. Jog an easy 5 minutes at the end and perhaps add some walking as well.

On Wednesday of Week 14, the bike includes 4 × 90 sec., building heart rate into Zones 4 to 5a (3 min. RI). The brick that week is a negative-split workout, with both the bike and the run beginning in Zones 1 to 2. At the turnaround, bring both home at race pace. For both days, do A2 speed endurance workouts, increasing heart rate into Zone 5b in each 3-minute interval: 4–6 × 3 min. (3 min. RI).

## COMPETITIVE PREPARATION

In the few days preceding the race, reduce volume and include some segments of short speed work. The brick on Wednesday is to loosen the legs, but also to check equipment. Be sure that all race equipment is in working order and ready for the race. If repairs are necessary, you have a few days to get problems taken care of.

## RACE DAY

On race day, recall all of the successful workouts you had in the past 15 weeks. In particular, recall your negative-split workouts. Plan to finish each sport within the race slightly faster than you began. Also, try to finish the race at a higher intensity than you began. Make the race a negative-split effort.

Today is the day to enjoy the harvest of your hard work, a day to have fun. It is exciting to go fast, but going fast is uncomfortable. The fastest athletes manage that discomfort and enjoy the speed. Use the strategies you found useful in training to keep calm, motivated, and focused.

# 13

# FASTER OLYMPIC-DISTANCE PERFORMANCE

*Consistency, planning, and rest are the keys to successful training.*
—ALEXANDER DURST, USA

Perhaps it was a New Year's resolution or the lingering memory of how much fun that triathlon was last summer. For any number of reasons, it would be fun to do an Olympic-distance triathlon and try to race faster. The plan in this chapter is designed to help you do just that.

Table 13.1 gives an overview of the plan. The first column shows a plan length of 24 weeks, and the fourth column reveals weekly training hours ranging from 6:15 to a maximum of 13:00. The plan begins on the first Monday in January and ends with a race in June, but could just as easily start on the first Monday in February, with a race in July. In other words, the months are shown only as examples. Finally, the third column indicates which training period corresponds to each week.

If this plan looks manageable, read on.

| | | TABLE 13.1: PLAN OVERVIEW | |
|---|---|---|---|
| Week | Month | Period | Weekly Planned Hours |
| 1 | January | General Preparation | 07:30 |
| 2 | January | General Preparation | 07:30 |
| 3 | January | General Preparation | 07:30 |
| 4 | January | General Preparation | 06:15 |
| 5 | January/February | Specific Preparation 1 | 08:45 |
| 6 | February | Specific Preparation 1 | 10:45 |
| 7 | February | Specific Preparation 1 | 12:00 |
| 8 | February | Specific Preparation 1 | 06:15 |
| 9 | February/March | Specific Preparation 2 | 09:30 |
| 10 | March | Specific Preparation 2 | 11:15 |
| 11 | March | Specific Preparation 2 | 12:30 |
| 12 | March | Specific Preparation 2 | 06:15 |
| 13 | March/April | Specific Preparation 3 | 10:00 |
| 14 | April | Specific Preparation 3 | 12:00 |
| 15 | April | Specific Preparation 3 | 13:00 |
| 16 | April | Specific Preparation 3 | 06:15 |
| 17 | April/May | Pre-competitive 1 | 11:15 |
| 18 | May | Pre-competitive 1 | 11:15 |
| 19 | May | Pre-competitive 1 | 06:15 |
| 20 | May | Pre-competitive 2 | 10:45 |
| 21 | May | Pre-competitive 2 | 10:45 |
| 22 | May/June | Competitive | 10:00 |
| 23 | June | Competitive | 07:30 |
| 24 | June | Competitive | 03:00 + Race |

# PROFILE

You may or may not be an experienced triathlete. Either way, you are look-ing to do an Olympic-distance triathlon about six months in the future. You know how to swim and can comfortably get through about 30 min-utes in the pool. An hour bike ride or an hour run is not a stretch for you. Your total weekly training is around six hours prior to beginning the plan.

## GOAL

Your goal is to complete an Olympic-distance event that is about six months away. You want more than simple survival. You want to race at a fast pace.

## THE PLAN

Table 13.2 outlines the journey to a faster-paced Olympic-distance race. It begins with a General Preparation period, an overall conditioning phase. Specific Preparation 1 emphasizes strength training and begins to build overall training volume. Specific Preparation 2 reduces heavy strength training and adds more hills to cycling and running. Specific Preparation 3 begins lactate threshold training. Pre-competitive 1 and 2 have challenging days of anaerobic threshold training. Finally, in the Competitive period, a reduction in overall training volume and some fast workouts in the mix each week bring you to a fast race with a well-rested body. Let's look at each period in more detail.

## GENERAL PREPARATION

This period prepares the body for future stresses by introducing strength training and an opportunity to establish a routine. Week 1 has a time trial in each sport, which will be used as baseline measure for fitness. The rest of the General Preparation block contains a good deal of form and speed work in all three sports. Form work is included throughout the entire plan to emphasize good technique—its goal being "free" speed. Efficient form can reduce the effort it takes to travel at any given pace, while inefficient form can rob an athlete of precious energy.

There are numerous types of speed work, all intended to get you going faster. Short segments of speed, like those in the General Preparation period, help train the neuromuscular system to go fast without a huge tax on the aerobic system. The energy system needed for this type of speed is anaerobic, but the workouts are not intended to produce stores of lactate that the body must labor to process. This type of speed work, in addition to form work, is ideally continued throughout the season.

| Week | Sport | Mon. Time | Mon. Code | Tues. Time | Tues. Code | Wed. Time | Wed. Code | Thurs. Time |
|------|-------|-----------|-----------|------------|------------|-----------|-----------|-------------|
| 1 | Strength | 01:15 | AA | | | 01:15 | AA | |
| | Swim | | | 00:30 | E2 | 00:45 | T1 | |
| | Bike | | | | | | | 00:45 |
| | Run | | | 00:30 | E1 | | | 00:30 |
| 2 | Strength | 01:15 | AA | | | 01:15 | AA | |
| | Swim | | | 00:30 | E2 | | | 00:45 |
| | Bike | | | | | | | |
| | Run | | | 00:30 | E1 | | | 00:30 |
| 3 | Strength | 01:15 | AA | | | 01:15 | AA | |
| | Swim | | | 00:30 | E2 | | | 00:45 |
| | Bike | | | | | | | |
| | Run | | | 00:30 | E1 | | | 00:30 |
| 4 | Strength | 01:15 | AA | | | 01:15 | AA | |
| | Swim | | | 00:30 | E2 | | | 00:30 |
| | Bike | | | | | | | |
| | Run | | | 00:30 | E1 | | | |
| 5 | Strength | 01:30 | MS | | | 01:30 | MS | |
| | Swim | | | 00:45 | E (Form) | | | 00:45 |
| | Bike | | | | | | | |
| | Run | | | 00:30 | E1 | | | 00:30 |
| 6 | Strength | 01:30 | MS | | | 01:30 | MS | |
| | Swim | | | 01:00 | E (Speed) | | | 01:00 |
| | Bike | | | | | | | |
| | Run | | | 00:30 | E1 | | | 00:30 |
| 7 | Strength | 01:30 | MS | | | 01:30 | MS | |
| | Swim | | | 01:00 | E (Form) | | | 01:00 |
| | Bike | | | | | | | |
| | Run | | | 00:30 | E1 | | | 00:45 |
| 8 | Strength | 01:00 | MS | | | 01:00 | MS | |
| | Swim | | | 00:30 | E (Speed) | | | 00:30 |
| | Bike | | | | | | | 00:45 |
| | Run | | | 00:30 | S2 | | | |
| 9 | Strength | 01:15 | PE | | | 01:15 | PE | |
| | Swim | | | 01:00 | Force | | | 00:45 |
| | Bike | | | | | | | |
| | Run | | | 00:30 | E2 | | | 00:30 |
| 10 | Strength | 01:15 | PE | | | 01:15 | PE | |
| | Swim | | | 01:00 | Force | | | 01:00 |
| | Bike | | | | | | | |
| | Run | | | 00:30 | E2 | | | 00:30 |
| 11 | Strength | 01:15 | PE | | | 01:15 | PE | |
| | Swim | | | 01:00 | Force | | | 01:00 |
| | Bike | | | | | | | |
| | Run | | | 00:30 | E2 | | | 00:45 |

**TABLE 13.2: OLYMPIC-DISTANCE TRIATHLON PERFORMANCE PLAN**

FASTER OLYMPIC-DISTANCE PERFORMANCE

| Thurs. Code | Fri. Time | Fri. Code | Sat. Time | Sat. Code | Sun. Time | Sun. Code | Weekly Training Hours | Weekly Hours by Sport | |
|---|---|---|---|---|---|---|---|---|---|
| | | | | | | | | Strength | 02:30 |
| | | | | | | | | Swim | 01:15 |
| S1 | | | 01:00 | T1 | | | | Bike | 01:45 |
| S2 | | | 01:00 | T1 | | | 07:30 | Run | 02:00 |
| | | | | | | | | Strength | 02:30 |
| E (Form) | | | | | | | | Swim | 01:15 |
| | 00:30 | S2 | | | 01:15 | E2 | | Bike | 01:45 |
| S2 | | | 01:00 | E2 | | | 07:30 | Run | 02:00 |
| | | | | | | | | Strength | 02:30 |
| E (Form) | | | | | | | | Swim | 01:15 |
| | 00:30 | S1 | | | 01:15 | E2 | | Bike | 01:45 |
| S2 | | | 01:00 | E2 | | | 07:30 | Run | 02:00 |
| | | | | | | | | Strength | 02:30 |
| E (Speed) | | | | | | | | Swim | 01:00 |
| | 00:30 | S2 | | | 01:00 | E2 | | Bike | 01:30 |
| | | | 00:45 | S1 | | | 06:15 | Run | 01:15 |
| | | | | | | | | Strength | 03:00 |
| E3 | | | | | | | | Swim | 01:30 |
| | 00:45 | S1 | | | 01:30 | E3 | | Bike | 02:15 |
| S1 | | | 01:00 | S2 | | | 08:45 | Run | 02:00 |
| | | | | | | | | Strength | 03:00 |
| E3 | | | 00:30 | E1 | | | | Swim | 02:30 |
| | 01:00 | S2 | | | 02:00 | E2 | | Bike | 03:00 |
| S2 | | | 01:15 | E3 | | | 10:45 | Run | 02:15 |
| | | | | | | | | Strength | 03:00 |
| E3 | | | 00:45 | E1 | | | | Swim | 02:45 |
| | 01:00 | S1 | | | 02:30 | E3 | | Bike | 03:30 |
| S1 | | | 01:30 | E2 | | | 12:00 | Run | 02:45 |
| | | | | | | | | Strength | 02:00 |
| T1 | Day off | | | | | | | Swim | 01:00 |
| S3 | | | | | 01:00 | T1 | | Bike | 01:45 |
| | | | 01:00 | T1 | | | 06:15 | Run | 01:30 |
| | | | | | | | | Strength | 02:30 |
| E2 | | | 01:00 | E (Form) | | | | Swim | 02:45 |
| | 00:30 | S1 | | | 01:45 | E4 | | Bike | 02:15 |
| S2 | | | 01:00 | E2 | | | 09:30 | Run | 02:00 |
| | | | | | | | | Strength | 02:30 |
| E2 | | | 01:15 | M | | | | Swim | 03:15 |
| | 01:00 | S5 | | | 02:15 | E2 | | Bike | 03:15 |
| S2 | | | 01:15 | E4 | | | 11:15 | Run | 02:15 |
| | | | | | | | | Strength | 02:30 |
| E2 | | | 01:15 | E1 | | | | Swim | 03:15 |
| | 01:15 | S1 | | | 02:45 | E4 | | Bike | 04:00 |
| S2 | | | 01:30 | E4 | | | 12:30 | Run | 02:45 |

| | | Mon. Time | Mon. Code | Tues. Time | Tues. Code | Wed. Time | Wed. Code | Thurs. Time |
|---|---|---|---|---|---|---|---|---|
| Week | Sport | | | | | | | |
| 12 | Strength | 01:00 | PE | | | 01:00 | PE | |
| | Swim | | | 00:30 | E (Form) | | | 00:30 |
| | Bike | | | | | | | 00:45 |
| | Run | | | 00:30 | S2 | | | |
| 13 | Strength | 01:00 | SM | | | | | |
| | Swim | | | 01:00 | E2 | | | 00:45 |
| | Bike | | | | | 01:00 | M2 (4–5aZ) | |
| | Run | | | 00:30 | S1 | | | 00:30 |
| 14 | Strength | 01:00 | SM | | | | | |
| | Swim | | | 01:00 | E2 | | | 01:15 |
| | Bike | | | | | 01:00 | M2 (4–5aZ) | |
| | Run | | | 00:30 | S2 | | | 01:00 |
| 15 | Strength | 01:00 | SM | | | | | |
| | Swim | | | 01:15 | E2 | | | 01:15 |
| | Bike | | | | | 01:30 | E2 | |
| | Run | | | 00:30 | S1 | | | 01:00 |
| 16 | Strength | 01:00 | SM | | | | | |
| | Swim | | | 00:45 | E1 | | | 00:45 |
| | Bike | | | | | 01:00 | S5 | |
| | Run | | | | | | | 00:30 |
| 17 | Strength | 01:00 | SM | | | | | |
| | Swim | | | 01:00 | E2 | | | 01:00 |
| | Bike | | | | | 01:00 | S5 | |
| | Run | | | 01:00 | A2 (5bZ) | | | 00:30 |
| 18 | Strength | 01:00 | SM | | | | | |
| | Swim | | | 01:00 | E2 | | | 01:00 |
| | Bike | | | | | 01:00 | M4 (20) | |
| | Run | | | 01:00 | E2 | | | 00:30 |
| 19 | Strength | 01:00 | SM | | | | | |
| | Swim | | | 01:00 | E1 | | | 01:00 |
| | Bike | | | | | | | |
| | Run | | | | | 00:45 | E2 | |
| 20 | Strength | 01:00 | SM | | | | | |
| | Swim | | | 01:00 | E2 | | | 01:00 |
| | Bike | | | | | 01:00 | M5 (20) | |
| | Run | | | 00:4S | E2 | | | 00:30 |
| 21 | Strength | 01:00 | SM | | | | | |
| | Swim | | | 01:00 | E2 | | | 01:00 |
| | Bike | | | | | 01:00 | M5 (25–30) | |
| | Run | | | 00:45 | E2 | | | 00:30 |
| 22 | Strength | 01:00 | SM | | | | | |
| | Swim | | | 01:00 | M | | | 01:00 |
| | Bike | | | | | 01:00 | M5 (30–35) | |
| | Run | | | 00:30 | E2 | | | 00:30 |

TABLE 13.2: OLYMPIC-DISTANCE TRIATHLON PLAN PERFORMANCE (CONTINUED)

| Thurs. Code | Fri. Time | Fri. Code | Sat. Time | Sat. Code | Sun. Time | Sun. Code | Weekly Training Hours | Weekly Hours by Sport | |
|---|---|---|---|---|---|---|---|---|---|
|  | Day off |  |  |  |  |  |  | Strength | 02:00 |
| T1 |  |  |  |  |  |  |  | Swim | 01:00 |
| S3 |  |  |  |  | 01:00 | T1 |  | Bike | 01:45 |
|  | 01:00 |  |  | T1 |  |  | 06:15 | Run | 01:30 |
|  |  |  |  |  |  |  |  | Strength | 01:00 |
| M (Form) |  |  | 01:00 | E2 |  |  |  | Swim | 02:45 |
|  | 01:00 | S5 |  |  | 02:15 | E2 |  | Bike | 04:15 |
| E2 |  |  | 01:00 | M2 (4–5aZ) |  |  | 10:00 | Run | 02:00 |
|  |  |  |  |  |  |  |  | Strength | 01:00 |
| M (Speed) |  |  | 01:15 | E1 |  |  |  | Swim | 03:30 |
|  | 01:15 | E1 |  |  | 02:30 | E4 |  | Bike | 04:45 |
| M2 (4–5aZ) |  |  | 01:15 | E2 |  |  | 12:00 | Run | 02:45 |
|  |  |  |  |  |  |  |  | Strength | 01:00 |
| M (Form) |  |  | 01:15 | E1 |  |  |  | Swim | 03:45 |
|  | 01:00 | M2 (4–5aZ) |  |  | 03:00 | E4 |  | Bike | 05:30 |
| M2 (4–5aZ) |  |  | 01:15 | E2 |  |  | 13:00 | Run | 02:45 |
|  | Day off |  |  |  |  |  |  | Strength | 01:00 |
| E2 |  |  |  |  |  |  |  | Swim | 01:30 |
|  |  |  |  |  | 01:15 | E2 |  | Bike | 02:15 |
| S2 |  |  | 01:00 | A1c |  |  | 06:15 | Run | 01:30 |
|  |  |  |  |  |  |  |  | Strength | 01:00 |
| A |  |  | 01:00 | E1 |  |  |  | Swim | 03:00 |
|  | 00:45 | E2 |  |  | 03:00 | A1c |  | Bike | 04:45 |
| E1 |  |  | 01:00 | S2 |  |  | 11:15 | Run | 02:30 |
|  |  |  |  |  |  | Brick |  | Strength | 01:00 |
| A |  |  | 01:15 | E1 |  |  |  | Swim | 03:15 |
|  | 01:00 | E1 |  |  | 02:00 | E2 |  | Bike | 04:00 |
| S1 |  |  | 01:00 | A1c | 00:30 | E2 | 11:15 | Run | 03:00 |
|  | Day off |  |  |  |  | Brick |  | Strength | 01:00 |
| M (Speed) |  |  |  |  |  |  |  | Swim | 02:00 |
|  |  |  | 01:00 | T2 | 01:00 | S4 |  | Bike | 02:00 |
|  |  |  |  |  | 00:30 | S2 | 06:15 | Run | 01:15 |
|  |  |  |  |  |  |  |  | Strength | 01:00 |
| A |  |  | 01:00 | E (Speed) |  |  |  | Swim | 03:00 |
|  | 01:00 | S5 |  |  | 02:30 | A1c |  | Bike | 04:30 |
| S2 |  |  | 01:00 | A1c |  |  | 10:45 | Run | 02:15 |
|  |  |  |  |  |  |  |  | Strength | 01:00 |
| A |  |  | 01:00 | E1 |  |  |  | Swim | 03:00 |
|  | 01:00 | S2 |  |  | 02:30 | A1c |  | Bike | 04:30 |
| S2 |  |  | 01:00 | A2 (5bZ) |  |  | 10:45 | Run | 02:15 |
|  |  |  |  |  |  | Brick |  | Strength | 01:00 |
| E2 |  |  | 01:00 | E (Form) |  |  |  | Swim | 03:00 |
|  | 01:15 | S1 |  |  | 01:30 | Text |  | Bike | 03:45 |
| S2 |  |  | 00:45 | E1 | 00:30 | Text | 10:00 | Run | 02:15 |

155

**TABLE 13.2: OLYMPIC-DISTANCE TRIATHLON PLAN PERFORMANCE (CONTINUED)**

| Week | Sport | Mon. Time | Mon. Code | Tues. Time | Tues. Code | Wed. Time | Wed. Code | Thurs. Time |
|---|---|---|---|---|---|---|---|---|
| *23* | Strength | 01:00 | SM | | | | | |
| | Swim | | | 00:45 | M | | | |
| | Bike | | | | | 01:00 | M2 (4–5aZ) | |
| | Run | | | 00:30 | E2 | | | 00:45 |
| *24* | Strength | | | | | | | |
| | Swim | | | 00:45 | E (Form) | | | 00:30 |
| | Bike | 00:45 | A7 | | | | | |
| | Run | | | | | 00:30 | S1 | |

## SPECIFIC PREPARATION 1

This block of training begins the delicate balancing act of increasing volume and intensity. Certain workouts are intended to stress the body so that when followed by a period of rest, the body is stronger and/or faster. These stressful workouts are called "breakthrough" or BT workouts. As a general rule of thumb, a single week should not include more than four BT workouts total in all three sports; usually two or three BTs per week is a better idea. How the BT sessions are scheduled within a week depends on the intended benefit. If it becomes necessary to rearrange the daily schedule shown on the plan, be conscious of stacking stressful workouts together. Give thought to what you are doing and why.

For Specific Preparation 1, a maximum strength (MS) workout (see Chapter 22) is considered a BT session. If done correctly, this phase of strength training yields excellent results on the bike. Because this type of strength training involves building muscle, some athletes may gain small amounts of weight (two to five pounds), and may notice that their legs feel heavy while running and on the bike. This is normal, and positive changes—like fast and powerful-feeling legs—emerge as training progresses.

Low-end lactate threshold work begins in all three sports by spending time in Zone 3. Do not make it a goal to see how much time you can spend in Zone 3; rather, allow hills, wind, and strong arms or legs to dictate the amount of time spent in this higher zone.

| Thurs. Code | Fri. Time | Fri. Code | Sat. Time | Sat. Code | Sun. Time | Sun. Code | Weekly Training Hours | Weekly Hours by Sport | |
|---|---|---|---|---|---|---|---|---|---|
| | Day off | | | | | Brick | | Strength | 01:00 |
| | | | 01:00 | E (Speed) | | | | Swim | 01:45 |
| | | | 01:00 | E2 | 01:00 | Text | | Bike | 03:00 |
| A7 | | | | | 00:30 | Text | 07:30 | Run | 01:45 |
| | Day off | | | Brick | Race! | | | Strength | 00:00 |
| E (Speed) | | | | | | | | Swim | 01:15 |
| | | | 00:20 | S4 | | | | Bike | 01:05 |
| | | | 00:10 | S2 | | | 03:00 | Run | 00:40 |

# SPECIFIC PREPARATION 2

Strength was built in the weight room in Specific Preparation 1. Now we can apply that strength directly to each sport by adding paddles to swimming and more aggressive hills to cycling and running. If your city is pancake-flat, use the wind, a treadmill, or higher gears on the bike to simulate hills.

Paddles in the pool and more challenging terrain for cycling and running also provide a natural opportunity for lactate threshold training. Specific-sport strength and lactate threshold training are combined in a single workout for each sport. For swimming, this is the Tuesday workout, and in running and cycling, it is one or both weekend workouts. It is important to be rested for those workouts.

# SPECIFIC PREPARATION 3

Strength training in Specific Preparation 3, and for the rest of the plan, goes into a maintenance mode. Gains in the weight room (adding more plates to the stack) are no longer expected. Strength is simply maintained in the gym.

The energy that once went into weights is now going into sport. Lactate threshold intervals are scheduled in all three sports. During this training block, volume is still increasing, so be very conscientious about not overextending yourself. Here is more detail on the lactate threshold workouts in this training block.

## BIKE

*Week 13 (Wed.):* 5–6 × 3 min. into Zones 4 to 5a (1 min. RI)

*Week 14 (Wed.):* 4–6 × 4 min. into Zones 4 to 5a (1 min. RI)

*Week 15 (Fri.):* 4–5 × 5 min. into Zones 4 to 5a (2 min. RI)

## RUN

*Week 13 (Sat.):* 5–6 × 3 min. into Zones 4 to 5a (1 min. RI)

*Week 14 (Thurs.):* 4–6 × 4 min. into Zones 4 to 5a (1 min. RI)

*Week 15 (Thurs.):* 4–5 × 5 min. into Zones 4 to 5a (2 min. RI)

*Tip:* At the end of the rest week in this block, a 10K race or fast group run can be used as a new benchmark for progress.

# PRE-COMPETITIVE PREPARATION 1

For the remainder of the plan, training is either very fast or very easy. Avoid spending large amounts of training time in Zone 3 during this period. It is important for you to be well rested before workouts where top speed is important. If the workout does not include speed work, then it is either a recovery workout, a form workout, or is intended to maintain aerobic fitness.

This training block includes two bricks in Weeks 18 and 19. The first brick is endurance-based and trains your legs to run right after a bike ride. The second brick adds some short speed work.

# PRE-COMPETITIVE PREPARATION 2

In this block of training (Weeks 20–21), some athletes may need to modify the training plan due to fatigue. If you are struggling to recover and constantly feel fatigued, the intensity of the Wednesday or the Sunday bike ride may need to change to E2.

# COMPETITIVE PREPARATION

As you taper for the big race, you may experience strange feelings. Not all athletes experience the same feelings, but the typical "taper blues" include:

- *When beginning to taper volume, some athletes say they feel more tired than when they were putting in lots of training hours.*
- *As the taper continues, some athletes notice they are slightly grouchy—or their friends and family members notice it.*
- *Others report little aches and pains they never noticed before. The pains show up for no apparent reason. In other words, there were no incidents to cause a sore knee, so where did that come from?*
- *The last week before the race, some athletes begin feeling slightly blue or depressed. Others feel they have so much energy, they want to go work out or they will go nuts.*

While the taper blues are frustrating, they don't last forever. Within one or two days of the race, most athletes feel darn good. They are typically ready to go and eager for race day to come!

The short intervals done before the race should help legs and arms remain fast and feel strong. Here's some more detail on the fast workouts.

## BIKE

On Wednesday of Week 23, you can repeat one of the muscular endurance interval sessions listed in Specific Preparation 3.

## BRICKS

On Sunday of Week 22, begin with a 1.5-hour bike ride in which the first hour of the ride is mostly in Zones 1 to 2 and the last 30 minutes of the ride is at race pace, or Zones 4 to 5a. The run following the bike is 30 minutes on an out-and-back course. The first 15 minutes of the run is in Zones 1 to 2—

try to relax your shoulders and face. The last 15 minutes is at race pace or Zones 4 to 5a.

On Sunday of Week 23, begin with a 1-hour bike ride in which the first 30 minutes of the ride is mostly in Zones 1 to 2 and the last 30 minutes of the ride is at race pace, or Zones 4 to 5a. The run following the bike is 30 minutes on an out-and-back course. The first 15 minutes of the run is in Zones 1 to 2—try to relax your shoulders and face. The last 15 minutes is at race pace, or Zones 4 to 5a.

## RACE DAY

Calm your nerves and resist the temptation to do more training as race day approaches. Your work is complete, so now it's time to relax and enjoy the experience. Expect to feel good and go fast.

# 14

# FASTER DUATHLON PERFORMANCE

*The counterintuitive thing that I learned with a structured training plan is that you have to go easy to see how hard you can really go. Before working off a structured plan, I went too hard on my easy days and thus too easy on my hard days. As a result I was never really reaching peak performance. I needed a structured plan from an objective, knowledgeable trainer. Using this approach, I was able to meet my five-year-long goal to place in my age group at a World Championship Duathlon.*

—ROBIN STEELE, USA

The duathlon plans in Part III were for single-sport athletes making the change to multisport. This plan is for athletes who already have a good base in running and cycling and want to get faster in both sports, but are not sure what path to take.

## PROFILE

The athlete this plan is designed for is quite comfortable running three times per week for 30, 40, and 60 minutes per session before beginning the plan. It's also important to be comfortable cycling three days per week. Two of the cycling sessions are around 45 minutes long, with the third session at

90 minutes. After reading Chapter 2, you have determined that most of your training before entering this plan has been in Zones 1 to 3.

You want to get faster but without adding much more training time to your current routine. Also, your body responds best to only two stressful, or breakthrough (BT), workouts each week. A third BT workout each week is too much.

## GOAL

At the end of 11 weeks of training, it's your goal to complete a duathlon consisting of a 5K run, a 30K bike, and a second 5K run—at a fast clip.

## THE PLAN

Table 14.1 gives an overall snapshot of the plan, showing weekly training hours ranging from 2:45 to 6:15. As with all the plans in this book, the months are given for example only. Table 14.2 shows the plan in detail. Following this program will require running three days per week and cycling three days per week. The plan shows Monday as a day off; however, it could be used as a strength training day if that is already part of your routine.

If you have the time and energy to do so, each training day could be increased by 15 minutes. It is not necessary to increase all the days; for example, only increasing the Wednesday bike rides by 15 minutes is an option. Read on to examine the plan in more detail.

## SPECIFIC PREPARATION

The workouts needing special explanation in this period are the Thursday runs and the brick in Week 4. All other workouts are described in Chapters 20 and 21. For example, the Thursday run workouts in Week 1 should incorporate four to six sets of 3-minute intervals followed by a 1-minute rest interval (RI), or as follows:

| | | | Weekly Planned Hours |
|---|---|---|---|
| Week | Month | Period | |
| 1 | May | Specific Preparation | 05:15 |
| 2 | May | Specific Preparation | 05:45 |
| 3 | May | Specific Preparation | 06:15 |
| 4 | May | Specific Preparation | 02:45 |
| 5 | May/June | Pre-competitive 1 | 05:45 |
| 6 | June | Pre-competitive 1 | 05:45 |
| 7 | June | Pre-competitive 1 | 02:45 |
| 8 | June | Pre-competitive 2 | 05:45 |
| 9 | June/July | Pre-competitive 2 | 05:45 |
| 10 | July | Competitive | 05:05 |
| 11 | July | Competitive | 05:45 + Race |

*TABLE 14.1: PLAN OVERVIEW*

*Week 1:* 4–6 × 3 min. (1 min. RI)

*Week 2:* 4–6 × 4 min. (1 min. RI)

*Week 3:* 4–6 × 5 min. (2 min. RI)

All these intervals should be in Zones 4 to 5a. If you would rather run by pace, run these intervals at your open 10K race pace. (Open 10K means a running race only, no cycling or other sport performed before the run.)

For the brick scheduled on Saturday of Week 4, bike one hour and immediately transition to a 30-minute run. Both workouts are negative split. Split each workout time in half and go out at an intensity in Zones 1 to 2. Come back in Zones 4 to 5a.

# PRE-COMPETITIVE 1 PREPARATION

This block (Weeks 5–7) is three weeks long, and the two fast workouts are shown on Saturday and Sunday. Some athletes are better served by separating the fast training days. If this is the case for you, do the fast run on Thursday and make Saturday the E2 run.

Special instructions for Saturday run workouts in this block of training are:

## TABLE 14.2: FASTER DUATHLON PERFORMANCE PLAN

| Week | Sport | Mon. Code | Tues. Time | Tues. Code | Wed. Time | Wed. Code | Thurs. Time | Thurs. Code |
|---|---|---|---|---|---|---|---|---|
| 1 | | Day off | | | | | | |
| | Run | | 00:30 | S2 | | | 00:45 | M2 (4–5aZ) |
| | Bike | | | | 00:45 | S2 | | |
| 2 | | Day off | | | | | | |
| | Run | | 00:30 | S2 | | | 00:45 | M2 (4–5aZ) |
| | Bike | | | | 00:45 | S3 | | |
| 3 | | Day off | | | | | | |
| | Run | | 00:30 | S2 | | | 00:45 | M2 (4–5aZ) |
| | Bike | | | | 00:45 | S2 | | |
| 4 | | Day off | | | Day off | | | |
| | Run | | 00:30 | S2 | | | | |
| | Bike | | | | | | 00:45 | S3 |
| 5 | | Day off | | | | | | |
| | Run | | 00:30 | S2 | | | 00:45 | E2 |
| | Bike | | | | 00:45 | S3 | | |
| 6 | | Day off | | | | | | |
| | Run | | 00:30 | S2 | | | 00:45 | E2 |
| | Bike | | | | 00:45 | S5 | | |
| 7 | | Day off | | | | | | |
| | Run | | 00:30 | S2 | | | | |
| | Bike | | | | | | 00:45 | S3 |
| 8 | | Day off | | | | | | |
| | Run | | 00:30 | S2 | | | 00:45 | E2 |
| | Bike | | | | 00:45 | S3 | | |
| 9 | | Day off | | | | | | |
| | Run | | 00:30 | S2 | | | 00:45 | E2 |
| | Bike | | | | 00:45 | S5 | | |
| 10 | | Day off | | | | | | |
| | Run | | 00:30 | S2 | | | 00:45 | E2 |
| | Bike | | | | 00:45 | S3 | | |
| 11 | | Day off | | | Day off | | | Brick |
| | Run | | 00:30 | S2 | | | 00:30 | A7 |
| | Bike | | | | | | 00:15 | A7 |

*Week 5:* 3–4 × 3 min. (3 min. RI)
*Week 6:* 3–4 × 3 min. (3 min. RI)

These intervals should take your heart rate into Zone 5b. If you prefer to run by pace, make this interval equivalent to your open 5K running pace.

There are also special instructions for one of the bike workouts:

FASTER DUATHLON PERFORMANCE

| Fri. Time | Fri. Code | Sat. Time | Sat. Code | Sun. Time | Sun. Code | Training Hours | Weekly Hours by Sport | |
|---|---|---|---|---|---|---|---|---|
| | | 01:00 | E2 | | | | Run | 02:15 |
| 00:45 | E2 | | | 01:30 | E4 | 05:15 | Bike | 03:00 |
| | | 01:15 | E2 | | | | Run | 02:30 |
| 00:45 | E2 | | | 01:45 | E4 | 05:45 | Bike | 03:15 |
| | | 01:30 | E2 | | | | Run | 02:45 |
| 00:45 | E2 | | | 02:00 | E4 | 06:15 | Bike | 03:30 |
| Day off | | Brick | | Day off | | | | |
| | | 00:30 | Text | | | | Run | 01:00 |
| | | 01:00 | Text | | | 02:45 | Bike | 01:45 |
| | | 01:00 | A2 (5b) | | | | Run | 02:15 |
| 00:45 | E2 | | | 02:00 | M5(20–25) | 05:45 | Bike | 03:30 |
| | | 01:00 | A2 (5b) | | | | Run | 02:15 |
| 00:45 | E2 | | | 02:00 | M2(4–5aZ) | 05:45 | Bike | 03:30 |
| Day off | | . | Race sim. | | | | | |
| | | 00:30 | Text | | | | Run | 01:00 |
| | | 01:00 | | | | 02:45 | Bike | 01:45 |
| | | 01:00 | Text | | | | Run | 02:15 |
| 00:45 | E2 | | | 02:00 | M2(4–5aZ) | 05:45 | Bike | 03:30 |
| | | 01:00 | Text | | | | Run | 02:15 |
| 00:45 | E2 | | | 02:00 | M2(4–5aZ) | 05:45 | Bike | 03:30 |
| | | | Race sim. | | | | | |
| | | 00:50 | | | | | Run | 02:05 |
| 00:45 | S5 | 01:00 | | 00:30 | E1 | 05:05 | Bike | 03:00 |
| Day off | | | | Race! | | | | |
| | | | | | | | Run | 01:00 |
| | | 00:30 | S3 | | | 01:45 | Bike | 00:45 |

*Week 6 (Sunday):* 4–5 × 6 min. into Zones 4 to 5a (2 min. RI)

This training block has the first race simulation workout in Week 7. Total run time is shown as 30 minutes, but it is split as follows: Begin the workout by running for 15 minutes in Zones 1 to 2. Move right into a bike ride of 1 hour, including a 20-minute segment in Zones 4 to 5a near the end of the ride.

Transition back to a run. The last run is 15 minutes and steadily builds speed. Begin in Zone 1 and gently increase the speed throughout the 15 minutes so the last 3 to 5 minutes is in Zone 5a.

# PRE-COMPETITIVE 2 PREPARATION

Weeks 8 and 9 make up this block, and the two fast workouts are shown on Saturday and Sunday. As with Pre-competitive 1, some athletes are better served by separating the fast training days. If this is the case for you, complete the fast run on Thursday and make Saturday the E2 run.

## RUN

The run workouts in this block are both at the track. First, on Saturday in Week 8, warm up and include a few 20- to 30-second accelerations. Then:

*Run 2 × 800 meters,* checking pace at each 400 or 200 mark on the track. The goal is to run at your current 10K-race pace plus 1 to 5 seconds. For example, if your current 10K pace is 8 minutes per mile, your half-mile pace (800 meters) is 4 minutes, quarter-mile pace (400 meters) is 2 minutes, and 200 meters is 1 minute. In the example, this set would be run at a 2:01 to 2:05 pace per 400 meters. *Jog easy* in Zone 1 to recover. The rest interval should be equal to the run time. After the last recovery interval go right into the next run.

*Run 2 × 600 meters* at your current 10K-race pace.
*Jog easy* in Zone 1. The rest interval should be equal to the run time. After the last recovery interval, go right into the next run.

*Run 2 × 400 meters,* with each 400 at the current 10K race pace, minus 1 to 5 seconds (slightly faster than race pace). Check pace at each 200 meters or half-lap.
*Jog easy* in Zone 1. The rest interval should be equal to the run time. After the last recovery interval, go right into the next run.

*Run 2 × 200 meters,* with each 200 at 1 to 5 seconds faster than you ran the 200s in the previous 400 set.

*Jog easy* in Zone 1. The rest interval should be equal to the run time.

*Cool down* with easy jogging for 5 to 10 minutes and then stretching.

In Week 9, for the Saturday run, include in your warm-up a few 20- to 30-second accelerations. Then:

*Run 3 × 800 meters,* checking pace at each 400. The goal is to run at your current 10K race pace plus 1 to 5 seconds (slightly slower than race pace).

*Jog easy* in Zone 1. The rest interval should be equal to the run time. After the last recovery interval, go right into the next run.

*Run 3 × 600 meters* at current 10K race pace.

*Jog easy* in Zone 1. The rest interval should be equal to the run time. After the last recovery interval, go right into the next run.

*Run 3 × 400 meters* at current 10K-race pace, minus 1 to 5 seconds slightly faster than race pace. Check pace at each 200 meters or half-lap.

*Jog easy* in Zone 1. The rest interval should be equal to the run time. After the last recovery interval, go right into the next run.

*Run 3 × 200 meters,* with each 200 at 1 to 5 seconds faster than you ran the 200s in the previous 400 set.

*Jog easy* in Zone 1. The rest interval should be equal to the run time.

*Cool down* with easy jogging for 5 to 10 minutes and then stretching.

## BIKE

Two bike workouts in this block need special instruction. In Week 8, on Sunday, include two to three sets of 2-mile intervals, raising heart rate into Zones

4 to 5a. Note the time it takes you to cover 2 miles and make the recovery interval, in Zone 1, one-quarter the time of the work interval.

In Week 9, on Sunday, do three sets of 3-mile intervals (3 × 3 mi.), raising heart rate into Zones 4 to 5a. Note the time it takes you to cover 3 miles and make the recovery interval, in Zone 1, one-quarter the time of the work interval.

## COMPETITIVE PREPARATION

The competitive block will take you from Week 10 to race day. For the race simulation workout on Saturday of Week 10, begin with a 20-minute run in Zones 1 to 2. Transition to a 1:00 bike ride, beginning in Zones 1 to 2 and finishing the last 20 minutes at race pace, or roughly Zones 4 to 5a. Transition to a final run of 30 minutes, with 10 minutes in Zones 1 to 2 and the last 20 minutes at race pace.

Week 11 is race week and you need to rest. The only workout needing special instructions is the brick. Begin the brick by cycling for 30 minutes, and include three sets of 90-second taper intervals. Follow the bike ride with a short run of 15 minutes, with two sets of 90-second taper intervals.

## RACE DAY

With rest and proper nutrition, race day is greeted with eager, energized legs. After setting up your gear in the transition area, take an easy jog of 5 to 10 minutes to warm up. When the race begins, be patient during the first run. Open at a pace that feels like a Zone 1 to 2 intensity and make the run a negative-split effort. Transition to the bike and make the bike a negative-split effort as well.

The transition to the second run is always awkward; however, the beginning of the second run is at the same pace you finished the first run. The second run is also a negative-split effort. Increase your RPE over the last half of the race faster than you did in the first half. This strategy will help you have a successful race. Try to relax and take pleasure from the experience!

# 15

## 13 WEEKS TO A
## SUB-13-HOUR IRONMAN

*You are my new hero. I followed your plan "13 Weeks to a 13-Hour Ironman." As a 195-pound 50-year-old I had no real idea it would get me anywhere near the 13-hour mark—like most Ironman virgins I just wanted to finish and not hurt some part of my body. But it did work! I did an easy 12:55 at Florida Ironman, 20 minutes ahead of a man my age who trained at least twice as hard and long and who e-mailed you when he first read your article to tell you it wouldn't work! Thank you, I will use your plan when I enter Ironman Hawaii at age 60.*

—BRIAN DOWLING, USA

When I wrote a column titled "13 Weeks to a 13-Hour Ironman" for beginner Ironman-distance athletes with limited training time, it generated more positive reader response than any other column I've ever written. That column is now Chapter 7 of this book. Athletes in various age groups and with a range of initial ability wrote to tell me about their strong finishes in Ironman-distance races around the globe. If it is possible to train to successfully finish an Ironman-distance event in 13 hours with 13 weeks of preparation, not training over 13 hours in any given week, is it also possible to break the 13-hour mark in 13 weeks of training? It is that very question that inspired this chapter.

To help you decide if a sub-13 Ironman is in your future, take a look at Table 15.1. The chart displays split times by sport, given a particular pace during the Ironman event. These split times can be assembled into a total estimated finish time. Also, by combining different split times, it is possible to see there are different paths to a sub-13-hour Ironman race. For example, if an athlete happens to have the slowest swim time exhibited on the chart, at a 2 minute, 10 second pace per 100 meters, the swim-split time is 1:32. This athlete can really ride, able to average 19 mph on the bike. Add a swim of 1:32, a bike time of 5:54, and two transitions at 0:20 to total 7:46. This athlete can run slightly faster than a 5:14 marathon and be under 13 hours for the entire event.

A second athlete happens to be a faster runner and is confident she can clock a 3:30 pace on the marathon. Her bike, however, isn't as fast as she'd like at 7:28, average speed at 15 mph. Add her run, bike, and transition times together to total 11:18. She will need to swim slightly faster than 1:42, at a 2 minute, 25 second pace per 100 meters, to break 13 hours.

You can see from the two examples cited that there are different ways to complete an Ironman event in under 13 hours. In the examples given, the assumption was made that each athlete could hold the estimated paces for each leg of the entire event and the effort must be relatively easy, or mostly Zones 1 to 2 and limited Zone 3.

For your sub-13 Ironman, there are three key training areas to be aware of as you begin:

1. *Overall endurance (to go the distance)*
2. *High speed at an aerobic pace (high to average speed for a "relatively easy" effort)*
3. *Nutritional pacing*

Training in these three key areas will help you complete your sub-13 goal on race day.

| TABLE 15.1: SUB-13-HOUR RACE MIX AND MATCH | | | | | |
|---|---|---|---|---|---|
| SWIM 2.4 miles | | BIKE 112 miles | | RUN 26.2 miles | |
| Pace (100 m) | Split Time | Pace (mph) | Split Time | Pace (min./mi.) | Split Time |
| 02:10 | 1:32 | 15 | 7:28 | 12 | 5:14 |
| 02:00 | 1:25 | 16 | 7:00 | 11 | 4:48 |
| 01:50 | 1:17 | 17 | 6:35 | 10 | 4:22 |
| 01:40 | 1:00 | 18 | 6:13 | 9 | 3:56 |
| 01:30 | 1:03 | 19 | 5:54 | 8 | 3:30 |
| 01:20 | 0:56 | 20 | 5:36 | 7 | 3:03 |

Note: *Transitions can be estimated at 10 minutes each.*

## PROFILE

This plan is designed for an experienced triathlete who trains around 12 hours per week before beginning the program. You swim two to three times a week, and this may or may not be with a masters team. You ride a bike two to three days a week, and a 3-hour ride is normal for you. You run two to three days a week, with the long run of the week lasting between 1:30 and 1:45. Strength training may or may not be part of your weekly routine. In short, you are very fit with a good base of swimming, cycling, and running.

## GOAL

Swim 2.4 miles, bike 112 miles, and run 26.2 miles to complete an Ironman-distance triathlon, at the end of 13 weeks of preparation, finishing under 13 hours.

## THE PLAN

Your training plan is displayed in Table 15.2. There are one four-week cycle and three three-week cycles. The biggest training week is 18 hours. The plan includes building overall race endurance on the weekend workouts, which is where you will also practice nutritional pacing. There are interval sessions included to boost average speed.

The plan is written so that each week, one workout in each sport is intended to focus on the three key success areas. On some occasions one key area is worked on individually, while in other workouts, you'll work on some combination of the three key areas. The workouts most important for your success are also the ones that tend to be most stressful. These are called breakthrough (BT) workouts.

BT workouts are typically long or fast. Since most of an Ironman-distance event is raced below lactate threshold, one of the training goals is to see how fast you can go while keeping your heart rate below Zone 4 on the BT workouts. The fastest pace for the least cost (heart rate) is desirable.

In short, this plan is every busy, committed triathlete's dream because it is fast-track training for improved performance. Because each training period is compressed, I'll explain the plan by sport as I did in Part II on fast-track training. Be sure to read the full chapter before beginning the plan.

## STRENGTH TRAINING

If you have not been strength training, take Monday as a day off. If you are already strength training on your own program, keep lifting on Mondays. Strength training should not take the zip out of your arms and legs, so you may have to reduce the number of exercises you are doing or the repetitions of each exercise, or both.

If you are following your own strength training format, the most important exercises to keep in the mix are hip extension (squats, leg press, or step-ups), bent-arm lat pull-downs, abdominal and back extensions (or core body exercises), and seated rowing. If you have the time or personal need (injury prevention or area of weakness), include any of the following: hamstring curls, knee extension, adductors, abductors, or heel raises. Two or three sets of each exercise at around 12 repetitions (reps) work fine.

Be sure to do an aerobic warm-up of running or cycling before beginning a strength training session. Include an easy spin on a stationary bike to cool down after lifting, followed by stretching. Stretching suggestions and more detail on strength workouts are included in Chapter 22.

## SWIM

Although "meters" is used in the descriptions, if your pool is measured in yards, just substitute "yards" in the text. Four types of swim sessions are shown on the plan, including numbered, form, E2, and continuous workouts. The main set of the numbered swims (#1, #2, #3, etc.) is intended to be Zone 3 perceived exertion, up to T1 pace, depending on your swimming history. See Chapter 19 for a description of swimming paces. You can use the workouts in this chapter, swim with a masters group, or use *Workouts in a Binder®: Swim Workouts for Triathletes*. In all cases, try to keep the intensity of each swim as suggested in the training plan.

In all numbered workouts shown in this chapter, warm up with your choice of mixed swimming, drills, and kicks, totaling 800 to 1,500 meters. After the main set, cool down with a few hundred meters of easy swimming. The symbol (RI) means rest interval, so (:20 RI) means 20 seconds of rest between intervals. A second RI indicates the amount of rest you take before moving into the next segment of repeat intervals.

The numbered workouts are BT sessions and the major goal of each workout is to swim even splits for each segment. For example, in Swim #1, the 200 repeat times are within about 10 seconds of each other, followed by 100 repeats that are all within 5 seconds of each other. You're striving for a high average speed.

*Swim #1 main set:*  5–7 × 200 (:30 RI) at T1 pace, 1:00 RI
5–7 × 100 (:20 RI) at T1 pace

*Swim #2 main set:*  5–7 × 200 (:30 RI) at T1 pace, 1:00 RI
5–7 × 100 (:20 RI) at T1 pace, 1:00 RI
8–10 × 50 (:15 RI) at slightly faster than T1 pace

## TABLE 15.2: SUB-13-HOUR IRONMAN IN 13 WEEKS

| Week | Sport | Mon. Time | Mon. Code | Tues. Time | Tues. Code | Wed. Time | Wed. Code | Thurs. Time | Thurs. Code |
|---|---|---|---|---|---|---|---|---|---|
| 1 | Strength | 01:00 | SM | | | | | | |
| | Swim | or Day off | | 01:00 | #1 | | | 01:00 | E (Form) |
| | Bike | | | | | 01:00 | M2 (3Z) | | |
| | Run | | | 01:00 | M2 (3Z) | | | 00:30 | S3 |
| 2 | Strength | 01:00 | SM | | | | | | |
| | Swim | or Day off | | 01:00 | #2 | | | 01:00 | E (Form) |
| | Bike | | | | | 01:00 | M2 (3Z) | | |
| | Run | | | 01:00 | M2 (3Z) | | | 00:30 | S3 |
| 3 | Strength | 01:00 | SM | | | | | | |
| | Swim | or Day off | | 01:00 | #3 | | | 01:00 | E (Form) |
| | Bike | | | | | 01:00 | M2 (3Z) | | |
| | Run | | | 01:00 | M2 (3Z) | | | 00:30 | S3 |
| 4 | Strength | 01:00 | SM | | | | | | |
| | Swim | or Day off | | 00:45 | Text | | | 00:45 | E (Form) |
| | Bike | | | | | | | | |
| | Run | | | | | 00:45 | S3 | | |
| 5 | Strength | 01:00 | SM | | | | | | |
| | Swim | or Day off | | 01:00 | #4 | | | 01:00 | E (Form) |
| | Bike | | | | | 01:00 | S4 | | |
| | Run | | | 01:00 | M2 (3Z) | | | 00:30 | S3 |
| 6 | Strength | 01:00 | SM | | | | | | |
| | Swim | or Day off | | 01:00 | #5 | | | 01:00 | E (Form) |
| | Bike | | | | | 01:00 | M2 (3Z) | | |
| | Run | | | 01:00 | E2 | | | 00:30 | S3 |
| 7 | Strength | 01:00 | SM | | | | | | |
| | Swim | or Day off | | 00:45 | Text | | | 00:45 | E (Form) |
| | Bike | | | | | | | | |
| | Run | | | | | 00:45 | S3 | | |
| 8 | Strength | 01:00 | SM | | | | | | |
| | Swim | or Day off | | 01:15 | #6 | | | 01:00 | E (Form) |
| | Bike | | | | | 01:00 | S4 | | |
| | Run | | | 01:15 | M2 (3Z) | | | 00:30 | S3 |
| 9 | Strength | 01:00 | SM | | | | | | |
| | Swim | or Day off | | 01:30 | #7 | | | 01:00 | E (Form) |
| | Bike | | | | | 01:00 | M2 (3Z) | | |
| | Run | | | 01:15 | E2 | | | 00:30 | S3 |
| 10 | Strength | 01:00 | SM | | | | | | |
| | Swim | or Day off | | 00:45 | Text | | | 00:45 | E (Form) |
| | Bike | | | | | | | | |
| | Run | | | | | 00:45 | S3 | | |
| 11 | Strength | 01:00 | SM | | | | | | |
| | Swim | or Day off | | 00:45 | Text | | | 01:00 | E (Form) |
| | Bike | | | | | 01:00 | M1 (20) | | |
| | Run | | | 01:00 | S3 | | | 00:30 | E2 |

| Fri. Time | Fri. Code | Sat. Time | Sat. Code | Sun. Time | Sun. Code | Weekly Training Hours | Weekly Hours by Sport | |
|---|---|---|---|---|---|---|---|---|
| | | | | | | | Strength | 01:00 |
| | | 01:00 | E2 | | | | Swim | 03:00 |
| 01:00 | E1 | | | 03:00 | E2 | | Bike | 05:00 |
| | | 01:45 | E2 | | | 12:25 | Run | 03:15 |
| | | | | | | | Strength | 01:00 |
| | | 01:15 | E2 | | | | Swim | 03:15 |
| 01:00 | E1 | | | 03:00 | E2 | | Bike | 05:00 |
| | | 02:00 | E2 | | | 12:45 | Run | 03:30 |
| | | | | | | | Strength | 01:00 |
| | | 01:30 | E2 | | | | Swim | 03:30 |
| 01:00 | E1 | | | 03:00 | E2 | | Bike | 05:00 |
| | | 02:15 | E2 | | | 13:15 | Run | 03:45 |
| | | | | | | | Strength | 01:00 |
| | | | | | | | Swim | 01:30 |
| | | 02:00 | Brick (text) | 01:00 | E1 | | Bike | 03:00 |
| | | 01:00 | | | | 07:15 | Run | 01:45 |
| | | | | | | | Strength | 01:00 |
| | | 01:15 | E2 | | | | Swim | 03:15 |
| 01:00 | E1 | | | 04:30 | E3 | | Bike | 06:30 |
| | | 02:30 | E2 | | | 14:15 | Run | 04:00 |
| | | | | | | | Strength | 01:00 |
| | | 01:30 | E2 | | | | Swim | 03:30 |
| 01:00 | E1 | | | 05:00 | E2 | | Bike | 07:00 |
| | | 02:45 | E3 | | | 15:45 | Run | 04:15 |
| | | | | | | | Strength | 01:00 |
| | | | | | | | Swim | 01:30 |
| | | 03:00 | Brick (text) | 01:00 | E1 | | Bike | 04:00 |
| | | 02:00 | | | | 09:15 | Run | 02:45 |
| | | | | | | | Strength 01:00 | |
| | | 01:00 | E2 | | | | Swim | 03:15 |
| 01:00 | E1 | | | 05:30 | E3 | | Bike | 07:30 |
| | | 03:00 | E2 | | | 16:30 | Run | 04:45 |
| | | | | | | | Strength | 01:00 |
| | | 01:00 | E2 | | | | Swim | 03:30 |
| 01:00 | E1 | | | 06:00 | E2 | | Bike | 08:00 |
| | | 03:15 | E2 | | | 17:30 | Run | 05:00 |
| | | | | | | | Strength | 01:00 |
| | | | | | | | Swim | 01:30 |
| | | 02:00 | Brick (text) | 01:00 | E1 | | Bike | 03:00 |
| | | 01:00 | | | | 07:15 | Run | 01:45 |
| | | | | | | | Strength | 01:00 |
| | | 01:15 | #8 | | | | Swim | 03:00 |
| 01:00 | E1 | 04:30 | Brick (text) | | | | Bike | 06:30 |
| | | 01:30 | | 01:00 | S3 | 14:30 | Run | 04:00 |

| Week | Sport | Mon. Time | Mon. Code | Tues. Time | Tues. Code | Wed. Time | Wed. Code | Thurs. Time | Thurs. Code |
|------|-------|-----------|-----------|------------|------------|-----------|-----------|-------------|-------------|
| **TABLE 15.2: SUB-13-HOUR IRONMAN IN 13 WEEKS (CONTINUED)** | | | | | | | | | |
| 12 | Strength | Day off | | | | | | | |
| | Swim | | | 00:30 | text | | | 00:45 | E (Form) |
| | Bike | | | | | 01:00 | M1(20–30) | | |
| | Run | | | 00:30 | S3 | | | 00:30 | E2 |
| 13 | Strength | | | | | | | | |
| | Swim | | | | | | | 00:45 | #10 |
| | Bike | | | | | 01:00 | M6 | | |
| | Run | 00:30 | S3 | 00:30 | S3 | | | | |

*Swim #3 main set:* 5–7 × 300 (:30 RI) at T1 pace, 1:00 RI

10–12 × 50 (:15 RI) at slightly faster than T1 pace

*Swim #4 main set:* 10–15 × 100 (:15 RI) at T1 pace, 1:00 RI

5–8 × 100 (:10 RI) at T1 pace, 1:00 RI

10–15 × 50 (:15 RI) at slightly faster than T1 pace or build speed so each 50 is faster than the previous one

*Swim #5 main set:* 4–6 × 400 (:30 RI) at T1 pace, 1:00 RI

5–8 × 100 (:15 RI) at slightly faster average speed than previous set

*Swim #6 main set:* 10–15 × 200 (:20 RI) at T1 pace, 1:00 RI

6–10 × 50 (:15 RI), building speed throughout or at slightly faster average than T1 pace

*Swim #7 main set:* 4–6 × 500 (1:00 RI) at T1 pace, 2:00 RI

5–8 × 100 (:30 RI) at T1 pace, 1:00 RI

*Optional:* 6–10 × 50 (:30 RI), building speed throughout or at slightly faster average than T1 pace

| Fri. Time | Fri. Code | Sat. Time | Sat. Code | Sun. Time | Sun. Code | Weekly Training Hours | Weekly Hours by Sport | |
|---|---|---|---|---|---|---|---|---|
| Day off | | | | | | | Strength | |
| | | 01:00 | #9 | | | | Swim | 02:15 |
| | | 02:00 | Brick (text) | 01:15 | E1 | | Bike | 04:15 |
| | | | 02:00 | | | 09:30 | Run | 03:00 |
| Day off | | | | Race! | | | Strength | |
| | | | | | | | Swim | 00:45 |
| | | 00:20 | Brick (text) | | | | Bike | 01:20 |
| | | 00:10 | | | | 03:15 | Run | 01:10 |

*Swim #8 main set:* 5–8 × 200 (:20 RI) at T1 pace, 1:00 RI
8–10 × 100 (:10 RI) at T1 pace

*Swim #9 main set:* 5–8 × 100 (:10 RI) at T1 pace, 1:00 RI
5–8 × 100 (:20 RI) at T1 pace, 1:00 RI
5–8 × 100 (:30 RI), building speed on each 100 or
at slightly faster average than T1 pace for all 100s

*Swim #10 main set:* 1 × 500 at T1 pace, 2:00 RI
10 × 50 (:20 RI), building speed on each 50 or at
slightly faster average than T1 pace for all 50s

In general, use the lower number of repeats for the swim workouts early in the plan or if you are feeling tired. Add more repeats as the weeks progress and if you have the time and energy to do so. Advanced or fast swimmers can use the higher number of repeats.

For E2 swimming sessions, you will need to supplement this column with additional workouts from one of the many masters swimming Web sites, a workout book for swimmers, a masters group, or additional workouts from *Workouts in a Binder®: Swim Workouts for Triathletes,* available at www.VeloGear.com. If you use a masters group, try to control swimming speeds so intensity remains in the assigned zone for that day.

For an E (Form) workout in swimming, make the overall intensity Zone 1 with the focus on drills and good swimming technique.

A continuous session is completed by swimming for a continuous amount of time. This can be conducted in a safe open water situation or in a pool. If you do this in a pool, make it a "broken swim" by swimming 10 to 15 minutes continuously, then taking 1 or 2 minutes of recovery. Repeat the pattern until the assigned time is completed.

## CYCLING

Most of the Wednesday bike rides are designed to improve average speed. Friday bike rides are E1 for recovery and Sunday rides are either E2 or E3. To work on form, a few of the sessions are labeled S4 to improve your cadence.

For the numbered Wednesday workouts, begin in Zones 1 to 2, then proceed to the intervals after the warm-up. As soon as you increase speed, the interval time begins. Gently increase speed until your heart rate is in Zone 3 (Z3), then hold heart rate in that zone until the end of the interval. During the interval, speed may increase or decrease, depending on course conditions, but try to hold a steady Zone 3 heart rate once it has been achieved.

*Bike #1:*   4–6 × 4 min. Z3 (1:00 RI)
*Bike #2:*   4–6 × 5 min. Z3 (2:00 RI)
*Bike #3:*   4–6 × 6 min. Z3 (2:00 RI)
*Bike #4:*   3–5 × 8 min. Z3 (2:00 RI)
*Bike #5:*   3–5 × 10 min. Z3 (3:00 RI)
*Bike #6:*   After warm-up, ride 20 min. steady in Zone 3
*Bike #7:*   After warm-up, ride 20–30 min. steady in Zone 3
*Bike #8 (A7):*   After warm-up, ride 4 × 90 sec., allowing heart rate to climb into Zone 3 (1:30 RI)

## RUN

The run workouts are labeled E2 or E3, are numbered 1 through 5, or are noted as "Form." The numbered interval workouts are performed the same way as the bike intervals. Warm up in Zones 1 to 2, then proceed to the intervals. As soon as you increase speed, the interval time begins. Slowly increase speed until heart rate is in Zone 3 (Z3), then hold heart rate within Zone 3 until the end of the interval. The rest intervals are very easy jogging or walking. Form and numbered workouts follow (your choice of form workouts S1, S2, and S3 are described in Chapter 21):

*Run #1:* 4–6 × 4 min. Z3 (1:00 RI)
*Run #2:* 4–6 × 5 min. Z3 (2:00 RI)
*Run #3:* 4–6 × 6 min. Z3 (2:00 RI)
*Run #4:* 3–5 × 8 min. Z3 (2:00 RI)
*Run #5:* 3–4 × 10 min. Z3 (3:00 RI)

On long run workouts and in the race, consider using walking intervals as a strategy to increase average speed. A couple of athletes I coached, Jim and Janet Green, used a run 30 minutes, walk 10 minutes format to get 2 miles farther on their long training runs preparing for a marathon and eventually an Ironman. They used the walking time to recover, refuel, and rehydrate. These experienced athletes used the run-walk strategy to shave an entire hour off their Black Mountain Marathon trail run time.

Would you rather say, "I ran (or shuffled) the entire marathon, I didn't walk a single time!" or "I ran and walked my way to a personal best time"?

## BRICKS

Bricks are listed on the Saturdays of Weeks 4, 7, 10, 11, 12, and 13. Bike for the time shown below the total brick time, then transition to a run. The time for the run is displayed below the bike time. For each sport within the brick workouts, complete the first half of the time at intensity Zones 1 to 2 and the return trip in Zones 1 to 3. This is a negative-split strategy.

To use this strategy in Week 4, for example, begin with a 60-minute ride in Zones 1 to 2. Turn around and come home in Zones 1 to 3. If you feel good, push more Zone 3. Transition to a 30-minute run, going out in Zones 1 to 2, then run home in Zones 1 to 3. Again, go for more Zone 3 if you feel strong. Also, you can include a few 20- to 30-second accelerations (not all-out sprints) on the return trip. Performed correctly, it should take less time to return home than it takes to go out.

The only brick that should be performed differently than described in the last two paragraphs is the brick in Week 13. The overall intensity of the entire Week 13 brick is in Zones 1 to 2. Within the brick, include a few 20-second accelerations in each sport to help your legs feel light and fast.

## EATING AND DRINKING IN TRAINING AND RACING

You must, must, must eat and drink on a regular basis during long training sessions and during your sub-13 event. If you get lazy or sloppy about eating and drinking, chances are you will end up in the medical tent, above your sub-13 goal time, or perhaps in a ditch (I'm not kidding). An athlete I coach lost track of his eating and drinking pace during a half-Ironman event. Additionally, he was concerned about eating too much because of a fear he'd gain weight. This fear and inattention to detail ended his race. On the run portion of the race, he remembers waking up in a ditch with medical personnel around him. Minutes later he recalls a visit to the medical tent. His race ended with a rectal thermometer instead of a finisher's medal.

To help obtain a finisher's medal and a personal-best time, it is critical to practice eating and drinking at regular intervals during training sessions lasting over an hour, then use the same format during the race. As a rule of thumb, most people need to consume some 300 to 600 calories and drink one bottle of fluid each hour, during both training and racing. There are exceptions to this guideline, with some people being over or under those numbers. More calories are needed for larger people and for faster paces. The pace of fueling is as important as race pace. One strategy is to set the timer on your watch to chirp every 15 to 20 minutes to remind you to eat and drink.

## RACE DAY

When race day arrives, I hope you can enjoy each moment. Your body is in remarkable condition. Plan to do the race in a negative-split fashion, just like the brick workouts. Begin each sport in Zones 1 to 2 and plan to make the second half of each event slightly faster. Be cautious not to push the intensity too much on the last half of the bike ride. If you feel up to it, include a few 20-second accelerations throughout the event—just as you did in training. Keep your fuel pacing (eating and drinking at regular intervals) consistent throughout the event. By focusing on the three key success areas during training and racing, you can enjoy a sub-13 Ironman buffet.

# PART V

# Long-Term Training

The plans in Part V are 26 to 52 weeks in length. There are three plans in this part to accommodate serious multisport athletes, not beginners.

Because these plans span several months, each chapter includes a brief overview that displays the number of weeks in the plan, a suggested month to begin training, the phase of training for that month, and the total training hours each week. Any special instructions for each training phase are detailed in the chapter text.

Although it is highly unlikely you can use the plans exactly as they appear in this book, you can use the format and general design to tailor the plans to your personal needs. You may need to reduce the hours of one or more of the workouts. It may be necessary to reduce the intensity of one workout per week. You may need to put hill repeats in cycling instead of running, due to your personal race goals and performance limiters. Don't be afraid to make those design modifications, because the optimal plan is the one that meets your personal needs best.

# 16

## 27-WEEK PLAN TO
## A HALF-IRONMAN

*During the race I try to keep my motivation up by saying, "Anything can happen to anyone, so it ain't over 'til it's over!" Again I remind myself to "RACE YOUR RACE." After the race I don't dwell too long on the events of the race; instead, I try to draw on the experiences and lessons I learned from the race and move on to preparing myself for the next one.*

—GAIL LAURENCE, USA

The experienced triathlete using the half-Ironman plan in this chapter prefers a gentle increase in training hours. Weekly training hours during the early part of the year are somewhat limited by short days (and perhaps short desire). There is something about winter that turns normally enjoyable hours of endurance activities into arduous training.

The plan overview is shown in Table 16.1. Although the plan begins on the first Monday in January, the weeks could easily slide forward a month or two to prepare for a late July or August race. This plan is very similar to the Ironman plan in Chapter 15, and it may be helpful to read the instructions for that chapter as well. One of the major differences in format between the Ironman plan and this plan, besides volume, is the addition of a rest week at Week 24 and a full three-week taper. Both methods work, and the decision about which format to use depends on each individual athlete and the number of weeks available to train. Some athletes need that extra week of rest prior to a taper, while others prefer to head into a gentle tapering of volume after the largest training week. You need to decide what method works best for you.

## PROFILE

You are an experienced triathlete and maintain fitness throughout the year. Other commitments, such as holidays, and a conscious decision to take a break have you training between seven and eight hours each week. This training has been consistent for at least four weeks. The training has consisted of swimming once or twice a week, running three times a week, and cycling once or twice a week for an hour on a trainer or in a spin class. You may have done a bit of crosstraining, such as hiking, cross-country skiing, or snowshoeing. Week 1 on the first page of the detailed plan (Table 16.2) seems quite easy to accomplish. The long weekend workouts for the remainder of the plan, although challenging, seem doable.

## GOAL

Your goal is to complete a half-Ironman race that is about six months away.

## THE PLAN

The entire 27-week plan is shown in Table 16.2. In the first three months, overall training time builds over four-week blocks, rather than every week. Weekly training hours begin to build in late March as the days get warmer and longer. Those living in the Southern Hemisphere might begin Week 1 in May. The longest training week on the plan is around 15:30, four weeks before race week. The structure of the plan typically puts long runs on Saturday and long bike rides on Sunday. One benefit of this kind of structure is that athletes run on relatively rested legs and reduce their risk of injury. Some would argue that athletes run on tired legs after a bike ride of 56 miles on race day, and that therefore the long bike in training should be on Saturday and the long run on

| | | | Weekly Planned |
|---|---|---|---|
| Week | Month | Period | Hours |
| 1 | January | Specific Preparation 1 | 09:30 |
| 2 | January | Specific Preparation 1 | 09:45 |
| 3 | January | Specific Preparation 1 | 09:45 |
| 4 | January | Specific Preparation 1 | 07:15 |
| 5 | January/February | Specific Preparation 2 | 10:30 |
| 6 | February | Specific Preparation 2 | 10:30 |
| ⑦ | February | Specific Preparation 2 | 10:30 |
| 8 | February | Specific Preparation 2 | 06:45 |
| 9 | February/March | Specific Preparation 3 | 11:00 |
| 10 | March | Specific Preparation 3 | 11:00 |
| 11 | March | Specific Preparation 3 | 11:00 |
| 12 | March | Specific Preparation 3 | 06:45 |
| 13 | March/April | Pre-competitive 1 | 10:15 |
| 14 | April | Pre-competitive 1 | 11:45 |
| 15 | April | Pre-competitive 1 | 12:45 |
| 16 | April | Pre-competitive 1 | 07:00 |
| 17 | April/May | Pre-competitive 2 | 11:45 |
| 18 | May | Pre-competitive 2 | 13:30 |
| 19 | May | Pre-competitive 2 | 14:15 |
| 20 | May | Pre-competitive 2 | 07:00 |
| 21 | May | Pre-competitive 3 | 12:45 |
| 22 | May/June | Pre-competitive 3 | 14:30 |
| 23 | June | Pre-competitive 3 | 15:30 |
| 24 | June | Pre-competitive 3 | 07:00 |
| 25 | June | Competitive | 12:15 |
| 26 | June/July | Competitive | 08:15 |
| 27 | July | Competitive | 03:45 + Race |

TABLE 16.1: PLAN OVERVIEW

Sunday. Either way will work, so choose the format that suits your personal needs.

As you progress through the plan, notice that leg and arm speed drills are included throughout the 27 weeks. Too often, athletes who train for a long event slog through endless, slow miles. While that strategy does build endurance, constantly swimming, cycling, or running at a sauntering pace teaches the body to function at that one speed. To enhance endurance training, form work is included, because it is neuromuscular in nature and is intended to improve economy. Form work sessions give you more gears, so to speak. The fast segments are high-speed movements with good form, for short duration. After finishing a form session, you should feel fast and eager to do more, not exhausted.

| Week | Sport | Mon. Time | Mon. Code | Tues. Time | Tues. Code | Wed. Time | Wed. Code | Thurs. Time |
|------|-------|-----------|-----------|------------|------------|-----------|-----------|-------------|
| *1* | Strength | 01:15 | AA | | | 01:15 | AA | |
| | Swim | | | 01:00 | E2 | | | 01:00 |
| | Bike | | | | | | | |
| | Run | | | 00:30 | S2 | | | 00:30 |
| *2* | Strength | 01:15 | AA | | | 01:15 | AA | |
| | Swim | | | 01:00 | E2 | | | 01:00 |
| | Bike | | | | | | | |
| | Run | | | 00:45 | S2 | | | 00:30 |
| *3* | Strength | 01:15 | AA | | | 01:15 | AA | |
| | Swim | | | 01:00 | E2 | | | 01:00 |
| | Bike | | | | | | | |
| | Run | | | 00:45 | S2 | | | 00:30 |
| *4* | Strength | 01:15 | AA | | | 01:15 | AA | |
| | Swim | | | | | | | 01:00 |
| | Bike | | | | | | | |
| | Run | | | 00:45 | S2 | | | |
| *5* | Strength | 01:15 | MS | | | 01:30 | MS | |
| | Swim | | | 01:00 | E (Form) | | | 01:00 |
| | Bike | | | | | | | |
| | Run | | | 00:45 | S2 | | | 00:30 |
| *6* | Strength | 01:15 | MS | | | 01:30 | MS | |
| | Swim | | | 01:00 | E (Speed) | | | 01:00 |
| | Bike | | | | | | | |
| | Run | | | 00:45 | S2 | | | 00:30 |
| *7* | Strength | 01:15 | MS | | | 01:30 | MS | |
| | Swim | | | 01:00 | E (Form) | | | 01:00 |
| | Bike | | | | | | | |
| | Run | | | 00:45 | S2 | | | 00:30 |
| *8* | Strength | 01:00 | MS | | | 01:00 | MS | |
| | Swim | | | | | | | 01:00 |
| | Bike | | | | | | | |
| | Run | | | 00:45 | S2 | | | |
| *9* | Strength | 01:00 | PE | | | 01:15 | PE + Plyo #1 | |
| | Swim | | | 01:00 | E (Speed) | | | 01:00 |
| | Bike | | | | | | | |
| | Run | | | 00:45 | TM #1 or S2 | | | 00:30 |
| *10* | Strength | 01:00 | PE | | | 01:15 | PE + Plyo #2 | |
| | Swim | | | 01:00 | Force | | | 01:00 |
| | Bike | | | | | | | |
| | Run | | | 00:45 | TM #2 or S2 | | | 00:30 |
| *11* | Strength | 01:00 | PE | | | 01:15 | PE + Plyo #3 | |
| | Swim | | | 01:00 | Force | | | 01:00 |
| | Bike | | | | | | | |
| | Run | | | 00:45 | TM #3 or S2 | | | 00:30 |

**TABLE 16.2: 27-WEEK HALF-IRONMAN PERFORMANCE PLAN**

| Thurs. Code | Fri. Time | Fri. Code | Sat. Time | Sat. Code | Sun. Time | Sun. Code | Weekly Training Hours | Weekly Hours by Sport | |
|---|---|---|---|---|---|---|---|---|---|
| | | | | | | | | Strength | 02:30 |
| T1b | | | 01:00 | E (Form) | | | | Swim | 03:00 |
| | 01:00 | S1 | | | 01:00 | T1 (5) | | Bike | 02:00 |
| E1* | | | 01:00 | T1 (3) | | | 09:30 | Run | 02:00 |
| | | | | | | | | Strength | 02:30 |
| E (Speed) | | | 01:00 | E (Form) | | | | Swim | 03:00 |
| | 01:00 | S2 | | | 01:00 | E2* | | Bike | 02:00 |
| E1* | | | 01:00 | E2 | | | 09:45 | Run | 02:15 |
| | | | | | | | | Strength | 02:30 |
| E (Speed) | | | 01:00 | E (Form) | | | | Swim | 03:00 |
| | 01:00 | S1 | | | 01:00 | E2* | | Bike | 02:00 |
| E1* | | | 01:00 | E2 | | | 09:45 | Run | 02:15 |
| | | | | | | | | Strength | 02:30 |
| E (Speed) | | | 00:45 | E (Form) | | | | Swim | 01:45 |
| | 00:30 | S2 | | | 01:00 | S5 | | Bike | 01:30 |
| | | | 00:45 | S1 | | | 07:15 | Run | 01:30 |
| | | | | | | | | Strength | 02:45 |
| E2 | | | 01:15 | E3 | | | | Swim | 03:15 |
| | 01:00 | S1 | | | 01:15 | E3 | | Bike | 02:15 |
| E1* | | | 01:00 | E2 | | | 10:30 | Run | 02:15 |
| | | | | | | | | Strength | 02:45 |
| E2 | | | 01:15 | E3 | | | | Swim | 03:15 |
| | 01:00 | S2 | | | 01:15 | E2* | | Bike | 02:15 |
| E2 | | | 01:00 | E3 | | | 10:30 | Run | 02:15 |
| | | | | | | | | Strength | 02:45 |
| E2 | | | 01:15 | E3 | | | | Swim | 03:15 |
| | 01:00 | S1 | | | 01:15 | E3 | | Bike | 02:15 |
| E1* | | | 01:00 | E2 | | | 10:30 | Run | 02:15 |
| | | | | | | | | Strength | 02:00 |
| T1b | | | 00:45 | E (Form) | | | | Swim | 01:45 |
| | 00:30 | S2 | | | 01:00 | T1 (5) | | Bike | 01:30 |
| | | | 00:45 | T1(3) | | | 06:45 | Run | 01:30 |
| | | | | | | | | Strength | 02:15 |
| M | | | 01:15 | E2 | | | | Swim | 03:15 |
| | 01:00 | S1 | | | 02:00 | E2 | | Bike | 03:00 |
| E2 | | | 01:15 | E4 | | | 11:00 | Run | 02:30 |
| | | | | | | | | Strength | 02:15 |
| E2 | | | 01:15 | E2 | | | | Swim | 03:15 |
| | 01:00 | S2 | | | 02:00 | E2* | | Bike | 03:00 |
| E2 | | | 01:15 | E2 | | | 11:00 | Run | 02:30 |
| | | | | | | | | Strength | 02:15 |
| M | | | 01:15 | E2 | | | | Swim | 03:15 |
| | 01:00 | S1 | | | 02:00 | E2* | | Bike | 03:00 |
| E2 | | | 01:15 | E4 | | | 11:00 | Run | 02:30 |

| Week | Sport | Mon. Time | Mon. Code | Tues. Time | Tues. Code | Wed. Time | Wed. Code | Thurs. Time |
|------|-------|-----------|-----------|------------|------------|-----------|-----------|-------------|
| | | | | | **TABLE 16.2: 27-WEEK HALF-IRONMAN PERFORMANCE PLAN (CONTINUED)** | | | |
| 12 | Strength | 01:00 | PE | | | 01:15 | PE + Plyo #4 | |
| | Swim | | | | | | | 00:45 |
| | Bike | | | | | | | |
| | Run | | | 00:45 | TM #4 or S2 | | | 00:30 |
| 13 | Strength | 01:00 | SM | | | | | |
| | Swim | | | 01:00 | E (Speed) | | | 01:00 |
| | Bike | | | | | 01:00 | M1 (20) | |
| | Run | | | 00:45 | S2 | | | 00:30 |
| 14 | Strength | 01:00 | SM | | | | | |
| | Swim | | | 01:00 | E (Form) | | | 01:00 |
| | Bike | | | | | 01:00 | E2 | |
| | Run | | | 00:45 | S1 | | | 01:00 |
| 15 | Strength | 01:00 | SM | | | | | |
| | Swim | | | 01:00 | E (Speed) | | | 01:00 |
| | Bike | | | | | 01:30 | M1 (30) | |
| | Run | | | 00:30 | S2 | | | 01:00 |
| 16 | Strength | 01:00 | SM | | | | | |
| | Swim | | | | | | | 01:00 |
| | Bike | | | | | 01:00 | S5 | |
| | Run | | | 00:45 | S1 | | | |
| 17 | Strength | 01:00 | SM | | | | | |
| | Swim | | | 01:00 | E (Form) | | | 01:00 |
| | Bike | | | | | 00:45 | E2 | |
| | Run | | | 00:30 | S2 | | | 00:30 |
| 18 | Strength | 01:00 | SM | | | | | |
| | Swim | | | 01:00 | E (Speed) | | | 01:15 |
| | Bike | | | | | 01:15 | M1 (40) | |
| | Run | | | 00:30 | E2 | | | 01:00 |
| 19 | Strength | 01:00 | SM | | | | | |
| | Swim | | | 01:00 | E (Form) | | | 01:00 |
| | Bike | | | | | 01:15 | E2 | |
| | Run | | | 01:00 | M2 (3Z) | | | 00:30 |
| 20 | Strength | 01:00 | SM | | | | | |
| | Swim | | | | | | | 01:00 |
| | Bike | | | | | 01:00 | S5 | |
| | Run | | | 00:45 | S1 | | | |
| 21 | Strength | 01:00 | SM | | | | | |
| | Swim | | | 01:00 | E (Speed) | | | 01:00 |
| | Bike | | | | | 00:45 | E2 | |
| | Run | | | 00:30 | E2 | | | 00:30 |
| 22 | Strength | 01:00 | SM | | | | | |
| | Swim | | | 01:00 | E (Form) | | | 01:00 |
| | Bike | | | | | 01:30 | M1 (40–50) | |
| | Run | | | 01:00 | E2 | | | 00:30 |

| Thurs. Code | Fri. Time | Fri. Code | Sat. Time | Sat. Code | Sun. Time | Sun. Code | Weekly Training Hours | Weekly Hours by Sport | |
|---|---|---|---|---|---|---|---|---|---|
| | Day off | | | | | | | Strength | 02:15 |
| M (Speed) | | | 00:45 | E (Form) | | | | Swim | 01:30 |
| | | | | | 01:00 | S5 | | Bike | 01:00 |
| E2 | | | 00:45 | A1b | | | 06:45 | Run | 02:00 |
| | | | | | | | | Strength | 01:00 |
| E2 | | | 01:00 | M | | | | Swim | 03:00 |
| | 01:00 | E1 | | | 01:30 | E2 | | Bike | 03:30 |
| E2 | | | 01:30 | E3 | | | 10:15 | Run | 02:45 |
| | | | | Brick | | | | Strength | 01:00 |
| E2 | | | 01:15 | E3 | | | | Swim | 03:15 |
| | 01:15 | S4 | 01:00 | E2 | 02:00 | E3 | | Bike | 05:15 |
| M2 (3Z) | | | 00:30 | E2 | | | 11:45 | Run | 02:15 |
| | | | | | | | | Strength | 01:00 |
| E2 | | | 01:15 | E3 | | | | Swim | 03:15 |
| | 01:30 | E1 | | | 02:30 | E2 | | Bike | 05:30 |
| E2 | | | 01:30 | E3 | | | 12:45 | Run | 03:00 |
| | Day off | | | | | | | Strength | 01:00 |
| T1b | | | 01:00 | E (Form) | | | | Swim | 02:00 |
| | | | | | 01:30 | T1 (6–10) | | Bike | 02:30 |
| | | | 00:45 | E2 | | | 07:00 | Run | 01:30 |
| | | | | | | | | Strength | 01:00 |
| E2 | | | 01:15 | E3 | | | | Swim | 03:15 |
| | 01:00 | S5 | | | 03:00 | E3 | | Bike | 04:45 |
| E1 | | | 01:45 | E3 | | | 11:45 | Run | 02:45 |
| | | | | Brick | | | | Strength | 01:00 |
| E3 | | | 01:00 | E1 | | | | Swim | 03:15 |
| | 01:15 | S4 | 01:00 | Text | 03:30 | E2 | | Bike | 07:00 |
| E2 | | | 00:45 | Text | | | 13:30 | Run | 02:15 |
| | | | | | | | | Strength | 01:00 |
| E2 | | | 01:15 | E3 | | | | Swim | 03:15 |
| | 01:30 | S4 | | | 04:00 | E3 | | Bike | 06:45 |
| S2 | | | 01:45 | E2 | | | 14:15 | Run | 03:15 |
| | Day off | | | | | | | Strength | 01:00 |
| T1b | | | 01:00 | E (Form) | | | | Swim | 02:00 |
| | | | | | 01:30 | E2 | | Bike | 02:30 |
| | | | 00:45 | T1 (3) | | | 07:00 | Run | 01:30 |
| | | | | | | | | Strength | 01:00 |
| E2 | | | 01:00 | E3 | | | | Swim | 03:00 |
| | 01:00 | S2 | | | 04:00 | E3 | | Bike | 05:45 |
| E1 | | | 02:00 | E3 | | | 12:45 | Run | 03:00 |
| | | | | Brick | | | | Strength | 01:00 |
| E2 | | | 01:30 | E3 | | | | Swim | 03:30 |
| | 00:30 | S1 | 01:00 | Text | 04:30 | E2 | | Bike | 07:30 |
| E1 | | | 01:00 | Text | | | 14:30 | Run | 02:30 |

| | | TABLE 16.2: 27-WEEK HALF-IRONMAN PERFORMANCE PLAN (CONTINUED) | | | | | | |
|---|---|---|---|---|---|---|---|---|
| Week | Sport | Mon. Time | Mon. Code | Tues. Time | Tues. Code | Wed. Time | Wed. Code | Thurs. Time |
| 23 | Strength | 01:00 | SM | | | | | |
| | Swim | | | 01:00 | E (Speed) | | | 01:00 |
| | Bike | | | | | 01:15 | E2 | |
| | Run | | | 01:00 | E2 | | | 00:30 |
| 24 | Strength | 01:00 | SM | | | | | |
| | Swim | | | | | | | 01:00 |
| | Bike | | | | | 01:00 | S5 | |
| | Run | | | 00:45 | S1 | | | |
| 25 | Strength | 01:00 | SM | | | | | |
| | Swim | | | 01:00 | E (Form) | | | 01:00 |
| | Bike | | | | | 01:00 | E2 | |
| | Run | | | 01:00 | S1 | | | 00:30 |
| 26 | Strength | 01:00 | SM | | | | | |
| | Swim | | | 00:45 | E (Speed) | | | 00:45 |
| | Bike | | | | | 01:00 | S5 | |
| | Run | | | 00:30 | E2 | | | 00:45 |
| 27 | Strength | | | | | | | |
| | Swim | | | 00:45 | E (Speed) | | | |
| | Bike | | | | | 00:45 | M1 (15) | |
| | Run | 00:45 | M1 (20) | | | | | 00:30 |

For the first few weeks, include at least one 800- to 1,000-meter main set in your swim workouts. The swim can be continuous or broken. If broken, make the rest intervals no greater than 10 seconds. Slowly increase the distance of this main set over the course of several weeks to 1,500 to 2,000 meters. Some athletes may reach a main set of 2,500 meters, but much over that is not necessary. If you have accomplished the main-set goals, add some Zone 3 intensity to segments of the main set to increase muscular endurance.

# SPECIFIC PREPARATION 1

The first week of the plan includes a baseline time trial in each sport. It goes without saying that if you have not been training consistently, do not begin

| Thurs. Code | Fri. Time | Fri. Code | Sat. Time | Sat. Code | Sun. Time | Sun. Code | Weekly Training Hours | Weekly Hours by Sport | |
|---|---|---|---|---|---|---|---|---|---|
| | | | | | | | | Strength | 01:00 |
| E2 | | | 01:30 | E3 | | | | Swim | 03:30 |
| | 01:15 | S5 | | | 05:00 | E3 | | Bike | 07:30 |
| E1 | | | 02:00 | E3 | | | 15:30 | Run | 03:30 |
| | Day off | | | | | | | Strength | 01:00 |
| T1b | | | 01:00 | E (Form) | | | | Swim | 02:00 |
| | | | | | 01:30 | T1 (6–10) | | Bike | 02:30 |
| | | | 00:45 | E2 | | | 07:00 | Run | 01:30 |
| | | | | | | | | Strength | 01:00 |
| E2 | | | 01:15 | E3 | | | | Swim | 03:15 |
| | 01:00 | S4 | 02:15 | Text | 01:00 | E1 | | Bike | 05:15 |
| E2 | | | 01:15 | Text | | | 12:15 | Run | 02:45 |
| | Day off | | | Brick | | | | Strength | 01:00 |
| E2 | | | 01:00 | M | | | | Swim | 02:30 |
| | | | 01:00 | Text | 01:00 | E1 | | Bike | 03:00 |
| E2 | | | 00:30 | Text | | | 08:15 | Run | 01:45 |
| | Day off | | | Brick | Race! | | | Strength | 00:00 |
| | | | 00:30 | E (Speed) | | | | Swim | 01:15 |
| | | | 00:20 | S4 | | | | Bike | 01:05 |
| S2 | | | 00:10 | S2 | | | 03:45 | Run | 01:25 |

the plan—especially time trials—until you have achieved some foundation conditioning. That foundation is described in the Profile section.

This plan allows for crosstraining. An asterisk (*) beside the code of any workout, such as the run on Thursday of Week 1, means crosstraining is an option. Because heart rate ranges vary for different sports, use rate of perceived exertion (RPE) to determine the correct training zones. Suggestions for crosstraining include aerobics classes, circuit training, kickboxing, snowshoeing, cross-country skiing, and hiking, to name a few. Athletes using crosstraining in this plan are blending general and specific phases of training until the crosstraining is eliminated.

Spin classes can also serve as excellent sources of winter training. A few words of caution: Do not let the instructor or other students in the class determine the intensity of your session, but work out at your own pace.

For all Friday bike rides for Weeks 1 through 12, ride time can be between 30 and 60 minutes.

## SPECIFIC PREPARATION 2

This first block of Specific Preparation 2 training includes two maximum strength (MS) training days per week, which are particularly helpful to build strength for hilly bike courses. Some athletes find that two days of MS strength training fatigue their legs and that they need to reduce the intensity of one of the weekend workouts. If this is the case for you, reduce the intensity of the sport that is already your strength.

## SPECIFIC PREPARATION 3

The first Specific Preparation 3 block has several options. The first option is the Tuesday run. For experienced athletes, I recommend doing the treadmill workouts found in Appendix G. Choose the lower number of repetitions in each set. I have found no better training tool to improve running speed and pace perception than a treadmill. People who are uncomfortable getting on and off a running treadmill are better off sticking to simple pickups.

The second option during this block is the plyometric workouts shown with the Wednesday strength training session and found in Appendix F. Chapter 22, which covers strength training, explains why plyometrics enhance an endurance athlete's training program. If you are in the first season of plyometric work, select the lowest number of sets and repetitions. Also, if you are in your first year of plyometrics, include one plyo workout per week.

Both plyometrics and the treadmill sessions are not intended to be exceptionally difficult workouts. If you are exhausted or extremely sore after either workout, it is a message to back off on speed or intensity of the sessions.

This is the last training block that includes optional crosstraining.

## PRE-COMPETITIVE PREPARATION 1

The second block of Pre-competitive Preparation 1 is when weekly endurance volume begins to build and strength training is reduced to one day for strength maintenance (SM). The intensity of workouts remains in Zones 1 to 3, where most of a half-Ironman race will occur. Hilly races will solicit some time in Zones 4 and above, but keep this time very minimal.

Week 14 of the plan has a Zone 3 run on Thursday that should be three to four sets of 6-minute intervals with 2-minute rest intervals (RI), or 3–4 × 6 min. (2 min. RI). All Wednesday bike rides that do not include Zone 3 time should be considered optional. Cut the ride time down or eliminate the ride altogether if you are feeling excessive fatigue.

Saturday of Week 14 has the first brick of the schedule, which can be done immediately after the swim or later in the day. Both bike and run segments are in Zones 1 and 2.

Once athletes begin to increase training volume, many find that more than two aerobic time trials within the rest week are too much. So with that in mind, there are only two time trials in Week 16; notice that the distance of the bike time trial is increased.

## PRE-COMPETITIVE PREPARATION 2

Weekly volume continues to build during this block. This is a perfect opportunity to establish the eating and drinking format you will use on race day. Take the time to figure out a nutritional plan—in detail—and write it down. What will you eat and drink each 15 to 20 minutes of the entire race? Do not take this lightly; many half-Ironman races have been spoiled by not eating or drinking properly. Make a plan and practice it.

The workouts needing additional explanation during this block include the brick on Saturday of Week 18 and the run in Week 19. For the Week 18 Saturday brick, both sports are controlled at Zones 1 to 2 for the first half of the assigned time. The second half of the time can go at Zones 1 to 3. It is not a goal to maximize time in Zone 3. For the Week 19 Tuesday run, do 3–5 × 6 min. (2 min. RI).

## PRE-COMPETITIVE PREPARATION 3

The most important workouts of Weeks 21 through 24 are scheduled on the weekends. Other workouts during the week should be reduced, if necessary, to allow for full recovery for the weekend sessions. For the Week 22 Saturday brick, both sports are controlled at Zones 1 to 2 for the first half of the assigned time. The second half of the time can go in Zones 1 to 3. It is not a goal to maximize time in Zone 3.

## COMPETITIVE PREPARATION

All of the hard work is complete; it is time to enjoy. Weeks 25, 26, and 27 have reduced volume and some intensity to keep legs and arms feeling rested and fresh for race day. The bricks in Weeks 25 and 26 are negative-split efforts; that is, the first half of time for the bike and run are at Zones 1 to 2 intensity. The second half is at Zones 1 to 3, and should be slightly faster. Two to three weeks prior to the race is a good time for a total bike tune-up. This allows enough time for new cables to stretch and any problems to appear so they can be addressed before the bike is racked in the transition area on race day.

## RACE DAY

On race day, pace yourself and recall your practice sessions: long runs, long bike rides, long swims, and bricks. Those workouts were all simply dress rehearsals for race day. Race pace should be no faster than what was practiced in training. This can be difficult to control with surging adrenaline and a rested body that wants to take off like a thoroughbred coming out of the gate.

To help control that thoroughbred impulse, recall the negative-split workouts, where the first half of the session was done at a lower intensity than the second half of the workout. Try to make each individual sport, and the entire race, a negative split. This means that the swim will be at a lower RPE and relative speed than the last half of the run. Each leg of the race—

swim, bike, and run—should be split in half as well. The first half of each event is a bit slower, or at a lower intensity, than the second half. These increases in speed are subtle.

At the end of the race, celebrate—and don't make that subtle!

# 17

# 26-WEEK PLAN TO
# AN IRONMAN

*I have loved training and racing in endurance sports, especially run-*
*ning, since I was 14. Long, intense workouts were enjoyable, so hard*
*work came naturally. However, constant injury disrupted my training*
*continuity, causing regression and frustration. Training with a great*
*coach is teaching me that part of discipline is training intelligently.*
*Hard work alone can be a powerfully destructive force without a well-*
*focused plan based on knowledge.*
  *And I am finally getting the joke on pace. Controlling the pace within*
*each sport, so I don't start too fast, is critical for Ironman training*
*and racing—this goes for eating and drinking as well.*

—PAUL O'BRIEN, USA

It is the post-holiday, northern-latitude Ironman who appreciates the plan
in this chapter. Cold, short winter days keep bike rides at a two-hour limit
on the indoor trainer. There are stories of people spending inhuman
amounts of time on an indoor trainer watching multiple tapes of old Ironman races—but that is not for you, thank you.

The plan overview is shown in Table 17.1. Although the plan begins on
the first Monday in January, the weeks could easily slide forward a month
or two to prepare for a late July or August race. The plan in this chapter is
similar to the Chapter 16 plan for a half-Ironman, so you may find it beneficial to read that chapter as well.

| | | TABLE 17.1: PLAN OVERVIEW | |
|---|---|---|---|
| Week | Month | Period | Weekly Planned Hours |
| 1 | January | Specific Preparation 1 | 09:30 |
| 2 | January | Specific Preparation 1 | 10:30 |
| 3 | January | Specific Preparation 1 | 11:15 |
| 4 | January | Specific Preparation 1 | 07:30 |
| 5 | January/February | Specific Preparation 2 | 12:30 |
| 6 | February | Specific Preparation 2 | 12:45 |
| 7 | February | Specific Preparation 2 | 12:45 |
| 8 | February | Specific Preparation 2 | 07:30 |
| 9 | February/March | Specific Preparation 3 | 12:15 |
| 10 | March | Specific Preparation 3 | 12:15 |
| 11 | March | Specific Preparation 3 | 12:15 |
| 12 | March | Specific Preparation 3 | 08:00 |
| 13 | March/April | Pre-competitive 1 | 12:45 |
| 14 | April | Pre-competitive 1 | 14:45 |
| 15 | April | Pre-competitive 1 | 16:00 |
| 16 | April | Pre-competitive 1 | 08:30 |
| 17 | April/May | Pre-competitive 2 | 13:30 |
| 18 | May | Pre-competitive 2 | 16:00 |
| 19 | May | Pre-competitive 2 | 17:00 |
| 20 | May | Pre-competitive 2 | 08:30 |
| 21 | May | Pre-competitive 3 | 14:45 |
| 22 | May/June | Pre-competitive 3 | 16:30 |
| 23 | June | Pre-competitive 3 | 18:15 |
| 24 | June | Competitive | 14:30 |
| 25 | June | Competitive | 10:30 |
| 26 | June/July | Competitive | 04:15 + Race |

# PROFILE

You are an experienced triathlete and maintain fitness throughout the year. Other commitments, such as the holidays, and a conscious decision to take a break have you training between 7.5 and 8.5 hours each week. This has been consistent for at least four weeks. Training has been swimming once or twice a week, running three times a week, and cycling for an hour on a trainer or in a spin class. You may have done a bit of crosstraining, such as hiking, cross-country skiing, or snowshoeing. Week 1 on the first page of the detailed plan (Table 17.2) seems easy to accomplish. The long weekend workouts for the remainder of the plan, although challenging, seem doable.

## GOAL

Your goal is to complete an Ironman-distance race that is about six months away.

## THE PLAN

The entire 26-week plan is shown in Table 17.2. In the first three months, overall training time does not build significantly. Weekly training hours begin to build in late March as the days get warmer and longer. The longest training week on the plan is around 18 hours; this is three weeks before race week.

The structure of the plan typically puts long runs on Saturday and long bike rides on Sunday. One benefit of this kind of structure is that athletes run on relatively rested legs and reduce the risk of injury. Some would argue that Ironman athletes run on tired legs after a bike ride of 112 miles on race day, and that therefore the long bike in training should be on Saturday and the long run on Sunday. Either way will work, so choose the format that suits your personal needs.

As you progress through the plan, notice that leg and arm speed drills are included throughout the 26 weeks. Too often, athletes training for an Ironman event slog through endless slow miles. It is critical to include some form work in training, as it is intended to improve economy, that is, the cost of oxygen needed to produce any given speed. Do not be tempted to make a form session killer-hard; that is not the goal. The goal is to feel fast and light.

For the first few weeks, include at least one 1,000-meter main set. The swim can be continuous or broken. If broken, make the rest intervals no

| Week | Sport | Mon. Time | Mon. Code | Tues. Time | Tues. Code | Wed. Time | Wed. Code | Thurs. Time |
|------|-------|-----------|-----------|------------|------------|-----------|-----------|-------------|
| | | | | | | | **TABLE 17.2: 26-WEEK IRONMAN PERFORMANCE PLAN** | |
| *1* | Strength | 01:15 | AA | | | 01:15 | AA | |
| | Swim | | | 01:00 | E2 | | | 01:00 |
| | Bike | | | | | | | |
| | Run | | | 00:30 | S2 | | | 00:30 |
| *2* | Strength | 01:15 | AA | | | 01:15 | AA | |
| | Swim | | | 01:00 | E2 | | | 01:15 |
| | Bike | | | | | | | |
| | Run | | | 00:45 | S2 | | | 00:30 |
| *3* | Strength | 01:15 | AA | | | 01:15 | AA | |
| | Swim | | | 01:15 | E2 | | | 01:15 |
| | Bike | | | | | | | |
| | Run | | | 00:45 | S2 | | | 00:30 |
| *4* | Strength | 01:15 | AA | | | 01:15 | AA | |
| | Swim | | | | | | | 01:00 |
| | Bike | | | | | | | |
| | Run | | | 00:45 | S2 | | | |
| *5* | Strength | 01:30 | MS | | | 01:30 | MS | |
| | Swim | | | 01:15 | E (Form) | | | 01:00 |
| | Bike | | | | | | | |
| | Run | | | 01:00 | S2 | | | 00:30 |
| *6* | Strength | 01:30 | MS | | | 01:30 | MS | |
| | Swim | | | 01:15 | E (Speed) | | | 01:15 |
| | Bike | | | | | | | |
| | Run | | | 01:00 | S2 | | | 00:30 |
| *7* | Strength | 01:30 | MS | | | 01:30 | MS | |
| | Swim | | | 01:15 | E (Form) | | | 01:15 |
| | Bike | | | | | | | |
| | Run | | | 01:00 | S2 | | | 00:30 |
| *8* | Strength | 01:00 | MS | | | 01:00 | MS | |
| | Swim | | | | | | | 01:00 |
| | Bike | | | | | | | |
| | Run | | | 01:00 | S2 | | | |
| *9* | Strength | 01:00 | PE | | | 01:30 | PE + Plyo #1 | |
| | Swim | | | 01:15 | E (Speed) | | | 01:15 |
| | Bike | | | | | | | |
| | Run | | | 01:00 | TM #1 or S2 | | | 00:30 |
| *10* | Strength | 01:00 | PE | | | 01:30 | PE + Plyo #2 | |
| | Swim | | | 01:15 | Force | | | 01:15 |
| | Bike | | | | | | | |
| | Run | | | 01:00 | TM #2 or S2 | | | 00:30 |
| *11* | Strength | 01:00 | PE | | | 01:30 | PE + Plyo #3 | |
| | Swim | | | 01:15 | Force | | | 01:15 |
| | Bike | | | | | | | |
| | Run | | | 01:00 | TM #3 or S2 | | | 00:30 |

| Thurs. Code | Fri. Time | Fri. Code | Sat. Time | Sat. Code | Sun. Time | Sun. Code | Weekly Training Hours | Weekly Hours by Sport | |
|---|---|---|---|---|---|---|---|---|---|
| | | | | | | | | Strength | 02:30 |
| T1b | | | 01:00 | E (Form) | | | | Swim | 03:00 |
| | 01:00 | S1 | | | 01:00 | T1 (5) | | Bike | 02:00 |
| E1* | | | 01:00 | T1 (3) | | | 09:30 | Run | 02:00 |
| | | | | | | | | Strength | 02:30 |
| E (Speed) | | | 01:00 | E (Form) | | | | Swim | 03:15 |
| | 01:00 | S2 | | | 01:15 | E2* | | Bike | 02:15 |
| E1* | | | 01:15 | E2 | | | 10:30 | Run | 02:30 |
| | | | | | | | | Strength | 02:30 |
| E (Speed) | | | 01:00 | E (Form) | | | | Swim | 03:30 |
| | 01:00 | S1 | | | 01:30 | E2* | | Bike | 02:30 |
| E1* | | | 01:30 | E2 | | | 11:15 | Run | 02:45 |
| | | | | | | | | Strength | 02:30 |
| E (Speed) | | | 01:00 | E (Form) | | | | Swim | 02:00 |
| | 00:30 | S2 | | | 01:00 | S5 | | Bike | 01:30 |
| | | | 00:45 | E2 | | | 07:30 | Run | 01:30 |
| | | | | | | | | Strength | 03:00 |
| E2 | | | 01:15 | E3 | | | | Swim | 03:30 |
| | 01:00 | S1 | | | 02:00 | E3 | | Bike | 03:00 |
| E1* | | | 01:30 | E2 | | | 12:30 | Run | 03:00 |
| | | | | | | | | Strength | 03:00 |
| | | | 01:15 | E3 | | | | Swim | 03:45 |
| | 01:00 | S2 | | | 02:00 | E2* | | Bike | 03:00 |
| E2 | | | 01:30 | E3 | | | 12:45 | Run | 03:00 |
| | | | | | | | | Strength | 03:00 |
| E2 | | | 01:15 | E3 | | | | Swim | 03:45 |
| | 01:00 | S1 | | | 02:00 | E3 | | Bike | 03:00 |
| E1* | | | 01:30 | E2 | | | 12:45 | Run | 03:00 |
| | | | | | | | | Strength | 02:00 |
| T1b | | | 01:00 | E (Form) | | | | Swim | 02:00 |
| | 00:30 | S2 | | | 01:00 | T1 (5) | | Bike | 01:30 |
| | | | 01:00 | T1 (3) | | | 07:30 | Run | 02:00 |
| | | | | | | | | Strength | 02:30 |
| M | | | 01:15 | E2 | | | | Swim | 03:45 |
| | 01:00 | S1 | | | 02:00 | E2 | | Bike | 03:00 |
| E2 | | | 01:30 | E4 | | | 12:15 | Run | 03:00 |
| | | | | | | | | Strength | 02:30 |
| E2 | | | 01:15 | E2 | | | | Swim | 03:45 |
| | 01:00 | S2 | | | 02:00 | E2* | | Bike | 03:00 |
| E2 | | | 01:30 | E2 | | | 12:15 | Run | 03:00 |
| | | | | | | | | Strength | 02:30 |
| M | | | 01:15 | E2 | | | | Swim | 03:45 |
| | 01:00 | S1 | | | 02:00 | E2* | | Bike | 03:00 |
| E2 | | | 01:30 | E4 | | | 12:15 | Run | 03:00 |

| Week | Sport | Mon. Time | Mon. Code | Tues. Time | Tues. Code | Wed. Time | Wed. Code | Thurs. Time |
|------|-------|-----------|-----------|------------|------------|-----------|-----------|-------------|
| | | | | | | | TABLE 17.2: 26-WEEK IRONMAN PERFORMANCE PLAN (CONTINUED) | |

| Week | Sport | Mon. Time | Mon. Code | Tues. Time | Tues. Code | Wed. Time | Wed. Code | Thurs. Time |
|------|-------|-----------|-----------|------------|------------|-----------|-----------|-------------|
| 12 | Strength | 01:00 | PE | | | 01:30 | PE + Plyo #4 | |
| | Swim | | | | | | | 01:00 |
| | Bike | | | | | | | |
| | Run | | | 01:00 | TM #4 or S2 | | | 00:30 |
| 13 | Strength | 01:00 | SM | | | | | |
| | Swim | | | 01:15 | E (Speed) | | | 01:15 |
| | Bike | | | | | 01:00 | M1 (20) | |
| | Run | | | 00:45 | S2 | 00:30 | E1** | 00:30 |
| 14 | Strength | 01:00 | SM | | | | | |
| | Swim | | | 01:15 | E (Form) | | | 01:15 |
| | Bike | | | | | 01:00 | E2 | |
| | Run | | | 00:45 | S1 | 00:30 | E1** | 01:00 |
| 15 | Strength | 01:00 | SM | | | | | |
| | Swim | | | 01:15 | E (Speed) | | | 01:15 |
| | Bike | | | | | 01:30 | M1 (30) | |
| | Run | | | 00:30 | S2 | 00:30 | E1** | 01:00 |
| 16 | Strength | 01:00 | SM | | | | | |
| | Swim | | | | | | | 01:00 |
| | Bike | | | | | 01:00 | S5 | |
| | Run | | | 00:45 | S1 | | | 00:30 |
| 17 | Strength | 01:00 | SM | | | | | |
| | Swim | | | 01:00 | E (Form) | | | 01:00 |
| | Bike | | | | | 00:45 | E2 | |
| | Run | | | 00:30 | S2 | | | 00:30 |
| 18 | Strength | 01:00 | SM | | | | | |
| | Swim | | | 01:00 | E (Speed) | | | 01:30 |
| | Bike | | | | | 01:30 | M1 (40) | |
| | Run | | | 01:00 | E2 | 00:30 | E2** | 01:00 |
| 19 | Strength | 01:00 | SM | | | | | |
| | Swim | | | 01:15 | E (Form) | | | 01:15 |
| | Bike | | | | | 01:30 | E2 | |
| | Run | | | 01:00 | M2 (3Z) | | | 00:30 |
| 20 | Strength | 01:00 | SM | | | | | |
| | Swim | | | | | | | 01:00 |
| | Bike | | | | | 01:00 | S5 | |
| | Run | | | 00:45 | S1 | | | 00:30 |
| 21 | Strength | 01:00 | SM | | | | | |
| | Swim | | | 01:00 | E (Speed) | | | 01:00 |
| | Bike | | | | | 00:45 | E2 | |
| | Run | | | 00:30 | E2 | | | 00:30 |
| 22 | Strength | 01:00 | SM | | | | | |
| | Swim | | | 01:15 | E (Form) | | | 01:15 |
| | Bike | | | | | 01:30 | M1 (40–50) | |
| | Run | | | 01:00 | E2 | | | 00:30 |

| Thurs. Code | Fri. Time | Fri. Code | Sat. Time | Sat. Code | Sun. Time | Sun. Code | Weekly Training Hours | Weekly Hours by Sport | |
|---|---|---|---|---|---|---|---|---|---|
| | Day off | | | | | | | Strength | 02:30 |
| M (Speed) | | | 01:00 | E (Form) | | | | Swim | 02:00 |
| | | | | | 01:00 | S5 | | Bike | 01:00 |
| E2 | | | 01:00 | A1b | | | 08:00 | Run | 02:30 |
| | | | | | | | | Strength | 01:00 |
| E2 | | | 01:15 | M1 | | | | Swim | 03:45 |
| | 01:00 | E1 | | | 02:30 | E2 | | Bike | 04:30 |
| E2 | | | 01:45 | E3 | | | 12:45 | Run | 03:30 |
| | | | | Brick | | | | Strength | 01:00 |
| E2 | | | 01:30 | E3 | | | | Swim | 04:00 |
| | 01:30 | S4 | 01:00 | E2 | 03:00 | E3 | | Bike | 06:30 |
| M2 (3Z) | | | 01:00 | E2 | | | 14:45 | Run | 03:15 |
| | | | | | | | | Strength | 01:00 |
| E2 | | | 01:30 | E3 | | | | Swim | 04:00 |
| | 02:00 | E1 | | | 03:30 | E2 | | Bike | 07:00 |
| E2 | | | 02:00 | E3 | | | 16:00 | Run | 04:00 |
| | Day off | | | | | | | Strength | 01:00 |
| T1b | | | 01:15 | E (Form) | | | | Swim | 02:15 |
| | | | | | 02:00 | T1 (6–10) | | Bike | 03:00 |
| E1 | | | 01:00 | E2 | | | 08:30 | Run | 02:15 |
| | | | | | | | | Strength | 01:00 |
| E2 | | | 01:30 | E3 | | | | Swim | 03:30 |
| | 01:00 | S5 | | | 04:00 | E3 | | Bike | 05:45 |
| E1 | | | 02:15 | E3 | | | 13:30 | Run | 03:15 |
| | | | | Brick | | | | Strength | 01:00 |
| E3 | | | 01:00 | E1 | | | | Swim | 03:30 |
| | 01:00 | S4 | 01:00 | Text | 04:30 | E2 | | Bike | 08:00 |
| E2 | | | 01:00 | Text | | | 16:00 | Run | 03:30 |
| | | | | | | | | Strength | 01:00 |
| E2 | | | 01:30 | E3 | | | | Swim | 04:00 |
| | 01:30 | S4 | | | 05:00 | E3 | | Bike | 08:00 |
| S2 | | | 02:30 | E2 | | | 17:00 | Run | 04:00 |
| | Day off | | | | | | | Strength | 01:00 |
| T1b | | | 01:15 | E (Form) | | | | Swim | 02:15 |
| | | | | | 02:00 | E2 | | Bike | 03:00 |
| E2 | | | 01:00 | T1 (4–6) | | | 08:30 | Run | 02:15 |
| | | | | | | | | Strength | 01:00 |
| E2 | | | 01:00 | E3 | | | | Swim | 03:00 |
| | 01:00 | S2 | | | 05:00 | E3 | | Bike | 06:45 |
| E1 | | | 03:00 | E3 | | | 14:45 | Run | 04:00 |
| | | | | Brick | | | | Strength | 01:00 |
| E2 | | | 01:30 | E3 | | | | Swim | 04:00 |
| | 00:30 | S1 | 01:00 | Text | 05:30 | E2 | | Bike | 08:30 |
| E1 | | | 01:30 | Text | | | 16:30 | Run | 03:00 |

| | | Mon. | Mon. | Tues. | Tues. | Wed. | Wed. | Thurs. |
|---|---|---|---|---|---|---|---|---|
| Week | Sport | Time | Code | Time | Code | Time | Code | Time |
| 23 | Strength | 01:00 | SM | | | | | |
| | Swim | | | 01:15 | E (Speed) | | | 01:15 |
| | Bike | | | | | 01:15 | E2 | |
| | Run | | | 01:00 | E2 | | | 00:30 |
| 24 | Strength | 01:00 | SM | | | | | |
| | Swim | | | 01:15 | E (Form) | | | 01:15 |
| | Bike | | | | | 01:00 | E2 | |
| | Run | | | 01:00 | S1 | | | 01:00 |
| 25 | Strength | 01:00 | SM | | | | | |
| | Swim | | | 01:00 | E (Speed) | | | 00:45 |
| | Bike | | | | | 01:00 | S5 | |
| | Run | | | 00:45 | E2 | | | 00:45 |
| 26 | Strength | | | | | | | |
| | Swim | | | 00:45 | E (Speed) | | | |
| | Bike | | | | | 01:00 | M1 (15) | |
| | Run | 01:00 | M1 (20) | | | | | 00:30 |

TABLE 17.2: 26-WEEK IRONMAN PERFORMANCE PLAN (CONTINUED)

greater than 10 seconds. Slowly increase the distance of this main set over the course of several weeks to 2,000 to 3,000 meters. Some athletes may reach a main set of 2,500 to 3,500 meters. Look in *Workouts in a Binder®: Swim Workouts for Triathletes* for specific, detailed swimming workouts designed for Ironman athletes.

# SPECIFIC PREPARATION 1

The first week of the plan includes a baseline time trial in each sport. It goes without saying that if you have not been training consistently, do not begin the plan—especially these time trials—until some foundation conditioning has been achieved. That foundation is described in the Profile section.

| Thurs. Code | Fri. Time | Fri. Code | Sat. Time | Sat. Code | Sun. Time | Sun. Code | Weekly Training Hours | Weekly Hours by Sport | |
|---|---|---|---|---|---|---|---|---|---|
| | | | | | | | | Strength | 01:00 |
| E2 | | | 01:30 | E3 | | | | Swim | 04:00 |
| | 01:30 | S5 | | | 06:00 | E3 | | Bike | 08:45 |
| E1 | | | 03:00 | E3 | | | 18:15 | Run | 04:30 |
| | | | | Brick | | | | Strength | 01:00 |
| E2 | | | 01:30 | E3 | | | | Swim | 04:00 |
| | 01:00 | S4 | 03:00 | Text | 01:00 | E1 | | Bike | 06:00 |
| E2 | | | 01:30 | Text | | | 14:30 | Run | 03:30 |
| | Day off | | | Brick | | | | Strength | 01:00 |
| E2 | | | 01:15 | M | | | | Swim | 03:00 |
| | | | 02:00 | Text | 01:00 | E1 | | Bike | 04:00 |
| E2 | | | 01:00 | Text | | | 10:30 | Run | 02:30 |
| | Day off | | | Brick | Race! | | | Strength | 00:00 |
| | | | | | | | | Swim | 00:45 |
| | | | 00:45 | S4 | | | | Bike | 01:45 |
| S2 | | | 00:15 | S2 | | | 04:15 | Run | 01:45 |

This plan allows for crosstraining. An asterisk (*) beside the code of any workout, such as the run on Thursday of Week 1, means crosstraining is an option. Because heart rate ranges vary for different sports, use rate of perceived exertion (RPE) to determine the correct training zones. Suggestions for crosstraining include aerobics classes, circuit training, kickboxing, snowshoeing, cross-country skiing, and hiking, to name a few. Athletes using crosstraining in this plan are blending general and specific phases of training until the crosstraining is eliminated.

Spin classes can also serve as excellent sources of winter training. A few words of caution, however: Make the intensity of a spin class suit your personal goals. Some athletes have a difficult time controlling intensity and allow the instructor or others in the class to tempt them into a workout that becomes cough-up-a-lung hard. Have enough self-esteem to work out at your own pace.

## SPECIFIC PREPARATION 2

This first block of Specific Preparation 2 training includes two maximum strength (MS) training days each week. This is particularly helpful for building strength for hilly bike courses. Some athletes find that two days of MS training fatigues their legs and that they need to reduce the intensity of one of the weekend workouts. If this is the case for you, reduce the intensity of the sport that is already your strong suit.

## SPECIFIC PREPARATION 3

This block has several options. The first option is on the Tuesday runs. For experienced athletes, I recommend doing the treadmill workouts found in Appendix G. I have found no better training tool to improve form, running speed, and pace perception than a treadmill. The treadmill workouts in Appendix G are excellent for form. People who are uncomfortable getting on and off a running treadmill are better off sticking to simple pick-ups.

The second option during this block is the plyometric workouts shown with the Wednesday strength training session and found in Appendix F. Chapter 22, which covers strength training, explains why plyometrics will enhance an endurance athlete's training program. If you are in your first season of plyometric work, include plyo workouts only once per week and select the lowest number of sets and repetitions.

Both plyometrics and the treadmill sessions are not intended to be exceptionally difficult workouts. If you are exhausted or extremely sore after either workout, reduce the intensity of these sessions.

This is the last block that includes crosstraining.

## PRE-COMPETITIVE PREPARATION 1

The second week of the Pre-competitive Preparation 1 phase of training is when overall weekly volume begins to build and strength training is reduced to one day of strength maintenance. The intensity of the workouts remains in Zones 1 to 3, where most of an Ironman race will occur. Hilly races may solicit some time in Zone 4s and above, but keep this time very minimal.

Week 14 of the plan has a Zone 3 run on Thursday that should be 3 to 4 sets of 6-minute intervals with 2-minute rest intervals (RI), or 4–6 × 6 min. (2 min. RI). Also beginning in Week 14, any workout with a double asterisk (**) is optional.

Saturday of Week 14 has the first brick of the schedule, which can be done immediately after the swim or later in the day. Both bike and run segments are in Zones 1 and 2.

There are four tempo, or M1 workouts scheduled on the bike in the remaining weeks. These workouts help improve muscular endurance and can be done as steady-state rides or broken into intervals with work-to-rest ratios of 3:1 or 4:1.

Once athletes begin to increase training volume, many find that more than two aerobic time trials within a rest week are too much. So with that in mind, there are only two time trials in Week 16. Notice that the distance of the bike time trial is increased.

## PRE-COMPETITIVE PREPARATION 2

Weekly volume continues to build during this block. This is a perfect opportunity to establish the eating and drinking format you will use on race day. Take the time to figure out a nutritional plan—in detail—and write it down. What will you eat and drink each 15 to 20 minutes throughout the race? Do not take this lightly, as many Ironman races have been spoiled by eating or drinking improperly. Make a plan, practice it, modify it, and continue to refine it until you find what works for you.

The workouts needing additional explanation during this block include the brick in Week 18, a run in Week 19, and the run time trial in Week 20. For the Week 18 Saturday brick, both sports are controlled at Zones 1 to 2 for the first half of the assigned time. The second half of the time can go at Zones 1 to 3. It is not a goal to maximize time in Zone 3. For Week 18's Tuesday run, do 3–5 × 6 min. (2 min. RI) in Zone 3. For the Week 20 Saturday run time trial, notice the change in distance: Anywhere between 4 and 6 miles is fine.

## PRE-COMPETITIVE PREPARATION 3

The most important workouts are scheduled on the weekend during this block. Other workouts during the week should be reduced, if necessary, to allow for full recovery for the weekend sessions. For the Saturday brick in Week 22, both sports are controlled at Zones 1 to 2 for the first half of the assigned time. The second half of the time can go at Zones 1 to 3. It is not a goal to maximize time in Zone 3.

## COMPETITIVE PREPARATION

All of the hard work is done; it is time to enjoy. Weeks 24, 25, and 26 have reduced volume and some intensity to keep legs and arms feeling rested and fresh for race day. The bricks shown in Weeks 24 and 25 are done exactly like the brick in Week 22. The bike and run in Zones 1 and 2 for the first half of the assigned time. Bring it back home in Zones 1 to 3. Two to three weeks prior to the race is a good time for a total bike tune-up.

## RACE DAY

When race day finally arrives, take a deep breath at the starting line. You are ready. Relax any tight muscles, especially your neck and shoulders, and plan to enjoy your race.

# 18

## 52-WEEK PLAN TO AN OLYMPIC-DISTANCE TRIATHLON

*Racing hurts. Prior to a race I usually dread the pain that I will have to push through. But once the gun goes off, my fears vanish. It is that transformation in my mind from fear and doubt into determination and desire that makes racing so attractive for me.*

—DOUG FRIMAN, USA

2003 PAN-AMERICAN TEAM MEMBER,

FIRST ALTERNATE 2004 OLYMPIC TEAM

It is difficult to assemble a plan for an entire year that fits most athletes; in fact, it is impossible. So why include a yearlong plan? The goal of this chapter is to show how an annual plan might be designed and to give athletes a framework they can modify to meet their personal needs. Let's look at the big picture. An overview is shown in Table 18.1.

A brief description of each training period follows this paragraph. Each period will be explained in more detail within the chapter. The plan spans 52 weeks and begins with time for recovery. The recovery period shown is four weeks long; it could easily be slightly longer or shorter. Recovery is a time for transition following a long season of racing. It is very unstructured in nature, with the goal being rejuvenation of the body and mind.

| Week | Month | Period | Weekly Planned Hours | Activities | Race Priority |
|------|-------|--------|----------------------|------------|---------------|
| | | **TABLE 18.1: PLAN OVERVIEW** | | | |
| 1 | September | Recovery | 03:00–06:00 | | |
| 2 | October | Recovery | 03:00–06:00 | | |
| 3 | October | Recovery | 03:00–06:00 | | |
| 4 | October | Recovery | 03:00–06:00 | | |
| 5 | October | General Preparation | 08:30 | | |
| 6 | October/November | General Preparation | 08:30 | | |
| 7 | November | General Preparation | 08:30 | | |
| 8 | November | General Preparation | 07:00 | | |
| 9 | November | Specific Preparation 1 | 10:00 | | |
| 10 | November/December | Specific Preparation 1 | 11:30 | | |
| 11 | December | Specific Preparation 1 | 07:00 | | |
| 12 | December | Specific Preparation 2 | 12:00 | | |
| 13 | December | Specific Preparation 2 | 13:30 | | |
| 14 | December | Specific Preparation 2 | 07:00 | Holiday | |
| 15 | January | Specific Preparation 3 | 10:30 | | |
| 16 | January | Specific Preparation 3 | 12:30 | | |
| 17 | January | Specific Preparation 3 | 13:45 | | |
| 18 | January | Specific Preparation 3 | 07:00 | Business trip | 5–10K, C |
| 19 | January/February | Pre-competitive 1 | 11:00 | | |
| 20 | February | Pre-competitive 1 | 13:30 | | |
| 21 | February | Pre-competitive 1 | 15:00 | | |
| 22 | February | Pre-competitive 1 | 07:00 | ½ Marathon | C |
| 23 | February/March | Pre-competitive 2 | 12:30 | | |
| 24 | March | Pre-competitive 2 | 12:30 | | |
| 25 | March | Pre-competitive 2 | 07:30 | Triathlon | B |
| 26 | March | Pre-competitive 3 | 12:00 | | |

Recovery is followed by the more structured General Preparation period that begins building the foundation for higher levels of training. It is also four weeks long, but could be a few weeks more or less. The training periods shown in this particular plan follow a pattern of two or three weeks of increasing volume or intensity, followed by a rest week. The rest week allows the athlete to get stronger—to rebuild from the tearing-down process of training.

The General Preparation period is followed by Specific Preparation 1. Notice that Specific Preparation 1 and 2 are three weeks each. They follow the pattern of two weeks of increasing volume and one week of rest. The biggest reason for this pattern at this time of the year is to enforce

| Week | Month | Period | Weekly Planned Hours | Activities | Race Priority |
|---|---|---|---|---|---|
| | | | **TABLE 18.1: PLAN OVERVIEW (CONTINUED)** | | |
| 27 | March/April | Pre-competitive 3 | 12:00 | | |
| 28 | April | Pre-competitive 3 | 07:15 | Triathlon | B |
| 29 | April | Competitive | 10:30 | | |
| 30 | April | Competitive | 08:30 | | |
| 31 | April | Competitive | 04:10 | Triathlon | A |
| 32 | April/May | Recovery | 03:00–07:00 | | |
| 33 | May | Pre-competitive 1 | 11:00 | | |
| 34 | May | Pre-competitive 1 | 13:30 | | |
| 35 | May | Pre-competitive 1 | 15:00 | | |
| 36 | May/June | Pre-competitive 1 | 07:00 | | |
| 37 | June | Pre-competitive 2 | 12:30 | | |
| 38 | June | Pre-competitive 2 | 12:30 | | |
| 39 | June | Pre-competitive 2 | 07:00 | Vacation | 5–10K, C |
| 40 | June/July | Pre-competitive 3 | 12:00 | | |
| 41 | July | Pre-competitive 3 | 12:00 | | |
| 42 | July | Pre-competitive 3 | 12:00 | | |
| 43 | July | Pre-competitive 3 | 04:00 | Triathlon | B |
| 44 | July | Pre-competitive 4 | 12:00 | | |
| 45 | July/August | Pre-competitive 4 | 12:00 | | |
| 46 | August | Pre-competitive 4 | 04:00 | Triathlon | B |
| 47 | August | Competitive | 10:30 | 5K | C |
| 48 | August | Competitive | 08:30 | | |
| 49 | August/September | Competitive | 04:00 | Triathlon | A |
| 50 | September | Competitive | 07:00+ | | |
| 51 | September | Competitive | 07:00+ | | |
| 52 | September | Competitive | 07:00+ | | |

rest during the holiday season. If you do not celebrate the Christmas holiday, use this format and strategy to enforce rest when you celebrate a holiday period. As a rule of thumb, I plan an athletic rest week during times of high personal stress or other life commitments. The plan shown in this chapter adds a rest week during the Christmas holiday. Some athletes need two weeks of reduced volume during that time of the year. If that sounds like you, modify the plan accordingly.

After the beginning of the year, Specific Preparation 3 is followed by three Pre-competitive Preparation periods; the first period is four weeks in length, and Pre-competitive Preparation 2 and 3 are each three weeks long.

Notice the second phase of Pre-competitive Preparation training in Weeks 33 to 46 has four Pre-competitive periods, and they vary in length from three to four weeks. This format illustrates that there is more than one way to assemble periods or phases of training. In my experience, lengthening the periods to five or more weeks results in greater risk of illness or injury.

Those are some of the major items to notice on the overview of the plan. Now let's get into more detail about the type of athlete this plan was designed for and the specifics of the training plan.

## PROFILE

This plan is designed for an experienced triathlete looking for off-season and in-season conditioning. You train about 500 hours per year and have the ability to train from 7 to 15 hours a week.

## GOALS

Goals include peaking for two major Olympic-distance races this season; you consider these "A-priority" races. For these important events, you taper volume and rest so the races produce personal-best fitness levels and fast times. A "B-priority" race is important and will be scheduled at the end of a rest week. A "C-priority" race is for fun and may be skipped if it interferes with proper rest.

## THE PLAN

Table 18.2 lists training instructions for 52 weeks. Instructions for Weeks 1 to 4 are included, as are those for Weeks 32 and 50 to 52. Although this table details the overall plan shown in Table 18.1, some of the workouts in each period require special instructions. Those details follow.

## RECOVERY

As previously mentioned, recovery is a time for rejuvenation. Only work out when you feel like it, but do try to stay active. Sports other than swimming, cycling, and running are acceptable and encouraged. I recommend athletes try to run a couple of times per week during this time to make the transition back to run training easier.

## GENERAL PREPARATION

This is the beginning of structured training. Sport-specific training during this phase is mostly aerobic and includes a good deal of form work. Form work is important for the development of economy and will remain in the plan all season. There is also an emphasis on strength training in the weight room, which prepares the body for more difficult training to come. During each rest week, when aerobic training decreases, also decrease the number of sets or repetitions, or both, in the weight room.

If a lactate threshold test has not been completed yet, Week 8 would be a good time to do so, replacing one of the time trials.

On days when running and strength training are shown, if you decide to do both activities within a single workout, run first.

## SPECIFIC PREPARATION 1 AND 2

In these two periods, strength training changes to the maximum strength (MS) phase. Most triathletes find MS difficult, as it seems to remove that light, fast feeling from the legs. To help minimize this effect, use the treadmill workouts found in Appendix H. Those with only 20-second run times will help you maintain your running form. These workouts are particularly useful for people who may normally slog along in the dark or on slick streets in the evening after work. If you would rather do fast drills, use the S2 pick-up drills found in Chapter 21. Drills are also used on the bike and are designed to improve form.

## TABLE 18.2: OLYMPIC-DISTANCE ONE-YEAR PLAN

| Week | Sport | Mon. Time | Mon. Code | Tues. Time | Tues. Code | Wed. Time | Wed. Code | Thurs. Time |
|------|-------|-----------|-----------|-----------|-----------|-----------|-----------|-------------|
| 1–4 | Strength | | Weeks' goals: | | | | | |
| | Swim | | 1) Fun activities yielding 3–6 hours of physical activity per week. | | | | | |
| | Bike | | 2) Usually run two times per week, 30–45 min. each. | | | | | |
| | Run | | | | | | | |
| 5 | Strength | 01:15 | AA | | | 01:00 | AA | |
| | Swim | | | 01:00 | E (Form) | | | 01:00 |
| | Bike | | | | | | | 00:30 |
| | Run | | | | | 00:30 | S2 | |
| 6 | Strength | 01:15 | AA | | | 01:00 | AA | |
| | Swim | | | 01:00 | E (Form) | | | 01:00 |
| | Bike | | | | | | | 00:30 |
| | Run | | | | | 00:30 | S2 | |
| 7 | Strength | 01:15 | AA | | | 01:00 | AA | |
| | Swim | | | 01:00 | E (Form) | | | 01:00 |
| | Bike | | | | | | | 00:30 |
| | Run | | | | | 00:30 | S2 | |
| 8 | Strength | 01:00 | AA | | | 01:00 | AA | |
| | Swim | | | 00:45 | T1b | | | 00:45 |
| | Bike | | | | | | | |
| | Run | | | | | | | 00:30 |
| 9 | Strength | 01:30 | MS | | | 01:30 | MS | |
| | Swim | | | 01:00 | E (Form) | | | 01:00 |
| | Bike | | | | | | | |
| | Run | | | 00:45 | TM #1 | | | |
| 10 | Strength | 01:30 | MS | | | 01:30 | MS | |
| | Swim | | | 01:00 | E (Form) | | | 01:00 |
| | Bike | | | | | | | |
| | Run | | | 00:45 | TM #2 | | | 00:30 |
| 11 | Strength | 01:00 | MS | | | 01:00 | MS | |
| | Swim | | | 00:45 | E (Form) | | | 00:45 |
| | Bike | | | | | | | |
| | Run | | | | | | | 00:30 |
| 12 | Strength | 01:30 | MS | | | 01:30 | MS | |
| | Swim | | | 01:00 | E (Form) | | | 01:00 |
| | Bike | | | | | | | |
| | Run | | | 01:00 | TM #3 | | | 00:30 |
| 13 | Strength | 01:30 | MS | | | 01:30 | MS | |
| | Swim | | | 01:15 | E (Form) | | | 01:15 |
| | Bike | | | | | | | |
| | Run | | | 01:00 | TM #4 | | | 00:30 |
| 14 | Strength | 01:00 | MS | | | 01:00 | MS | |
| | Swim | | | 00:45 | T1b | | | 00:45 |
| | Bike | | | | | | | |
| | Run | | | | | | | 00:30 |

| Thurs. Code | Fri. Time | Fri. Code | Sat. Time | Sat. Code | Sun. Time | Sun. Code | Weekly Training Hours | Weekly Hours by Sport | |
|---|---|---|---|---|---|---|---|---|---|
| | | | | | | | | Strength | TBD |
| | 3) Bike or hike about an hour per week. | | | | | | | Swim | TBD |
| | 4) Swim, row, or rock climb for upper body. | | | | | | | Bike | TBD |
| | | | | | | | 03:00–06:00 | Run | TBD |
| | 01:00 | AA | | | | | | Strength | 03:15 |
| E2 | | | | | | | | Swim | 02:00 |
| S5 | | | | | 01:15 | E2 | | Bike | 01:45 |
| | | | 01:00 | E2 | | | 08:30 | Run | 01:30 |
| | 01:00 | AA | | | | | | Strength | 03:15 |
| E2 | | | | | | | | Swim | 02:00 |
| S5 | | | | | 01:15 | E2 | | Bike | 01:45 |
| | | | 01:00 | E2 | | | 08:30 | Run | 01:30 |
| | 00:45 | AA | | | | | | Strength | 03:00 |
| E2 | | | | | | | | Swim | 02:00 |
| S5 | | | | | 01:30 | E2 | | Bike | 02:00 |
| | | | 01:00 | E2 | | | 08:30 | Run | 01:30 |
| | | | | | | | | Strength | 02:00 |
| E (Form) | | | | | | | | Swim | 01:30 |
| | 01:00 | S5 | | | 01:00 | T1 (5 mi.) | | Bike | 02:00 |
| E2 | | | 01:00 | T1 (3 mi.) | | | 07:00 | Run | 01:30 |
| | | | | | | | | Strength | 03:00 |
| E (Speed) | | | 01:00 | M | | | | Swim | 03:00 |
| | 01:00 | S1 | | | 01:30 | E3 | | Bike | 02:30 |
| | | | 00:45 | E2 | | | 10:00 | Run | 01:30 |
| | | | | | | | | Strength | 03:00 |
| E (Speed) | | | 01:15 | M | | | | Swim | 03:15 |
| | 01:00 | S2 | | | 02:00 | E3 | | Bike | 03:00 |
| E1 | | | 01:00 | E2 | | | 11:30 | Run | 02:15 |
| | | | | | | | | Strength | 02:00 |
| E (Speed) | | | | | | | | Swim | 01:30 |
| | 01:00 | S1 | | | 01:00 | M1 (20–30) | | Bike | 02:00 |
| E2 | | | 01:00 | S2 | | | 07:00 | Run | 01:30 |
| | | | | | | | | Strength | 03:00 |
| E (Speed) | | | 01:15 | M | | | | Swim | 03:15 |
| | 01:00 | S2 | | | 02:00 | E2 | | Bike | 03:00 |
| E2 | | | 01:15 | E3 | | | 12:00 | Run | 02:45 |
| | | | | | | | | Strength | 03:00 |
| E (Speed) | | | 01:15 | M | | | | Swim | 03:45 |
| | 01:15 | S5 | | | 02:30 | E2 | | Bike | 03:45 |
| E2 | | | 01:30 | E3 | | | 13:30 | Run | 03:00 |
| | | | | | | | | Strength | 02:00 |
| E (Form) | | | | | | | | Swim | 01:30 |
| | 01:00 | S5 | | | 01:00 | T1 (5 mi.) | | Bike | 02:00 |
| E2 | | | 01:00 | T1 (3 mi.) | | | 07:00 | Run | 01:30 |

| Week | Sport | Mon. Time | Mon. Code | Tues. Time | Tues. Code | Wed. Time | Wed. Code | Thurs. Time |
|------|-------|-----------|-----------|------------|------------|-----------|-----------|-------------|
| **TABLE 18.2: OLYMPIC-DISTANCE ONE-YEAR PLAN (CONTINUED)** | | | | | | | | |
| 15 | Strength | 01:15 | PE | | | 01:30 | PE + Plyo #1 | |
| | Swim | | | 01:00 | E (Form) | | | 01:00 |
| | Bike | | | | | | | |
| | Run | | | 00:45 | M2 (4–5aZ) | | | 00:30 |
| 16 | Strength | 01:15 | PE | | | 01:30 | PE + Plyo #2 | |
| | Swim | | | 01:15 | E (Speed) | | | 01:15 |
| | Bike | | | | | | | |
| | Run | | | 01:00 | M2 (4–5aZ) | | | 00:30 |
| 17 | Strength | 01:15 | PE | | | 01:30 | PE + Plyo #3 | |
| | Swim | | | 01:15 | E (Form) | | | 01:15 |
| | Bike | | | | | | | |
| | Run | | | 01:00 | M2 (4–5aZ) | | | 00:45 |
| 18 | Strength | Day off | | | | 01:30 | PE + Plyo #4 | |
| | Swim | | | 01:00 | E (Speed) | | | 01:00 |
| | Bike | | | | | | | |
| | Run | | | | | | | 00:30 |
| 19 | Strength | 01:15 | SM | | | | | |
| | Swim | | | 00:45 | E (Form) | | | 01:00 |
| | Bike | | | | | 01:00 | M2 (4–5aZ) | |
| | Run | | | 00:45 | S1 (4–6 × 20) | | | 00:30 |
| 20 | Strength | 01:15 | SM | | | | | |
| | Swim | | | 01:15 | E (Speed) | | | 01:15 |
| | Bike | | | | | 01:00 | M2 (4–5aZ) | |
| | Run | | | 01:00 | S1 (6–8 × 20) | | | 00:30 |
| 21 | Strength | 01:15 | SM | | | | | |
| | Swim | | | 01:15 | E (Form) | | | 01:15 |
| | Bike | | | | | 01:30 | E2 | |
| | Run | | | 01:00 | S1 (6–8 × 20) | | | 01:00 |
| 22 | Strength | 01:00 | SM | | | | | |
| | Swim | | | 00:45 | E (Speed) | | | 00:45 |
| | Bike | | | | | | | |
| | Run | | | | | 00:30 | S2 | |
| 23 | Strength | 01:15 | SM | | | | | |
| | Swim | | | 01:00 | E1 | | | 01:15 |
| | Bike | | | | | 01:00 | E2 | |
| | Run | | | 00:45 | E1 | | | 01:00 |
| 24 | Strength | 01:15 | SM | | | | | |
| | Swim | | | 01:00 | E (Form) | | | 01:15 |
| | Bike | | | | | 01:00 | E2 | |
| | Run | | | 01:00 | TM (Track #1) | | | 00:45 |
| 25 | Strength | 01:00 | SM | | | | | |
| | Swim | | | 01:00 | E (Speed) | | | 00:45 |
| | Bike | | | | | | | |
| | Run | | | | | 00:45 | S2 | |

| Thurs. Code | Fri. Time | Fri. Code | Sat. Time | Sat. Code | Sun. Time | Sun. Code | Weekly Training Hours | Weekly Hours by Sport | |
|---|---|---|---|---|---|---|---|---|---|
| | | | | | | | | Strength | 02:45 |
| Force | | | 01:00 | E2 | | | | Swim | 03:00 |
| | 00:45 | E2 | | | 01:30 | E4 | | Bike | 02:15 |
| E1 | | | 01:15 | E2 | | | 10:30 | Run | 02:30 |
| | | | | | | | | Strength | 02:45 |
| Force | | | 01:15 | E2 | | | | Swim | 03:45 |
| | 01:00 | E2 | | | 02:00 | E4 | | Bike | 03:00 |
| E1 | | | 01:30 | E2 | | | 12:30 | Run | 03:00 |
| | | | | | | | | Strength | 02:45 |
| Force | | | 01:15 | E2 | | | | Swim | 03:45 |
| | 01:15 | E2 | | | 02:30 | E4 | | Bike | 03:45 |
| E1 | | | 01:45 | E2 | | | 13:45 | Run | 03:30 |
| | | | | | | | | Strength | 01:30 |
| M (Form) | | | | | | | | Swim | 02:00 |
| | 01:00 | S5 | | | 01:00 | E2 | | Bike | 02:00 |
| E1 | | | 01:00 | A1b | | | 07:00 | Run | 01:30 |
| | | | | | | | | Strength | 01:15 |
| A | | | 01:00 | E2 | | | | Swim | 02:45 |
| | 00:30 | E1 | | | 02:30 | E2 | | Bike | 04:00 |
| E1 | | | 01:45 | E4 | | | 11:00 | Run | 03:00 |
| | | | | | | | | Strength | 01:15 |
| A | | | 01:15 | E2 | | | | Swim | 03:45 |
| | 01:00 | S5 | | | 03:00 | E4 | | Bike | 05:00 |
| E1 | | | 02:00 | E2 | | | 13:30 | Run | 03:30 |
| | | | | | | | | Strength | 01:15 |
| A | | | 01:15 | E2 | | | | Swim | 03:45 |
| | 01:30 | E2 | | | 03:30 | E4 | | Bike | 06:30 |
| M1 (20–25) | 00:30 | E1 | 01:00 | E2 | | | 15:00 | Run | 03:30 |
| | | | | | | | | Strength | 01:00 |
| A | | | | | | | | Swim | 01:30 |
| | 01:00 | E1 | | | 01:00 | E1 | | Bike | 02:00 |
| | | | 02:00 | Race | | | 07:00 | Run | 02:30 |
| | | | | | | | | Strength | 01:15 |
| E2 | | | 01:00 | M (OW) | | | | Swim | 03:15 |
| | 01:00 | S1 | | | 03:00 | M3 (4Z) | | Bike | 05:00 |
| S2 | | | 01:15 | E2 | | | 12:30 | Run | 03:00 |
| | | | | | | | | Strength | 01:15 |
| E2 | | | 01:00 | M (OW) | | | | Swim | 03:15 |
| | 01:00 | S1 | | | 03:00 | M4 (20–30) | | Bike | 05:00 |
| S2 | | | 01:15 | E2 | | | 12:30 | Run | 03:00 |
| | | | | | | Brick or Race | | Strength | 01:00 |
| T1b | | | | | | | | Swim | 01:45 |
| | | | 01:00 | S5 | 01:45 | Text | | Bike | 02:45 |
| | 00:30 | E1 | | | 00:45 | Text | 07:30 | Run | 02:00 |

| Week | Sport | Mon. Time | Mon. Code | Tues. Time | Tues. Code | Wed. Time | Wed. Code | Thurs. Time |
|---|---|---|---|---|---|---|---|---|
| | | | | | | | TABLE 18.2: OLYMPIC-DISTANCE ONE-YEAR PLAN (CONTINUED) | |
| 26 | Strength | 01:00 | SM | | | | | |
| | Swim | | | 01:00 | E (Form) | | | 01:00 |
| | Bike | | | | | 01:00 | E1 | |
| | Run | | | 01:00 | TM (Track #2) | | | 00:45 |
| 27 | Strength | 01:00 | SM | | | | | |
| | Swim | | | 01:00 | E (Speed) | | | 01:00 |
| | Bike | | | | | 01:00 | E1 | |
| | Run | | | 01:00 | TM (Track #3) | | | 00:45 |
| 28 | Strength | 01:00 | SM | | | | | |
| | Swim | | | 01:00 | E (Speed) | | | 00:45 |
| | Bike | | | | | | | |
| | Run | | | | | 00:45 | E2 | |
| 29 | Strength | 01:00 | SM | | | | | |
| | Swim | | | 01:00 | E (Form) | | | 00:45 |
| | Bike | | | | | 01:00 | E1 | |
| | Run | | | 01:00 | TM (Track #4) | | | 00:30 |
| 30 | Strength | 00:45 | SM | | | | | |
| | Swim | | | 00:45 | E (Speed) | | | 00:45 |
| | Bike | | | | | 00:45 | E1 | |
| | Run | | | 00:45 | S2 | | | 00:30 |
| 31 | Strength | | | | | | | |
| | Swim | | | 01:00 | E (Speed) | | | 00:45 |
| | Bike | 01:00 | S4 | | | | | |
| | Run | | | | | 00:45 | S2 | |
| 32 | Strength | | | Week's goals: | | | | |
| | Swim | | | 1) All workouts are 2 hours or less. | | | | |
| | Bike | | | 2) Spend minimal time in Zones 3 and above. | | | | |
| | Run | | | 3) Take a minimum of 2 days off. | | | | |
| 33 | Strength | 01:15 | SM | | | | | |
| | Swim | | | 00:45 | E (Form) | | | 01:00 |
| | Bike | | | | | 01:00 | E2 | |
| | Run | | | 00:45 | S2 | | | 00:30 |
| 34 | Strength | 01:15 | SM | | | | | |
| | Swim | | | 01:00 | E (Form) | | | 01:15 |
| | Bike | | | | | 01:15 | E2 | |
| | Run | | | 01:00 | S2 | | | 00:45 |
| 35 | Strength | 01:15 | SM | | | | | |
| | Swim | | | 01:15 | E (Form) | | | 01:15 |
| | Bike | | | | | 01:30 | E2 | |
| | Run | | | 01:00 | S2 | | | 01:00 |
| 36 | Strength | 01:00 | SM | | | | | |
| | Swim | | | 01:00 | E (Speed) | | | 01:00 |
| | Bike | | | | | | | |
| | Run | | | | | 00:45 | E1 | |

| Thurs. Code | Fri. Time | Fri. Code | Sat. Time | Sat. Code | Sun. Time | Sun. Code | Weekly Training Hours | Weekly Hours by Sport | |
|---|---|---|---|---|---|---|---|---|---|
| | | | | | | | | Strength | 01:00 |
| E2 | | | 01:15 | M (OW) | | | | Swim | 03:15 |
| | 01:00 | S1 | | | 03:00 | A1c | | Bike | 05:00 |
| S2 | | | 01:00 | E2 | | | 12:00 | Run | 02:45 |
| | | | | | | | | Strength | 01:00 |
| E2 | | | 01:15 | M (OW) | | | | Swim | 03:15 |
| | 01:00 | S2 | | | 03:00 | A1c | | Bike | 05:00 |
| S2 | | | 01:00 | E2 | | | 12:00 | Run | 02:45 |
| | | | | Brick or Race | | | | Strength | 01:00 |
| T1b | | | | | | | | Swim | 01:45 |
| | | | 01:00 | S5 | 01:30 | S4 | | Bike | 02:30 |
| | 00:45 | E1 | | | 00:30 | S2 | 07:15 | Run | 02:00 |
| | | | | | | | | Strength | 01:00 |
| E2 | | | 01:00 | M (Speed) | | | | Swim | 02:45 |
| | 00:45 | S1 | | | 02:30 | Text | | Bike | 04:15 |
| E1 | | | 01:00 | E2 | | | 10:30 | Run | 02:30 |
| | | | | Brick | | | | Strength | 00:45 |
| E2 | | | 01:00 | A (Form) | | | | Swim | 02:30 |
| | 01:00 | S2 | | | 01:00 | Text | | Bike | 02:45 |
| E1 | | | 00:45 | E2 | 00:30 | Text | 08:30 | Run | 02:30 |
| | Day off | | | Brick | Race! | | | Strength | 00:00 |
| E (Speed) | | | | | | | | Swim | 01:45 |
| | | | 00:30 | S4 | | | | Bike | 01:30 |
| | | | 00:10 | S2 | | | 04:10 | Run | 00:55 |
| | 4) Work out only if you feel like it. | | | | | | | Strength | TBD |
| | 5) Relax, have fun. | | | | | | | Swim | TBD |
| | 6) At the end of the week, feel eager and ready to | | | | | | 03:00– | Bike | TBD |
| | resume structured training. | | | | | | 07:00 | Run | TBD |
| | | | | | | | | Strength | 01:15 |
| E2 | | | 01:00 | M | | | | Swim | 02:45 |
| | 01:00 | S5 | | | 02:30 | E4 or A1b | | Bike | 04:30 |
| E1 | | | 01:15 | E2 | | | 11:00 | Run | 02:30 |
| | | | | | | | | Strength | 01:15 |
| E2 | | | 01:15 | M | | | | Swim | 03:30 |
| | 01:15 | S3 (6–8) | | | 03:00 | E4 or A1c | | Bike | 05:30 |
| E2 | | | 01:30 | E4 | | | 13:30 | Run | 03:15 |
| | | | | | | | | Strength | 01:15 |
| E2 | | | 01:15 | M | | | | Swim | 03:45 |
| | 01:30 | S5 | | | 03:30 | E4 or A1b | | Bike | 06:30 |
| E2 | | | 01:30 | E4 | | | 15:00 | Run | 03:30 |
| | | | | | | | | Strength | 01:00 |
| T1b | | | | | | | | Swim | 02:00 |
| | 01:15 | E1 | | | 01:00 | T1(5 mi.) | | Bike | 02:15 |
| | | | 01:00 | T1 (3 mi.) | | | 07:00 | Run | 01:45 |

| Week | Sport | Mon. Time | Mon. Code | Tues. Time | Tues. Code | Wed. Time | Wed. Code | Thurs. Time |
|------|-------|-----------|-----------|------------|------------|-----------|-----------|-------------|
| | | | | **TABLE 18.2: OLYMPIC-DISTANCE ONE-YEAR PLAN (CONTINUED)** | | | | |
| 37 | Strength | 01:15 | SM | | | | | |
| | Swim | | | 01:00 | Force | | | 01:00 |
| | Bike | | | | | 01:00 | M3 (4–5aZ) | |
| | Run | | | 01:00 | E2 | | | 00:45 |
| 38 | Strength | 01:15 | SM | | | | | |
| | Swim | | | 01:00 | Force | | | 01:00 |
| | Bike | | | | | 01:00 | M3 (4–5aZ) | |
| | Run | | | 01:00 | E2 | | | 00:45 |
| 39 | Strength | 01:00 | SM | | | | Brick | |
| | Swim | | | 00:45 | E (Speed) | | | 00:45 |
| | Bike | | | | | 01:00 | S5 | |
| | Run | | | | | 00:30 | S2 | |
| 40 | Strength | 01:15 | SM | | | | | |
| | Swim | | | 01:00 | A | | | 01:00 |
| | Bike | | | | | 01:00 | M4 (20) | |
| | Run | | | 01:00 | S1 | | | 00:45 |
| 41 | Strength | 01:15 | SM | | | | | |
| | Swim | | | 01:00 | A | | | 01:00 |
| | Bike | | | | | 01:00 | M5 (20–25) | |
| | Run | | | 01:00 | S1 | | | 00:45 |
| 42 | Strength | 01:15 | SM | | | | | |
| | Swim | | | 01:00 | A | | | 01:00 |
| | Bike | | | | | 01:00 | M5 (20–30) | |
| | Run | | | 01:00 | S1 | | | 00:45 |
| 43 | Strength | 01:00 | SM | | | | Brick | |
| | Swim | | | 00:45 | M | | | 00:30 |
| | Bike | | | | | 00:45 | A7 | |
| | Run | | | | | 00:30 | S2 | |
| 44 | Strength | 01:15 | SM | | | | | |
| | Swim | | | 01:00 | E (Form) | | | 01:00 |
| | Bike | | | | | 01:00 | E2 | |
| | Run | | | 00:45 | E2 | | | 01:00 |
| 45 | Strength | 01:15 | SM | | | | | |
| | Swim | | | 01:00 | E (Form) | | | 01:00 |
| | Bike | | | | | 01:00 | E2 | |
| | Run | | | 00:45 | E2 | | | 01:00 |
| 46 | Strength | 01:00 | SM | | | | Brick | |
| | Swim | | | 00:45 | Text | | | 00:30 |
| | Bike | | | | | 00:45 | Text | |
| | Run | | | | | 00:30 | Text | |
| 47 | Strength | 01:00 | SM | | | | | |
| | Swim | | | 01:00 | E2 | | | 00:45 |
| | Bike | | | | | 01:00 | E2 | |
| | Run | | | 01:00 | E2 | | | 00:30 |

| Thurs. Code | Fri. Time | Fri. Code | Sat. Time | Sat. Code | Sun. Time | Sun. Code | Weekly Training Hours | Weekly Hours by Sport | |
|---|---|---|---|---|---|---|---|---|---|
| | | | | | | | | Strength | 01:15 |
| E (Speed) | | | 01:15 | E2 | | | | Swim | 03:15 |
| | 01:00 | S5 | | | 03:00 | E2 | | Bike | 05:00 |
| S2 | | | 01:15 | M2 (4–5aZ) | | | 12:30 | Run | 03:00 |
| | | | | | | | | Strength | 01:15 |
| E (Speed) | | | 01:15 | E2 | | | | Swim | 03:15 |
| | 01:00 | S5 | | | 03:00 | E2 | | Bike | 05:00 |
| S2 | | | 01:15 | M2 (4–5aZ) | | | 12:30 | Run | 03:00 |
| | Day off | | | | | | | Strength | 01:00 |
| E (Form) | | | | | | | | Swim | 01:30 |
| | | | | | 02:00 | E2 | | Bike | 03:00 |
| | | | 01:00 | A1c | | | 07:00 | Run | 01:30 |
| | | | | | | | | Strength | 01:15 |
| E2 | | | 01:00 | E (Speed) | | | | Swim | 03:00 |
| | 01:00 | E1 | | | 03:00 | E2 | | Bike | 05:00 |
| E3 | | | 01:00 | A2 (5b) | | | 12:00 | Run | 02:45 |
| | | | | | | | | Strength | 01:15 |
| E2 | | | 01:00 | E (Speed) | | | | Swim | 03:00 |
| | 01:00 | E1 | | | 03:00 | E2 | | Bike | 05:00 |
| E3 | | | 01:00 | A2 (5b) | | | 12:00 | Run | 02:45 |
| | | | | | | | | Strength | 01:15 |
| E2 | | | 01:00 | E (Speed) | | | | Swim | 03:00 |
| | 01:00 | E1 | | | 03:00 | E2 | | Bike | 05:00 |
| E3 | | | 01:00 | A2(5b) | | | 12:00 | Run | 02:45 |
| | Day off | | | | Race! | | | Strength | 01:00 |
| E (Speed) | | | | | | | | Swim | 01:15 |
| | | | 00:30 | Text | | | | Bike | 01:15 |
| | | | | | | | 04:00 | Run | 00:30 |
| | | | | | | | | Strength | 01:15 |
| E2 | | | 01:00 | A | | | | Swim | 03:00 |
| | 01:00 | S2 | | | 03:00 | A1c | | Bike | 05:00 |
| S2 | | | 01:00 | M5 (15–20) | | | 12:00 | Run | 02:45 |
| | | | | | | | | Strength | 01:15 |
| E2 | | | 01:00 | A | | | | Swim | 03:00 |
| | 01:00 | S1 | | | 03:00 | A1c | | Bike | 05:00 |
| S2 | | | 01:00 | A2 (5b) | | | 12:00 | Run | 02:45 |
| | Day off | | | | Race! | | | Strength | 01:00 |
| E (Speed) | | | | | | | | Swim | 01:15 |
| | | | 00:30 | S4 | | | | Bike | 01:15 |
| | | | | | | | 04:00 | Run | 00:30 |
| | | | | | | | | Strength | 01:00 |
| E (Speed) | | | 01:00 | M (OW) | | | | Swim | 02:45 |
| | 00:45 | S5 | | | 02:30 | A1d | | Bike | 04:15 |
| S2 | | | 01:00 | A1c | | | 10:30 | Run | 02:30 |

| Week | Sport | Mon. Time | Mon. Code | Tues. Time | Tues. Code | Wed. Time | Wed. Code | Thurs. Time |
|---|---|---|---|---|---|---|---|---|
| 48 | Strength | 00:45 | SM | | | | | |
| | Swim | | | 00:45 | E (Speed) | | | 00:45 |
| | Bike | | | | | 01:00 | E2 | |
| | Run | | | 00:45 | E2 | | | 00:30 |
| 49 | Strength | | | | | | | |
| | Swim | | | 01:00 | E (Speed) | | | 00:45 |
| | Bike | 01:00 | A7 | | | | | |
| | Run | | | | | 00:30 | A7 (3 × 90) | 00:15 |
| 50–52 | Strength | | Weeks' goals: | | | | | |
| | Swim | | 1) Do what you want, when you feel like it. Be sure to rest. | | | | | |
| | Bike | | Fitness is quite high now, so enjoy. | | | | | |
| | Run | | | | | | | |

**TABLE 18.2: OLYMPIC-DISTANCE ONE-YEAR PLAN (CONTINUED)**

In Specific Preparation 1, Weeks 9 through 11, the breakthrough workouts (BTs) are the two strength training days each week in Weeks 9 and 10 and one muscular endurance day in the pool. The treadmill workouts, although challenging, should not be extremely difficult.

In Specific Preparation 2, Weeks 12 through 14, some Zone 3 work is allowable on the long run. If this tends to be too much for you, reduce the intensity of the long run to Zones 1 and 2. If you do not want to build running volume toward a half-marathon, keep all Saturday runs in the 1:30 range, while the plan shows training hours building. Keep the intensity as shown on the plan.

Week 14 for this plan happens to be Christmas week. All intensity may have to be removed from the week, as personal commitments become priority. Not to worry—you will be fine. Reduce intensity and perhaps volume so you can enjoy family and friends. If you do not celebrate Christmas but rather another holiday, the same comments apply for that time of the year.

| Thurs. Code | Fri. Time | Fri. Code | Sat. Time | Sat. Code | Sun. Time | Sun. Code | Weekly Training Hours | Weekly Hours by Sport | |
|---|---|---|---|---|---|---|---|---|---|
| | | | | | | Brick | | Strength | 00:45 |
| E2 | | | 01:00 | M (Speed) | | | | Swim | 02:30 |
| | 00:45 | S5 | | | 01:00 | Text | | Bike | 02:45 |
| E1 | | | 00:45 | S2 | 00:30 | Text | 08:30 | Run | 02:30 |
| | Day off | | | | Race! | | | Strength | 00:00 |
| E (Speed) | | | | | | | | Swim | 01:45 |
| | | | 00:30 | S4 | | | | Bike | 01:30 |
| E2 | | | | | | | 04:00 | Run | 00:45 |
| | | | | | | | | Strength | TBD |
| | 2) Race shape can be maintained for a few weeks with low- | | | | | | | Swim | TBD |
| | volume weekday recovery and weekend racing. | | | | | | | Bike | TBD |
| | 3) Consider doing fun events. | | | | | | 07:00+ | Run | TBD |

# SPECIFIC PREPARATION 3

Strength training moves from maximum strength to power endurance (PE). An option for this period is to use the plyometric drills found in Appendix F. If you decide not to do plyometrics, simply follow the instructions for PE strength training found in Chapter 22.

Some of the Tuesday run workouts require more explanation:

*Week 15:* 4–6 × 3 min. (1 min. RI)
*Week 16:* 4–5 × 4 min. (1 min. RI)
*Week 17:* 4–5 × 5 min. (1 min., 30 sec. RI)
*Tip:* All of these intervals should take you into Zones 4 to 5a.

In Week 18, on the Saturday run, run with a fast group or do a 10K or 5K race. Always warm up before racing, with more warm-up time for shorter races.

Week 18 on the overview shows a "business trip." Any of the workouts shown on the plan can be done while traveling, if you have access to a gym.

Swimming with a new masters group can be fun as well. For running, some athletes like to jump into a weekend race in a new city. Bike rides may be done on a spin bike or exercise bike found at most gyms. If you have to miss workouts during this week, do not fret; it is a rest week anyway.

## PRE-COMPETITIVE PREPARATION 1

In Pre-competitive Preparation 1, strength training moves to the strength maintenance (SM) phase. As implied, this workout is intended to maintain strength. Do not make the strength training so difficult that it causes lingering soreness.

Several run workouts need more detail. On the Saturday runs in Weeks 19 and 20, continuous motion is not necessary during the long runs; walking breaks are fine. On Saturday in Week 22, do a half-marathon race for fun or do a fast group run.

Wednesday bike workouts needing more explanation are:

*Week 19:* 3–4 × 6 min. (2 min. RI)
*Week 20:* 3–4 × 6–8 min. (2 min. RI)
*Tip:* Heart rate should increase to Zones 4 to 5a during these intervals, but limit the amount of work in Zones 4 and above.

## PRE-COMPETITIVE PREPARATION 2

Intensity is removed from the beginning of Week 23 to allow for recovery from the half-marathon. The fast swim and fast bike that week should be done only if you are recovered from the race.

In this period, you will begin to work on speed or anaerobic endurance. My favorite way to improve speed is using a treadmill. It is very difficult, if not impossible, for athletes to have enough self-control to run a track workout at the same intensity as the treadmill workouts provided in Appendix H. If the thought of running on a treadmill is appalling, try to do the same workouts—using the time and pace designated in the appendix—on the track. If you do choose to do the workouts on the treadmill, you may find an entirely new level of speed and mental toughness.

If you have a safe way to execute an open-water swim for the muscular endurance (open-water) workouts during this block, swim the first half of the time at Zones 1 to 2 and the second half of the time fartlek. Make the fartlek portions at race pace. If you do not have access to open water, do a similar effort in the pool. If you decide to race this week, make the Week 25 Thursday swim an endurance (speed) workout.

On the Sunday bike in Week 23, do four to six sets of 4-minute intervals followed by 4-minute rest intervals (4–6 × 4 min. (4 min. RI)). The rest interval is equivalent to an easy spin downhill. On Sunday in Week 25, you can schedule the first race of the season, or do a brick. If a brick is chosen, ride 1:45 and run 45 minutes. The ride should begin in Zones 1 and 2, finishing with a 30-minute time trial at race pace. The run should be split in half, with the first half in Zones 1 to 2 and the second half at race pace.

## PRE-COMPETITIVE PREPARATION 3

Minimal special instructions for workouts are necessary for this training block. You have the option to race at the end of Week 28 or complete the brick as shown on the plan. If you decide to race, make the Thursday swim workout of that week an endurance (speed) session rather than a fitness test.

## COMPETITIVE PREPARATION

As volume tapers during this period, extreme self-control will be necessary. Refrain from sneaking in extra workouts and increasing workout time. You need to rest so your body is fastest on race day, not in a training session with your buddies.

The only workout needing special instructions is the brick on Sunday of Week 30. Bike for 1 hour and run for 30 minutes. Both are negative-split workouts, going out at Zones 1 and 2, coming back in Zones 4 to 5a. Enjoy the race in Week 31; go fast.

## RECOVERY

I like to schedule a recovery week midseason for all athletes I work with. Relax, enjoy, and take a break from structured training. Follow the general guidelines shown for Week 32 in Table 18.2.

## PRE-COMPETITIVE PREPARATION 1

After the first peak and race period, a return to the Pre-competitive Preparation 1 period is scheduled. Here, fast workouts are grouped entirely on the weekend. This is done to show there are different methods for organizing fast workouts within a training block. Also, I have found that variety keeps training fun. Variety is why the S2 pick-up workouts are scheduled for Tuesday runs. You can, however, repeat the form treadmill workouts in Appendix H. Simply do them in sequence beginning with the first treadmill workout (TM#1) in Week 33. Athletes often find their E2 speed has increased since the first time they did these workouts back in Base 1.

## PRE-COMPETITIVE PREPARATION 2

Each period builds on the previous one. In this training period, the Wednesday bike workouts needing special instructions include:

*Week 37:* 3–4 × 4–6 min. uphill, with RI equivalent to an easy spin downhill

*Week 38:* 3–4 × 6–8 min. uphill, with RI equivalent to an easy spin downhill

*Tip:* These intervals should increase heart rate to Zones 4 to 5a.

Some of the Saturday run workouts need special instructions in this block:

*Week 37:* 3–5 × 6 min. (2 min. RI)

*Tip:* Inexperienced athletes should select the lower number of repetitions.

*Week 38:* 3–5 × 6 min. (2 min. RI)

*Tip:* Try to do one more repetition than last week. These Saturday intervals should increase heart rate to Zones 4 to 5a.

*Week 39:* Vacation. You may want to reduce intensity and perhaps volume for a holiday week, as you would in Week 14.

## PRE-COMPETITIVE PREPARATION 3

The workouts needing additional details for this block include the Saturday run sessions.

*Week 40:* 4–5 × 3 min. (3 min. RI)

*Week 41:* 5–6 × 3 min. (3 min. RI)

*Week 42:* 6–7 × 3 min. (3 min. RI)

*Tip:* The intervals for these run sessions should take you into Zone 5b.

The swim session on Tuesday of Week 43 should include a main set equal to half the race distance at race pace. It can be broken into intervals or done as a straight swim. On Saturday of Week 43, make the ride mostly easy, but run through all your gears to be sure your bike is in proper working order.

Sunday is race day, so have fun. If there is no race available, create your own brick or race simulation workout.

## PRE-COMPETITIVE PREPARATION 4

One of the run sessions in this period builds on the previous block. On Saturday of Week 45, do 6–7 × 3 min. (3 min. RI).

The swim on Tuesday of Week 46 can be mostly easy, but include 5 × 100 meters at race pace (:20 sec. RI), as the main set. The brick that week is a 45-minute bike, mostly in Zones 1 to 2, with the last 15 minutes at race pace. The run is 30 minutes, mostly in Zones 1 to 2, with the last 10 minutes at race pace. This is enough intensity to keep you feeling fresh for the race this weekend. Race day instructions are the same as those for first Pre-competitive Preparation 3.

# COMPETITIVE PREPARATION

This is the second Competitive phase of the season. Three workouts need extra comment. The Week 47 run on Saturday can be a fast group run or a 5K race. For the Week 48 brick on Sunday, bike one hour and run 30 minutes, both negative-split workouts—out at Zones 1 to 2 and back at race pace. On the Monday bike in Week 49, do four sets of 90-minute intervals, followed by 3-minute rest intervals.

The final race of the season is likely on Sunday of Week 49. Best wishes for fast racing.

Many athletes find their fitness is at an excitingly high level after the last race of the season and a bit of rest. Most athletes are able to maintain this high level of fitness for two to six weeks. Depending on your desire to race, you may want to have a racing block at the end of the season and race every weekend. Others cannot stand the thought of packing all that gear and traveling to another event. Those who no longer want to race can still have fun by allowing some training sessions to become races. Savor that hard-earned fitness. In a few weeks, you can begin the cycle all over again with a recovery period.

# PART VI

# Workouts and Workout Codes

This section of the book explains the workout codes used in each of the training plans. Chapter 19 is for swimming, again meters are used in the text, meters and yards being interchangeable. Chapter 20 for cycling, Chapter 21 for running, and Chapter 22 is for strength training. A few athletes prefer their own strength training program to the one in this book. If that is the case, be certain the program suits your goals. There are athletes who select a body-building program that does develop a chiseled physique but is not optimal for multisport training. At the same time, if physique development is a higher-priority goal than endurance performance, by all means use the program that helps you reach your goal. All workouts should start out and end with an RPE of 1. That means, do not bolt out of the starting gate and start swimming, cycling, or running as fast as you can. Allow your body a chance to warm up. Yes, that warm-up and cool-down time is included in the total workout time. I also recommend that athletes stretch following their cool-down period at the end of every workout.

An example of plan layout can be found in Table 6.1. The left column has the week number, but each day of the week has two columns. One column lists the time of the workout in a specific sport and the second column has the workout code. Each sport or activity is listed in a separate row and repeats for each week. For example, Wednesday of Week 3 will be a form workout on the bike lasting an hour and a half.

Tips for hydration and refueling are covered in Chapter 3 and apply to all the plans.

# 19

# SWIM WORKOUTS

*I have never seen a poor taper. It is simply poor training.*
—NICK HANSEN, USA
WORLD-CALIBER SWIM COACH AND ENDURANCE ATHLETE

Swimming is different from cycling or running. The swim course is usually the same: 25 meters of clear water with a black line on the bottom of the pool. A variety of courses can be used to eliminate boredom during an aerobic workout in cycling or running. In the pool, adding variety to your workouts can have the same effect, and will keep swimming interesting.

Too often, athletes mix and match workouts or workout segments with no particular workout goal in mind. They simply swim. This habit leads to mediocre swimming. The plans in this book use specific workout codes designed to help you change gears. Some days are for recovery, taking it easy in the pool; other days go fast, with no holding back.

## SPECIFIC WORKOUTS

The workouts are based on a combination of rate of perceived exertion (RPE) and the associated training zones in Table 2.1, as well as the results from an individual time trial (T1) detailed in this chapter. If you are just beginning to get into shape, use RPE until enough fitness has been built to do the time trial. If you have special health conditions, consult a physician about any restrictions you may need to place on exercise intensities.

# WORKOUT CODES

Sample swim workouts for each code are included in Appendix E. More workouts can be found in *Workouts in a Binder®: Swim Workouts for Triathletes*, one of two books of waterproof workouts available from VeloPress. The swimming workouts are coded and can be used in conjunction with this book, or as stand-alone swimming workouts.

Generally, all swimming workouts will have a warm-up, a main set, and a cool-down. Workouts are categorized by a main emphasis, often designed to enhance a particular energy system; however, some workouts will have multiple goals.

## TESTING

Testing will typically be done every three to four weeks, during a rest week. Some athletes prefer to test every other rest week, or every six to eight weeks. Improving T1 pace (or T-pace) over several weeks and months of training is a mark of improved fitness and certainly a goal to shoot for.

*T1.* After a warm-up of 10 to 20 minutes, do the following:

*T1a.* If training for a sprint-distance triathlon, swim 3 × 100 with 20 seconds of rest between sets. The goal of the set is to swim at the highest possible sustained speed in order to achieve the lowest average time. In other words, do not swim a fast first 100 and have the third 100 be 15 seconds slower. Watch the clock and get your time on each 100. Average the time for all three 100s to establish a T1 pace. For example, a reasonable swim might look like 1:25, 1:21, and 1:24; the T1 pace would be 1:23. You wouldn't want to swim 1:20, 1:25, and 1:35 for a 15-second difference between the first and third 100s. It is best if all three 100s are within 5 seconds of one another.

*T1b.* If training for an Olympic- or Ironman-distance triathlon, swim 3 × 300 with 30 seconds of rest between sets. As with the 100s in the previous paragraph, the goal of the set is to swim at the highest average speed possible. An accurate test is when all three 300s are within 15 seconds of each other. In other words, do not swim a fast first 300 and have the third 300 be 20 or more seconds slower. Watch the clock and get your time on each 300. Average the time for all three 300s and divide the average by three to establish a T1 pace for a 100-meter distance. For example, if you swam 3:30, 3:25, and 3:22, the average time for the 300s is 3:27. Divide that result by three to obtain a T1 pace of 1:09. A handy reference chart for average 300 pace and T1 pace is Table 19.1.

## ENDURANCE WORKOUTS

The main emphasis of an endurance workout (E) is aerobic work. The main set of the workout is typically 20 to 40 minutes long, containing broken sets with rest intervals of 15 seconds or less. One of the main goals of this type of workout is to keep swimming. Swim at a pace that allows you to complete the entire set without taking extra rest. This speed is typically 5 to 8 seconds per 100 slower than T1 pace.

*E1.* Control the intensity of any (E) workout so RPE is in Zone 1.

*E2.* Control the intensity of any (E) workout so RPE is in Zones 1 to 2.

*E3.* Control the intensity of any (E) workout so RPE is in Zones 2 to 3.

*E (Speed).* The main set will be mostly aerobic work; however, the end of the workout will include some very fast 25s or 50s, with an emphasis on high-speed arm turnover. Generally, there is ample rest between swim segments to allow full recovery. Neuromuscular training is more important than sustaining high heart rates during the speed segment.

*E (Form).* The main set will be mostly aerobic work; however, a good deal of form work will be included at the beginning or the end of the workout. Most often, speed is less important than good form. Some coaches refer to this as drill work. Again, neuromuscular training is important during the

| TABLE 19.1: 300 SWIM AND T1 PACE | | | |
|---|---|---|---|
| 300 Time | Average T1 Pace per 100 | 300 Time | Average T1 Pace per 100 |
| 02:39 | 00:53 | 04:21 | 01:27 |
| 02:42 | 00:54 | 04:24 | 01:28 |
| 02:45 | 00:55 | 04:27 | 01:29 |
| 02:48 | 00:56 | 04:30 | 01:30 |
| 02:51 | 00:57 | 04:33 | 01:31 |
| 02:54 | 00:58 | 04:36 | 01:32 |
| 02:57 | 00:59 | 04:39 | 01:33 |
| 03:00 | 01:00 | 04:42 | 01:34 |
| 03:03 | 01:01 | 04:45 | 01:35 |
| 03:06 | 01:02 | 04:48 | 01:36 |
| 03:09 | 01:03 | 04:51 | 01:37 |
| 03:12 | 01:04 | 04:54 | 01:38 |
| 03:15 | 01:05 | 04:57 | 01:39 |
| 03:18 | 01:06 | 05:00 | 01:40 |
| 03:21 | 01:07 | 05:03 | 01:41 |
| 03:24 | 01:08 | 05:06 | 01:42 |
| 03:27 | 01:09 | 05:09 | 01:43 |
| 03:30 | 01:10 | 05:12 | 01:44 |
| 03:33 | 01:11 | 05:15 | 01:45 |
| 03:36 | 01:12 | 05:18 | 01:46 |
| 03:39 | 01:13 | 05:21 | 01:47 |
| 03:42 | 01:14 | 05:24 | 01:48 |
| 03:45 | 01:15 | 05:27 | 01:49 |
| 03:48 | 01:16 | 05:30 | 01:50 |
| 03:51 | 01:17 | 05:33 | 01:51 |
| 03:54 | 01:18 | 05:36 | 01:52 |
| 03:57 | 01:19 | 05:39 | 01:53 |
| 04:00 | 01:20 | 05:42 | 01:54 |
| 04:03 | 01:21 | 05:45 | 01:55 |
| 04:06 | 01:22 | 05:48 | 01:56 |
| 04:09 | 01:23 | 05:51 | 01:57 |
| 04:12 | 01:24 | 05:54 | 01:58 |
| 04:15 | 01:25 | 05:57 | 01:59 |
| 04:18 | 01:26 | 06:00 | 02:00 |

Note: 300 swim times shown with their associated average T1 pace per 100.

drill segment. Any time a "Form" workout is referenced in one of the training plan charts, use the guidelines for E (Form).

*E (OW).* Swim for the designated time in open water. Emphasize sighting objects (like buoys or markers on shore) to aid in swimming a straight line. The plan may say E (OW) (30), which means to swim for 30 minutes in open water in training Zones 1 to 3. Of course, swimming in a safe situation is essential, with lifeguards or other rescue persons present.

## FORCE WORKOUTS

*Force.* These workouts use paddles; however, a good deal of form work will be included at the beginning or the end of the workout.

*Force (Speed).* The main set includes paddles; however, the end of the workout includes very fast 25s or 50s, with an emphasis on high-speed arm turnover. Generally, there is ample rest between swim segments to allow full recovery. Neuromuscular training is more important than sustaining high heart rates during the speed segment.

*PREP*

*Force (Form).* The main set includes paddles; however, a good deal of form work will be included at the beginning or the end of the workout. Generally, there is ample rest between swim segments to allow full recovery. Neuromuscular training is more important than sustained high heart rates during the drill segment.

## MUSCULAR ENDURANCE WORKOUTS

These workouts are often referred to as lactate threshold or anaerobic threshold workouts. It is important to be well rested heading into a muscular endurance session.

*M.* This workout utilizes your T1 pace for the main set. The main set is some combination of distances lasting 20 to 40 minutes, with a good portion of the set at T1 pace or slightly (2 to 5 seconds) faster. Swim segments might be 50 to 200 meters long, and depending on the length of each swim, rest intervals are 5 to 20 seconds long. The goal is to sustain T1 pace, or slightly faster.

*M (Speed)*. The main set includes swims at T1 pace; however, the end of the workout includes very fast 25s or 50s, with an emphasis on high-speed arm turnover. Generally, there is ample rest between swim segments to allow full recovery. Neuromuscular training is more important than sustaining high heart rates during the speed segment.

*M (Form)*. The main set is at T1 pace; however, a good deal of form work will be included at the beginning or the end of the workout. Generally, there is ample rest between swim segments to allow full recovery. Neuromuscular training is more important than sustaining high heart rates during the drill segment.

*M (OW)*. Swim for the designated time in open water, at race pace. Emphasize sighting objects (like buoys or markers on shore) to aid in swimming a straight line. The plan may say 00:45, M (OW) (15), which means to swim for 45 minutes in open water, 15 minutes of which is at T1 pace or slightly faster. Of course, swimming in a safe situation is essential, with lifeguards or other rescue persons present.

## ANAEROBIC ENDURANCE WORKOUTS

These sessions achieve the best results if you are well rested. The intention is to swim fast—very fast—faster than you thought possible. The main set may be quite short in yardage, but still take 20 to 40 minutes to complete.

*A.* The main set includes swims typically in the 50- to 100-meter range, with rest intervals of 30 to 60 seconds or longer. The main goal is to swim fast—no conserving, just go for it. In this type of work, you may

| TABLE 19.2: MICHELE'S SWIMS* | | | |
|---|---|---|---|
| Workout Code | Description | Main Set | Speed |
| T1 pace | Time Trial | 3 x 300 (00:30 RI)<br>Result: 04:17, 04:15, 04:13<br>Average time: 04:15 | Resulting T1 pace of 01:25 per 100 |
| E1 | Endurance | 8 x 200<br>Zone 1 | Goal: Ignore the clock, make RPE |
| E2 | Endurance | 8 x 200 on a 03:20 swim interval | Goal: Hold 01:30–01:35 pace per 100 |
| E3 | Endurance | 8 x 200 on a 03:15 swim interval<br>or 02:50–03:00 per 200 | Goal: Hold 01:25–01:30 pace per 100 |
| Force | Force | 5 x 200 with paddles on a 03:15 swim interval | Goal: Hold 01:20–01:25 pace per 100<br>or 02:40–02:50 per 200 |
| M | Muscular Endurance | 5–6 x 200 on a 03:05 swim interval | Goal: Hold 01:20–01:25 pace per 100<br>or 02:40–02:50 pace per 200 |
| A | Anaerobic Endurance | 8 x 50 on a 02:30 swim interval | Goal: Hold under 00:35 pace per 50 |

*Speeds are based on the results of the time trial above. When the time trial speed decreases, the goal speeds will decrease as well.

Note: Example 300 swim time and the associated T1 pace per 100.

find that speed decreases as the set goes on. That is okay. The fastest speed possible for that given swim is the goal. If you are unable to swim faster than T1 pace, stop the set, swim easy, and try it again another day.

*A (Form).* The main set will include swims faster than T1 pace; however, a good deal of form work will be included at the beginning or the end of the workout. Generally, there is ample rest between swim segments to allow full recovery. Neuromuscular training is more important than sustaining high heart rates during the drill segment.

# SAMPLE ATHLETE

To illustrate how to use the workouts to your advantage, we will follow a sample athlete, Michele. Michele swam her 3 × 300 time trial and achieved an average pace of 4:15. Her T1 pace is 1:25 per 100. In order for Michele to progress and swim faster speeds, it is important that she swim at certain goal paces for certain workouts while not compromising rest. That pace changes, depending on the goal of the workout. The pace will also change as she swims faster time trials, decreasing her T1 pace.

Table 19.2 gives examples of the pace Michele should swim for each workout code at her current T1 pace of 1:25. As previously mentioned, these goal times will decrease as she gains more fitness and speed.

# 20

# BIKE WORKOUTS

*Gale designed—and dynamically managed—my training program for the 2004 Hawaii Ironman. My experience in Kona was the best sports day of my life, and I attribute that to Gale. She provided a program that was challenging but realistic, given my work and family obligations. She knew exactly when I needed to crank it up a notch, and when to go easy. Leading into the race, I was 100 percent confident that my training had been spot on. You can't ask for more.*

—ROB KLINGENSMITH, USA

All of the workouts are based on the training zones determined by doing one of the tests in Appendix A. If you have zero fitness, do not do the lactate threshold test, and consult a physician before beginning any exercise program. If you have any special health conditions, it would be wise to consult a physician about restrictions that should be placed on your exercise intensities.

## WARM-UP AND COOL-DOWN

The workout time listed in any plan includes warm-up and cool-down. A warm-up is typically between 10 and 30 minutes, depending on the particular workout and how much time is assigned. If the ride is mostly at Zone 1 to Zone 2, begin and end the ride in Zone 1. Before beginning intervals, tempo rides, or races, be certain to include a good warm-up. If the workout is a high-intensity session, begin the ride in Zone 1 and slowly increase speed, so that your heart rate is close to the zone in which you will be doing the work intervals. If you are unable to get your heart rate into the specified zone by the third interval, quit trying, spin easy, and head home; it was not your day.

After all workouts and races, take an easy spin to cool down. By the end of the cool-down, heart rate should be in Zone 1 or less. Stretch your muscles shortly after cool-down.

# WORKOUT CODES

## ENDURANCE WORKOUTS

*E1.* Ride in the small chainring on a flat course, keeping heart rate in Zone 1.

*E2.* This level is used for aerobic maintenance and endurance training. Heart rate should stay primarily in Zones 1 to 2. How much time is spent in each zone depends on how you feel that day. The goal of an E2 ride is not to see how much time you can spend in Zone 2. Ride on a rolling course, if possible, with grades up to 4 percent. For reference, most highway off-ramps are 4 percent grade. Riding in a slightly larger gear can simulate a gentle hill, if there are no hills where you live. Remain in the saddle on the hills. If you ride with a group, inner discipline is necessary to let the group go if they want to hammer.

*E3.* This workout is used for endurance training and the beginning of lactate threshold training. Ride a rolling course in Zones 1 to 3. Stay seated on the hills to build or maintain hip power. Ride a course and use gearing that allows work intensity into Zone 3, but not so hard you get into Zones 4 and 5.

*E4.* This is a multifaceted workout for building endurance, speed, and strength. The first time you do an E4 workout, keep heart rate in Zone 1 to Zone 4. As training progress continues, and depending on the specifics of the plan, you can spend some time in Zone 5. As fitness increases, it is possible to spend progressively larger amounts of time in Zones 4 and 5. This progression is not detailed in the plans and is left to the individual athlete. Begin conservatively.

## FORM OR SPEED WORKOUTS

If "Form" is noted on any workout plan and a specific code is not listed, you may select any form workout in this section.

*S1—Spin Step-ups.* This workout focuses on pedaling form and neuromuscular coordination. On an indoor trainer, warm up with low resistance and a pedaling cadence of 90 rpm. After 15 to 20 minutes of warm-up, increase cadence to 100 rpm for 3 minutes, 110 rpm for 2 minutes, and 120+ rpm for 1 minute. If time allows, spin easy for 5 minutes to recover, and repeat. If you're just beginning to increase pedaling speed, it may be best to cut all of the times in half in order to maintain the recommended speeds. It is important that resistance is low to allow a focus on the speed of the feet and not force on the pedals. This workout can be done on the road if the road is flat or slightly downhill.

*S2—Isolated Leg.* This workout helps work the dead spot out of a pedal stroke. After a warm-up on an indoor trainer with light resistance, do 100 percent of the work with one leg while the other leg is resting on a stool. The bottom of the stroke is similar to the motion of scraping mud off the bottom of your shoe. The top of the stroke can be improved by driving toes forward. In all positions, keep the toes relaxed. Do not allow them to curl up and clench the bottom of your shoe.

This can be done outdoors by relaxing one leg while the other leg does 90 percent of the work. Change legs when fatigue sets in, or set a specific time interval to prevent excess fatigue. Work your way up to a work interval of 30 to 60 seconds per leg. After doing a work segment with each leg, spin easy with both legs for a minute and then go back to single leg work.

Stop pedaling with one leg when form becomes sloppy. Do not worry about achieving any particular heart rate; smooth pedaling form is most important. Begin with a cumulative time of 3 to 5 minutes on each leg and build time as you become stronger.

*S3—Accelerations.* This workout is intended to work on leg speed and neuromuscular pathways. Warm up well, then complete the specified number of 30-second accelerations, spinning an easy 2 minutes and 30 seconds (2' 30") between accelerations. The end of the 30 seconds should be faster than the beginning. On the plans, the code looks something like S3 (4–6), which means do 30-second accelerations four to six times, with 2-minute, 30-second rest intervals between accelerations. If only S3 appears on the plan, the total number of repeats is left to your discretion.

*S4—Fartlek.* Ride mostly in Zones 1 to 2 with a few 10- to 20-second accelerations placed throughout the workout—your choice. This workout can be used as a pre-race bike check. If using it as a pre-race bike check, run through all the gears at some point during the ride to ensure smooth shifting.

*S5—Cadence.* With heart rate in Zones 1 to 2, the entire ride is at 90 rpm or greater. If cadence is not at least 90, coast until legs are recovered. This is best done on a flat course.

## MUSCULAR ENDURANCE WORKOUTS

*M1—Tempo.* This workout is the beginning of lactate threshold speed work and is used for a good portion of training for events lasting more than three hours. After a warm-up on a mostly flat course, ride in Zone 3 for the time indicated on the plan. For example, M1 (15) means ride 15 minutes, steady, in Zone 3. Begin timing as soon as the effort begins; do not wait until the first moment you see Zone 3 on your heart rate monitor.

*M2 (3Z)—Cruise Intervals.* These intervals will also begin work on lactate threshold speed. On a mostly flat course or indoor trainer, complete the number of intervals given on the plan, allowing heart rate to rise into Zone 3 over the course of the interval. For example, 4–5 × 4' (1' RI) means after the warm-up, ride four or five 4-minute intervals, allowing pulse to rise into Zone 3 and no higher. After heart rate is in Zone 3, try to hold it there until the end of the interval. Begin timing the interval as soon as you begin an increased effort—do not wait to begin the clock until your heart rate reaches Zone 3. All work intervals begin when effort is increased and end when effort is decreased. Spin easy and recover for 1 minute between efforts.

*M2 (4–5aZ)—Cruise Intervals.* These intervals work on lactate threshold speed as the season and your fitness progress. On a mostly flat course or indoor trainer, complete the number of intervals shown on the plan (or detailed within each plan's chapter), allowing heart rate to rise into Zones 4 to 5a over the course of the interval. For example, 4–5 × 4' (1' RI) means after warm-up, ride four or five times for 4 minutes, allowing pulse to rise into Zones 4 to 5a and no higher. After heart rate is in Zones 4 to 5a, try to hold it there until the end of the interval. Take 1 minute of easy spinning between work intervals to recover.

*M3 (3Z)—Hill Cruise Intervals.* Same as M2 (3Z), except on a long hill with a 2 to 4 percent grade.

*M3 (4Z)—Hill Cruise Intervals.* Same as M2 (4–5aZ), except on a long hill with a 2 to 4 percent grade.

*M4—Crisscross Threshold.* On a mostly flat or rolling course, begin with a warm-up and slowly increase heart rate to Zone 4. Once Zone 4 is attained, begin timing. Gradually build speed until the top of Zone 5a is achieved. Then gradually reduce speed until the bottom of Zone 4 is achieved. The build and reduction time segments should take about 2 minutes. Continue to crisscross from low Zone 4 to high Zone 5a for the time specified on the plan. For example, the plan may say M4 (20), which means crisscross the indicated zones for 20 minutes.

*M5—Tempo.* This workout improves lactate threshold speed. After a warm-up on a mostly flat course, ride in Zones 4 to 5a for the time indicated on the plan. For example, M5 (15) means ride 15 minutes, steady, in Zones 4 to 5a. Begin timing as soon as the effort begins; do not wait until the first moment you see Zone 4 to 5a on your heart rate monitor.

## SPEED ENDURANCE (ANAEROBIC) AND TAPER WORKOUTS

Some of the workouts specify a rolling course or a hilly course. "Hilly" is relative to where you live. In general, a rolling course has grades up to about 4 percent and a hilly course has steeper grades. If you live in Flat City, simulate pedaling up hills by shifting up a gear or two.

*A1a—Easy Group Ride.* This particular workout is not anaerobic, but is part of a series of group rides. Ride with a group and stay mostly in Zones 1 to 3.

*A1b—Faster-paced Group Ride.* Ride with a group and stay mostly in Zones 1 to 4. Some time can be spent in Zone 5, but keep it minimal.

*A1c—Fast, Aggressive Group Ride.* Ride with a group, and ride in all zones. Be aggressive and power up the hills, chase riders who might have been faster than you in the past, and have fun.

*A1d—Ride as You Feel.* If you are feeling great, ride aggressively with some time in all zones; if tired, take it easy.

*A2 (5bZ)—Speed Endurance Intervals.* After a good warm-up on a mostly flat course, do the specified number of intervals, allowing heart rate to climb into Zone 5b. The intervals may be done on a flat course or slightly uphill. For example, 4–5 × 3' (3' RI) means ride four or five times three minutes, getting heart rate into Zone 5b and keeping it there until the end of the interval. Timing begins when effort is increased and ends when effort ends. Take 3 minutes between intervals.

*A6 (5b–cZ)—Hill Reps.* After a good warm-up, ride a 6 to 8 percent grade hill and complete the specified number of hill repetitions. Stay seated for the first 60 seconds as you build to Zone 5b, then shift to a higher gear, stand, and drive the bike to the top, allowing heart rate to climb into Zone 5c. Recover completely for 3 to 4 minutes between repetitions.

*A7—Taper Intervals.* After a good warm-up, complete the specified number of 90-second accelerations, getting heart rate into Zones 4 to 5a. Note that some training plans specify raising heart rate into Zone 3. Take 3 full minutes to recover and get heart rate back to Zone 1 before going to the next interval. On the plans, the intervals may look like 4–5 × 90" (3' RI). If the number is not specified on the plan, do three to five repeats. If no training zone is specified, raise intensity until heart rate is in Zones 4 to 5a. Remember that more is not necessarily better. These intervals help keep legs feeling fresh and speedy while volume is tapering prior to a race or important ride.

## TESTING

*T1 (5), T1 (8), T1 (10)—Aerobic Time Trial (ATT).* This is best done on a CompuTrainer or a trainer with a rear-wheel computer pick-up. It can also be done on a flat section of road, but weather conditions will affect the results. After a warm-up, ride 5, 8, or 10 miles with your heart rate 9 to 11 beats below lactate threshold heart rate. Distance of the time trial may be designated, or it may be left to your own discretion, by simply T1, on the plan. Use a single gear and do not shift during the test. In your training journal, record the gear used, time, and how you felt. Each time you repeat the test, try to make testing conditions the same. As aerobic fitness improves, the time should decrease.

*T2—As-Fast-as-You-Can-Go Time Trial (TT).* After a 15- to 30-minute warmup, complete a 5- to 8-mile time trial as fast as you can possibly ride. If you are a novice, use 5 miles. You may need to use a distance somewhere between 5 and 8 miles, because the available course dictates the exact length. Your course needs to be free of stop signs and heavy traffic. You can use a course with a turnaround point. Use any gear you wish and shift at any time. Each time you repeat the test, try to make testing conditions as similar as possible (this includes wind, temperature, subjective feelings, and outside stressors).

## CROSSTRAINING

*XT.* Some of the plans show an option of crosstraining with other sports, such as aerobics, cross-country skiing, and in-line skating, to name a few. Keep in mind your crosstraining sport heart rates should not match your cycling heart rate. Use rate of perceived exertion (RPE) to estimate correct training zones. These workouts should be mostly easy.

## 21 | RUN WORKOUTS

*If you keep running fun, you will remain a kid forever—at least on the inside.*

—DON LORENZEN (AKA GOATMAN), USA

All of the workouts are based on the training zones determined by doing one of the tests in Appendix B. If you have zero fitness, do not do the lactate threshold test, and consult a physician before beginning any exercise program. If you have any special health conditions, it would be wise to consult a physician about restrictions you may need to place on your exercise intensities.

## WARM-UP AND COOL-DOWN

The workout time displayed in any plan includes warm-up and cool-down. A warm-up is typically between 10 and 30 minutes, depending on the particular workout and how much time is assigned. If the run is mostly Zone 1 to Zone 2, begin and end the run in Zone 1. Before beginning intervals, tempo runs, or races, be certain to get a good warm-up. If the workout is a high-intensity session, begin the run in Zone 1 and slowly increase speed so that heart rate is close to the zone in which you will be doing the work intervals. If you are unable to get your heart rate into the specified zone by the third interval, quit trying, jog easy, and head home; it was not your day.

After all workouts and races, take an easy jog or walk to cool down. By the end of the cool-down, heart rate should be in Zone 1 or less. Stretch muscles shortly after cool-down.

# WORKOUT CODES

## ENDURANCE WORKOUTS

*E1.* Run on a flat course—a soft surface would be best (grass, dirt, or a treadmill)—keeping heart rate in Zone 1.

*E2.* This level is used for aerobic maintenance and endurance training. Heart rate should stay primarily in Zones 1 to 2. How much time is spent in each zone depends on how you feel that day. The goal of an E2 run is not to see how much time you can spend in Zone 2. Run a rolling course, if possible, with grades up to 4 percent. For reference, most highway off-ramps are 4 percent grades. For those living in flat cities, changing the grade on a treadmill can simulate hills. If you run with a group, inner discipline is necessary to let the group go if they turn a training run into a race.

*E3.* This workout is used for endurance training and the beginning of lactate threshold training. It is also used for a good portion of half- and full-marathon training. Run a rolling or hilly course in Zones 1 to 3. Allow heart rate to rise into Zone 3, but do not force it there. If running a mountainous course, walk the steep hills, if necessary, to keep heart rate out of Zones 4 and up.

*E4.* This is a multifaceted workout that is for building endurance, speed, and strength. Run a hilly course, allowing heart rate to rise into all zones. The first time you do an E4 workout, keep heart rate in Zones 1 to 4, and limit total Zone 4 time to 15 to 20 minutes. Be cautious on the downhill sections, keeping speed under control to minimize pounding on your knees. As fitness increases, it is possible to spend progressively larger amounts of time in Zones 4 and 5. This progression is not detailed in the plans and is left to the individual athlete. Begin conservatively.

## FORM OR SPEED WORKOUTS

*S1—Strides.* This workout is intended for improving running form and neuromuscular coordination. After 15 to 20 minutes of warm-up, do the fast run segments on a soft, flat surface, such as a grassy park or football field. Run 20 to 30 seconds four to eight times as indicated on the plan. For example, the plan may say 4–6 × 20 sec., which means do four to six 20-second runs. Walk or slowly jog back to the start position, taking a minute and a half to 2 minutes to do so. As you gain experience, an option is to run on a gentle downhill at a park or golf course. The emphasis is on quick cadence and proud posture. This workout is for form, so trying to spend every moment above Zone 1 is not important. If heart rate drops below Zone 1 during recovery, that's okay. Cool down with 5 to 10 minutes of easy jogging.

*S2—Pick-ups.* Within a run that is mostly in Zones 1 to 2, insert several 20- to 30-second accelerations. Finish the acceleration faster than you began. Quick cadence and proud posture are important. Jog easy for 2 or more minutes between accelerations.

*S3—Cadence.* Run a flat to gently rolling course in Zones 1 to 2 and check your leg speed a few times during the run by counting left foot strikes for 15 seconds—shoot for 21-plus strikes.

## MUSCULAR ENDURANCE WORKOUTS

*M1—Tempo.* This workout is the beginning of lactate threshold speed work. On a mostly flat course, after a warm-up, run in Zone 3 for the time indicated on the plan. For example, M1 (15) means run 15 minutes, steady, in Zone 3.

*PREP*

*M2 (3Z)—Cruise Intervals.* These intervals will also begin work on lactate threshold speed. On a mostly flat course or treadmill, complete the number of intervals given on the plan, allowing heart rate to rise into Zone 3 over the course of the interval. For example, 4–5 × 4' (1' RI) means after a warm-up, run four or five times for 4 minutes, allowing pulse to rise into Zone 3 and no higher. After heart rate is in Zone 3, hold it there until the end of the interval. Begin timing the interval as soon as effort is increased—do not wait to begin the clock when heart rate reaches Zone 3. All work intervals begin when effort is increased and end when effort is decreased. Jog easy and recover for 1 minute between efforts.

*M2 (4–5a)—Cruise Intervals.* These intervals improve lactate threshold speed as the season and your fitness progress. On a mostly flat course or treadmill, complete the number of intervals given on the plan, allowing heart rate to rise into Zones 4 to 5a over the course of the interval. For example, 4–5 × 4' (1' RI) means after warm-up, run four or five, 4-minute intervals, allowing pulse to rise into Zones 4 to 5a and no higher. After heart rate is in Zones 4 to 5a, try to hold it there until the end of the interval. Take one minute of easy jogging to recover between work intervals.

Advanced athletes can use pace instead of heart rate to guide the intervals. Run the intervals at an open 10K pace, which is roughly 20 seconds faster per mile than a 10K pace completed at the end of a triathlon.

*M3 (3Z)—Hill Cruise Intervals.* Same as M2 (3Z), except on a long hill with a 2 to 4 percent grade.

*M3 (4Z)—Hill Cruise Intervals.* Same as M2 (4–5a), except on a long hill with a 2 to 4 percent grade. Using 10K speed does not work well here.

*M5—Tempo.* This workout is for lactate threshold speed. After a warm-up on a mostly flat course, run in Zones 4 to 5a for the time indicated on the plan. For example, M5 (15) means run 15 minutes, steady, in Zones 4 to 5a.

## SPEED ENDURANCE (ANAEROBIC) ~~SPECIAL~~ AND TAPER WORKOUTS

Some of the workouts specify a rolling course or a hilly course, which is relative to where you live. In general, a rolling course has grades up to about 4 percent and a hilly course has steeper grades. If you live in Flat City, simulate hills by changing the incline on a treadmill.

*A1a—Easy Group Run.* This particular workout is not anaerobic, but is part of a series of group runs. Run with a group and stay mostly in Zones 1 to 3.

*A1b—Faster-paced Group Run.* Run with a group and stay mostly in Zones 1 to 4. Time can be spent in Zone 5, but keep it minimal.

*A1c—Fast, Aggressive Group Run or Race.* Run with a group in all zones. Be aggressive and power up the hills, chase runners who might have been faster than you in the past, and have fun. Or run a race of a distance around 50 to 75 percent of the total time indicated on the plan.

*A1d—Run as You Feel.* If you are feeling great, run aggressively with some time in all zones; if tired, take it easy.

*A2 (5bZ)—Speed Endurance Intervals.* After a good warm-up on a mostly flat course (a track or treadmill works well), do the specified number of intervals, allowing heart rate to climb into Zone 5b. The intervals may be done on a flat course or slightly uphill. For example, 4–5 × 3' (3' RI) means run four or five, 3-minute intervals, getting heart rate into Zone 5b and keeping it there until the end of the interval. Take 3 minutes to recover between intervals.

*A6 (5b–cZ)—Hill Reps.* After a good warm-up, run up a hill with a 6 to 8 percent grade and complete the specified number of hill repetitions. Recover completely for 3 to 4 minutes between repetitions.

*A7—Taper Intervals.* After a good warm-up, do the specified number of 90-second accelerations, getting heart rate into Zones 4 to 5a. Take 3 full minutes to recover and get heart rate back to Zone 1 before going to the next interval. On the plans, the intervals will look like 4–5 × 90" (3' RI). If the number is not specified on the plan, do three to five repeats. Remember that more is not necessarily better. These intervals help to keep your legs feeling fresh and speedy while volume is tapering prior to a race.

## TESTING

*T1—Aerobic Time Trial (ATT).* This is best done on a track or very flat section of road. After a warm-up, run 1 to 3 miles with heart rate 9 to 11 beats below your lactate threshold heart rate. The distance is typically specified on the schedule, such as T1 (3) for a 3-mile time trial. Record how you feel, the time, and the conditions in your journal. Each time you repeat the test, try to make test conditions the same, including the amount of time since the last BT workout. As aerobic fitness improves, the time should decrease.

*T2—As-Fast-as-You-Can-Go Time Trial (TT).* After a 15- to 30-minute warm-up, complete a 1.5-mile time trial as fast as you can possibly run. As with the aerobic time trial, record time and the conditions. Each time you repeat the test, try to make testing conditions the same, including the amount of time since the last BT workout. As race fitness improves, the time should decrease.

*TT.* Time trial of length designated within the text of each plan.

## CROSSTRAINING

*XT.* Some of the plans show an option of crosstraining with other sports, such as aerobics, cross-country skiing, and in-line skating, to name a few. Keep in mind your crosstraining sport heart rates should not match your running heart rate. Use rate of perceived exertion to estimate correct training zones. These workouts should be mostly easy.

# 22

# STRENGTH TRAINING AND STRETCHING

*Ve vaunt to pomp you awp!*
—HANS AND FRANZ,
PERSONAL TRAINERS FROM *SATURDAY NIGHT LIVE*

**M**any athletes turn to strength training to enhance their performance in endurance events. Others are still holdouts, fearing the gym may turn them into hulking human specimens, capable of power-lifting small cars. Not to worry; multisport athletes should not weight train like power lifters or bodybuilders because their fitness goals are different.

Consider that our natural maximal muscular strength is achieved somewhere in our twenties or early thirties. For this reason, I suggest that anyone over 30 years old invest some time in a strength training program. The older you are, the more you need the gym.

Women tend to be approximately 50 percent weaker in the upper body and 30 percent weaker in the lower body than men. This measure is for average males and average females and is in terms of absolute strength. Athletic women are generally stronger than nonathletic women; however, they are usually not as strong as athletic males in the same sport. Much of this strength difference is due to hormonal factors, which give males greater muscle mass. Although women may not have goals to be as strong as men within their sport, they can use a weight training program to increase their strength per pound of body mass and their lean muscle mass.

Some of the adaptations that occur when we strength train are increased muscle fiber size, increased muscle contractile strength, and increased tendon, bone, and ligament tensile strength. These changes are thought to improve physical capacity, economy, and metabolic function, decrease injury risk, and help you look darn good.

"I might look good, but will I be faster?" There have been studies on trained and untrained (sedentary) cyclists, with both groups experiencing positive results. In one study, untrained cyclists who strength trained for 12 weeks improved their cycling endurance by 33 percent and lactate thresholds by an average of 12 percent, while the control group, who did no training, made no gains.

In a separate study on trained cyclists, the addition of a strength training program increased their cycling endurance by 20 percent, allowing them to pedal 14 minutes longer before fatigue set in. They also increased short-term, high-intensity endurance (performance in the four- to eight-minute range) by 11 percent.

In addition to performance increases, a weight training program can prevent bone loss and even increase bone mass, which is critical to the prevention of osteoporosis in both men and women. How important a weight training program might be to multisport athletes is not quantitatively known at this time.

## STARTING A STRENGTH TRAINING PROGRAM

No one was born with the knowledge to use all the pieces of equipment in the gym, nor was anyone born with perfect weight-lifting form. When just beginning a weight training program, ask for help. Good form is critical. This book provides guidelines on which exercises to use. To find illustrations and specific instructions for doing each exercise, consult a qualified trainer at the gym or the illustrations and instructions in my book *The Female Cyclist* or Joe Friel's *The Triathlete's Training Bible*. When seeking help at the gym, ask someone you trust to recommend a trainer and ask the trainer for his or her credentials.

The strength training exercises in this book are intended to augment your multisport program, specifically triathlon or duathlon. Because multisport athletes are trying to juggle fitness, family, and job responsibilities, this particular strength training program minimizes weight-room time while maximizing the benefits to a multisport program. Some plans include provisions for other sports such as soccer, softball, racquetball, and others. This particular plan may not be optimal for those sports.

Here are some guidelines for this program:

- *Focus on the muscle groups that do the majority of work in swimming, cycling, and running.*
- *When appropriate, mimic the positions and movements of swimming, cycling, or running as closely as possible.*
- *Make multijoint exercises the priority and do single-joint exercises as time allows. For example, squats use three joints—the hip, knee, and ankle. Knee extensions use only the knee joint.*
- *Always include abdominal exercises to strengthen your torso.*
- *Include exercises to strengthen your lower back. Seated rowing works the lower back; however, some athletes find that including back extensions minimizes back fatigue—particularly on hills.*
- *Separate strength training sessions by at least 48 hours.*
- *Maintain good postural alignment whenever possible. This means when you're standing in a normal, relaxed position, the head is supported by the neck, which has a normal curvature. The neck, which is part of the spine, also has a curvature that is normal for you. For example, when you're doing squats, your head and neck should be in a position that allows the curvature of your neck to be normal. Your head is not craned toward the ceiling, nor is your chin pointed at your chest.*
- *Always, always, always maintain control of the weight on the concentric and the eccentric actions. This means using muscles, not momentum, to lift the weight. It means lowering the weight using muscles to control the speed, not allowing gravity to do most of the work, and only using muscles to stop the weight at the end of the motion.*

# THE PROGRAM IN DETAIL

Table 22.1 shows an overview of the strength training program. This table can be copied and taken to the gym for reference. It can be stored in the journal you use to track strength training progress.

## STRENGTH TRAINING PHASES

Only three exercises—a hip extension exercise, seated row, and standing bent-arm lat pull-down—change phases. The rest of the exercises remain at the low end of the range for a certain number of sets and loads as recommended in the AA phase. One option is to decrease the number of repetitions of these exercises to 12 to 15. To keep the load light to moderate, lowering the repetitions may require a slight increase in weight.

*AA—Anatomical Adaptation.* This is the initial phase of strength training, which is included at the beginning of a racing season or when someone is just beginning a strength training program. It is typically used in the General or Specific Preparation training periods. Its purpose is to prepare tendons and muscles for greater loads in the next strength training phases.

*MS—Maximum Strength.* This phase is used to teach the central nervous system to recruit high numbers of muscle fibers. For exercises designated MS, do one warm-up set with a light weight—something it is possible to lift around 15 or 20 times. As you add more weight, begin the first set conservatively. Use a weight you are certain you can lift six to eight times.

After a rest and stretching, add 5 to 10 pounds and lift again. Continue these sequences until up to six sets are completed. At some point, it may be impossible to add more weight and you'll top out, having to lift the final two or three sets at the same weight. That's fine. If you find the last set was easy, begin the entire sequence 5 to 10 pounds heavier at the next strength training session.

## TABLE 22.1: STRENGTH TRAINING

| PHASE | AA | MS | PE | ME | SM |
|---|---|---|---|---|---|
| Total sessions per phase | 8–12 | 8–12 | 6–8 | 4–8 | 4+ |
| Days per week | 2–3 | 2 | 1–2 | 1–2 | 1–2 |
| Exercises (in order of completion) | 1 2 3 4 5 6 7 8 Circuit | [1 2][7 6][5 8] | [1 2][7 6][5 8] | [1 2][7 6][5 8] | [1 2][7 6][5 8] |
| Load (percent of 1 Rep Max) | 40–60 | 80–95 | 65–85 | 30–50 | Sets 1–2 at 60; set 3 at 80 |
| Sets per session | 3–5 | 3–6 | 3–5 | 2–4 | 2–3 |
| Reps per set | 20–30 | 3–6 | 8–15 | 40–60 | Sets 1–2 at 12; set 3 at 6–8 |
| Speed of movement | Slow | Slow–Moderate | Moderately Fast–Explosive | Moderate | Slow–Moderate |
| Minutes of recovery (between sets) | 1–1.5 | 2–4 | 3–5 | 1–2 | 1–2 |

| TRIATHLON EXERCISES: (in order of completion) | DUATHLON EXERCISES: (in order of completion) |
|---|---|
| 1. Hip extension (squat, leg press, or step-up) | 1. Hip extension (squat, leg press, or step-up) |
| 2. Standing bent-arm lat pull-down | 2. Upper body choice—lat pull-down or standing row |
| 3. Hip extension (different from #1) | 3. Hip extension (different from #1) |
| 4. Chest press or push-ups | 4. Chest press or push-ups |
| 5. Seated row | 5. Seated row |
| 6. Personal weakness (hamstring curl, knee extension, or heel raise) | 6. Personal weakness (hamstring curl, knee extension, or heel raise) |
| 7. Abdominal exercise | 7. Abdominal exercise |
| 8. Optional—back extension | 8. Optional—back extension |

**Notes:**
- Bold-faced exercises follow the guidelines for each particular phase. All other exercises remain at AA sets and loads. Repetitions for all other exercises move to 15 to 20.
- Explosive movements are only done if equipment described in the chapter is available, otherwise movements are moderately fast speeds.
- Do not continue any exercise that causes pain. This includes joints that "pop" or "crack" and any exercise that causes sharp pain during the exercise or lasting for days after the strength training session.
- Before each strength training session, warm up with 10 to 20 minutes of aerobic activity. Cool down with 10 to 20 minutes of easy spinning on the bike. Do not use running to cool down.
- Exercises in brackets [ ] can be done in a superset manner, alternating between the two exercises.

As for form on the MS phase, slowly exert force on the weight to move it. Do not use an explosive force to move the weight, like a rocket booster on the leg press machine. Using explosive force to get a heavy weight up will more than likely lead to knee or back problems. Going slower may lead to a bit of a struggle to get the weight up the first time; that is okay.

Many athletes find this phase fun because strength gains come quickly as loads increase. Be cautious not to extend this phase beyond the recommended number of sessions. Continuation of this phase for too long may result in muscle imbalances, particularly in the upper leg, which could lead to hip or knee injuries.

*PE—Power Endurance.* The PE strength training phase is intended to combine strength with velocity. Making fast movements with weights, however, is controversial. At least one study has shown that when lifters were asked to move a weight as quickly as possible while maintaining contact with the weight bar, power actually decreased. On a separate occasion, the same group was asked to move the weight as quickly as possible, but to release the weight. Their power and speed of movement increased in the second scenario.

In theory, the body was trying to protect itself in the first scenario, attempting to keep joints from being injured. It appears that the body was using opposing muscles to slow the weight down, actually decreasing power. So when you begin the PE phase, you must ask yourself if the particular piece of equipment or exercise you are using will increase or decrease your power.

One of the best options for a hip extension exercise with fast movements is a leg press machine that allows you to explosively jump off the platform with a load and return to the start position at a moderate speed. In other words, it does not allow the entire load to come slamming down on your shoulders. The type of equipment I am most familiar with has the athlete on an incline bench, with the travel of the platform parallel to the ground. If your gym does not have such a leg press machine, it is best to moderate your speed to reduce the risk of injury and to be certain you are not losing power.

The jumping exercise explained in the last paragraph is a form of plyometrics. Plyometrics are exercises or drills aimed at linking strength with speed of movement to produce power. It used to be thought that plyometrics was only for sprinters and football players, but one study showed that 5K running performance was improved for well-trained endurance athletes using plyometrics. The principle behind plyometrics is rapid force development. A typical plyometric drill is a repetitive vertical jump within a specified time frame. Just as you land from one jump you must generate enough force to immediately jump again. This repetitive action overloads the muscle to develop and improve explosiveness, or power.

An example of a plyometric exercise for the upper body is using a medicine ball in place of lat pull-downs. While standing, hold the medicine ball above your head and, as fast and forcefully as possible, slam the ball to the ground. A plyometric exercise to mimic rowing is difficult to duplicate. One option is to lie facedown on a bench, hanging one side of the body off the bench. Quickly lift a medicine ball off the ground and release it at maximum height. Another upper body option is quickly tossing a medicine ball between two people, keeping the elbows high, similar to a chest press position.

There simply is not enough room in this book to go into multiple detailed plyometric programs. One option for plyometrics (for conditioned athletes) is included in Appendix F. Plyometrics are recommended only on particular plans. If the plan you are using does not call for plyometrics, simply do PE strength training exercises at a moderate speed. For more information on plyometrics, consult Donald A. Chu's *Jumping into Plyometrics*, published by Leisure Press.

*ME—Muscular Endurance.* The ME phase follows PE and trains the body to manage fatigue at moderately high load levels by increasing capillary density and the number and size of mitochondria (energy production sites within the muscle cells). While this phase is beneficial to some athletes who lack race endurance, I have found that most athletes can best develop muscular endurance more effectively by doing muscular endurance workouts in each particular sport. Still other athletes prefer one day of PE and one day of ME for a four-week period. Each plan will make recommendations on what format to use.

*SM—Strength Maintenance.* As the name implies, this phase is intended to maintain strength. A day of SM training should not be exhausting. Save your energy for sport-specific exercises.

## EXERCISES

The recommended exercises are listed in Table 22.1. Some exercises show more than one option. While it is not possible to show all available options for each exercise, it is advantageous for athletes to have more than one choice for each exercise, particularly for the times when the gym gets busy. Additionally, exercises that are slightly different, like the squat and leg press, stimulate muscles in different ways. The end result is a greater number of muscle fibers stimulated by slightly varying the routine either within a week or from week to week. For example, if you lift on Tuesday and Thursday, during the PE phase, use squats on Tuesday and the leg press on Thursday.

In the AA phase, lifting can be completed in a "circuit," which means completing the first set of all the exercises before completing the second set. Sometimes this is a problem in a busy weight room, particularly for hip extension exercises. For example, if people circle the squat machine like buzzards while you are trying to complete the program, go ahead and complete all of the sets of hip extension before moving to the next exercise.

The order of completion of exercises in the other phases is such that all sets and repetitions of each exercise are completed before moving on to the next exercise. The exceptions are the exercises in brackets that can be completed in "superset" format. Supersetting means alternating between the exercises within the brackets before moving on to the next group of exercises.

## LOAD

The load estimates are given in terms of 1 Rep Max, or the maximum weight you could lift only once. It is not recommended that you attempt to find 1 Rep Max; rather, estimate it by finding the amount of weight you can lift 10 times, then divide that number by 0.75. For example, if you can leg press 150 pounds 10 times, maybe 11, but no more, divide 150 by 0.75 to estimate 1 Rep Max as 200 pounds.

Another way to estimate load is to begin with a weight that is embarrassingly easy. Slowly keep increasing the weight until you can only lift the number of repetitions listed for any particular phase.

## SETS

This means the number of repeated lifting bouts done on any particular exercise.

## REPETITIONS PER SET

This is the number of repetitions done within each set for any particular exercise. For example, during the PE phase, complete a hip extension exercise set three to five times, and lift the weight eight to fifteen times each time the exercise is done.

## SPEED OF MOVEMENT

The recommended speed is subjective; however, the weight must be controlled in both directions of movement. The phase requiring the most concern is the PE phase; please refer to the PE details for more information. Novice athletes (those in their first two years of strength training) should not try for highly explosive moves.

## MINUTES OF RECOVERY

Each phase has recommended recovery times between sets. These times are important for each phase. For example, the MS phase is compromised if the athlete shortens the two- to four-minute recovery times. A shortened recovery time means the athlete would have to reduce the weight, not making full use of the MS phase.

During the recovery time, stretch. Stretching exercises are outlined later in the chapter.

## RECOVERY WEEKS

As part of your periodization plan, some weeks will reduce the volume of training to rest and recover. This can be applied to strength training by reducing the number of strength training days that week, reducing the time spent in each strength session by reducing the number of sets within a workout, slightly reducing the weight lifted on each exercise, or a combination of any of these three methods.

## ADDITIONAL RECOMMENDATIONS

Often athletes have one leg or arm that is stronger than the other limb. If you have the time, I recommend doing single-limb exercises. For example, you can do single-leg leg presses. You can use a cable machine to do single-arm lat pull-downs. A cable machine can also be used to do standing single-arm swim strokes, or a bench can be utilized to do prone single-arm strokes. Single-limb exercises can improve overall sports fitness by identifying and improving dominant side strength.

# STRETCHING

Those who stretch are religious about their routine. Those who do not stretch do not see any benefit to doing so, nor do they associate any negative consequences with not stretching. Flexibility has been shown to improve neuromuscular coordination and physical efficiency, increase the supply of blood and nutrients to joint structure, improve balance and muscular awareness, and improve performance and strength. Improve strength?

A study of swimmers, football players, and runners had them do contract-relax flexibility training for the knee extensors and flexors. Contract-relax flexibility training involves a passive stretch of a muscle after an isometric contraction. The athletes did flexibility training for eight weeks, three days per week. The researchers found flexibility training to increase the range of motion of the knee joint by about 6 percent. The scientists also found that stretching improves knee joint torque. Eccentric knee extension torque increased 19 to 25 percent, depending on the particular velocity of the measurement. Eccentric knee flexion torque increased 16 to 18 percent, again depending on the velocity of the measurement. Concentric knee flexion torque increased 8 to 10 percent, while knee flexion isometric torque increased 11 percent.

The contract-relax flexibility training increased the strength of the knee flexors and extensors (hamstrings and quadriceps, respectively, to name some of the major muscles involved) during eccentric actions. The training also increased the strength of the knee flexors during concentric actions.

While this study showed a positive correlation between stretching and sport strength, this is not true for all studies. Reviewing the literature, there does not seem to be enough evidence to endorse or discontinue a stretching routine.

Literature aside, several athletes have found themselves faced with an activity-limiting injury. Many times part of the rehabilitation and future prevention routine includes a stretching regimen. Because the research literature is inconclusive and many recreational and elite athletes have benefited from a stretching protocol, I continue to recommend stretching as part of your fitness routine. If you are an athlete who has never stretched and has not experienced any problems due to your lack of flexibility, I don't see a reason to add stretching to your routine until it is needed.

There are two basic types of flexibility: static flexibility and dynamic flexibility. Static flexibility is the range of motion relative to a joint, with little emphasis on speed of movement. An example is the combination of hamstring, back, and upper back flexibility needed by people riding in a time trial position or enduring a long ride. Dynamic flexibility is resistance to motion at the joint and involves speed during physical performance. An example of the use of dynamic flexibility is a cyclist jumping out of the saddle to aggressively climb a hill or sprint to catch an opponent. A good endurance athlete must have both types of flexibility.

## HOW TO STRETCH

There are many methods for stretching. The one recommended in this book is called "proprioceptive neuromuscular facilitation" (PNF). There are also many variations on this technique. One easy-to-follow version is this:

1. *Static-stretch (stretch and hold) the muscle for about 8 seconds. Remember to breathe.*
2. *Contract the same muscle for about 8 seconds. (Leave out the contraction step when stretching during the rest interval of strength training and just hold static stretches for about 15 seconds.)*
3. *Stretch and hold the stretch again for about 8 seconds. Breathe.*
4. *Continue alternating muscle contractions and stretches until you have completed four to eight static stretches. End with a stretch and not a contraction.*

You should find you are able to stretch farther, or increase your range of motion, each time you repeat the stretch.

## STRETCHES FOR MULTISPORT

Table 22.2 provides suggestions for muscle groups to stretch, including when to stretch them. To find illustrations and specific instructions stretching particular muscles and groups of muscles, consult a qualified trainer at the gym or the illustrations and instructions in my book *The Female Cyclist* or Joe Friel's *The Triathlete's Training Bible*. A couple of good resources for stretching exercises are *Sport Stretch* by Michael J. Alter and *Stretching* by Bob Anderson.

| TABLE 22.2: STRETCHING GUIDE | |
|---|---|
| **Stretching Exercises** | **Muscles Stretched** |
| 1. Hip extension (*squat, leg press, or step-up*) | Quadriceps, hamstrings, gluteus |
| 2. Standing bent-arm lat pull-down | Latissimus dorsi, biceps |
| 3. Hip extension (different from #1) | Quadriceps, hamstrings, gluteus |
| 4. Chest press or push-ups | Biceps, triceps, pectoralis |
| 5. Seated row | Upper and lower back, latissimus dorsi, biceps |
| 6. Personal weakness: | |
|     *hamstring curl* | Hamstrings |
|     *knee extension* | Quadriceps |
|     *calf raise* | Calves |
| 7. Abdominal exercise | Abdominals |
| 8. Optional—back extension | Back, particularly lower back |
| Stretching After Swimming | Select exercises that stretch arms and the entire shoulder area, including, but not limited to, triceps, latissimus dorsi, biceps, trapezius, and deltoids |
| Stretching After Cycling | Quadriceps, hamstrings, gluteus, calves, lower back, and muscles listed for swimming |
| Stretching After Running | Quadriceps, hamstrings, gluteus, calves, lower back, and optional stretches, including those listed for swimming |

# EPILOGUE

*Swimming will continue to be a huge challenge for me. I never find it easy, but I have gotten faster and it feels great to have overcome my fears and improved. I have a long way to go but am confident now that with a lot of hard work, dedication, and determination I can do it . . . so can you! As long as you have the courage, the belief in yourself, and the desire to get better, you can and will improve— with lots of hard work and persistence. Never give up, never stop believing, push your limits, and reach for the stars! Anything is possible!*

—SIRI LINDLEY, USA
FIRST ALTERNATE TO THE 2000 TRIATHLON OLYMPIC
TEAM, 2001 WORLD CHAMPION

To end this book, I go back to the beginning of my coaching experience. I recognize that the words between the covers would not have been possible without the trust of all the people who allowed me to help them along their athletic journey. I value their trust, and many of the lessons we learned together are reflected in each chapter.

When Siri forwarded her words of wisdom to me, I thought it was a fitting sentiment to close the book. The best athletes are always looking to make themselves just a fraction better. My desire is that this book will give you training ideas and abet you on your journey of continuous athletic improvement.

For more information on educational coaching seminars and certification, contact USA Triathlon at www.usatriathlon.org.

# APPENDIX A
## FIELD TESTS FOR ESTIMATING LACTATE THRESHOLD HEART RATE ON THE BIKE

## 10-MINUTE TIME TRIAL FOR BEGINNERS

If you are using one of the beginner plans in this book and have limited fitness, begin with this ten-minute test. After gaining some base fitness, conduct a short time trial to estimate your lactate threshold heart rate (LTHR). Warm up for 10 to 15 minutes at rate of perceived exertion (RPE) Zones 1 to 2. After the warm-up, run or ride for about 10 minutes, steadily increasing your pace each minute. If you expect to get beyond the first minute, it's obvious you can't start out at a sprint. As you increase pace, notice your heart rate at the end of each minute. How do you feel? What is your breathing rate?

When your breathing becomes noticeably labored, and soon after that, a burning sensation creeps into your legs, take note of your heart rate. Use this heart rate as your lactate threshold for now. Also take note of when you felt the burning sensation, since that sensation can occur several minutes after your change in breathing. If you use the burning sensation to estimate LTHR, you might be overestimating your threshold. Overestimating threshold overestimates all the training zones, which means you might be working anaerobically when you intended to work aerobically. The result could be overtraining and underdevelopment of your aerobic system.

| Zone | | RPE | Description |
|------|---|-----|-------------|
| 1 | Recovery | 6 | |
| 1 | Recovery | 7 | Very, very light |
| 1 | Recovery | 8 | |
| 2 | Extensive endurance | 9 | Very light |
| 2 | Extensive endurance | 10 | |
| 2 | Extensive endurance | 11 | Fairly light |
| 3 | Intensive endurance | 12 | |
| 3 | Intensive endurance | 13 | Somewhat hard |
| 3 | Intensive endurance | 14 | |
| 4 | Threshold | 15 | Hard |
| 5a | Threshold | 16 | |
| 5b | Anaerobic endurance | 17 | Very hard |
| 5b | Anaerobic endurance | 18 | |
| 5c | Power | 19 | Very, very hard |
| 5c | Power | 20 | |

**TABLE A.1: THE BORG RATE OF PERCEIVED EXERTION (RPE) SCALE AND TRAINING ZONES**

As you gain more sport experience and fitness, your estimated lactate threshold number can be further refined.

## INDOOR TEST FOR ESTIMATING CYCLING LACTATE THRESHOLD HEART RATE

One way to estimate LTHR involves a CompuTrainer. The newer models of CompuTrainers have a calibration feature, so the instrument can be calibrated for each test and accurate retesting can be done at a later date. The use of the CompuTrainer method makes it easy for a coach or assistant to note athletes' ventilatory threshold (VT) and perceived exertion by standing next to them. Exertion and noticeable change in ventilation are best recorded while the test is in progress, instead of trying to recall the information later.

## EQUIPMENT, SETUP, AND ASSISTANCE

*1.* Recruit an assistant with clipboard, paper, pencil, a heart rate monitor, and a CompuTrainer. It is best to position the heart rate monitor readout where both the athlete and the assistant can see it. You can create your own data sheet using the piece of paper, or make a copy of the Lactate Threshold Test Data Sheet in this appendix (see Figure A.3).

*2.* Warm up on the CompuTrainer for around 10 minutes and calibrate according to the instructions in the manual.

*3.* Set "Program" to "Road Races/Courses," program 70.

*4.* Program the course to 10 miles, although you will not use the entire distance.

*5.* Input your body weight plus the bike weight and record this data on the log sheet for later reference.

*6.* Turn "Drafting" off.

## PROCEDURE

*1.* During the test, hold a predetermined power level (plus or minus 5 watts) as displayed on the screen. Begin the test at 50 watts and increase by 20 watts every minute, until you can no longer continue—meaning you cannot sustain the power plus or minus 5 watts or the rating of perceived exertion is too high. Stay seated throughout the test. You can change gears at any time. Highly fit or professional athletes may need to begin the test at more than 50 watts; around 110 watts may be more appropriate.

*2.* At the end of each minute, tell the assistant how your RPE is for the particular wattage just completed. Use the Borg scale in Table A.1; in other words, on a scale of 6 to 20, 6 being very easy and 20 being very, very hard, how difficult is it for you to hold a particular wattage? Keep the scale easily visible so you can grade your exertion.

*3.* The assistant will record your exertion rating and your heart rate at the end of the minute and instruct you to increase power to the next level. She or he can also encourage you to keep your power at the designated intensity. If you have no assistant, but do have a heart rate monitor that records data, store your heart rate at each "lap" minute. Mentally note perceived exertion or, better yet, jot it down on a copy of the data sheet.

*4.* The assistant will listen closely to your breathing to detect when it becomes labored and shallow. She or he will note the associated heart rate with the beginning of labored breathing and note VT.

NAME _____ BG

DATE _____ September 6

BIKE AND RIDER WEIGHT _____ 128 + 23 = 154

| WATTS | HEART RATE | RATE OF PERCEIVED EXERTION |
|---|---|---|
| 50 | 106 | 6 |
| 70 | 109 | 7 |
| 90 | 118 | 7 |
| 110 | 125 | 9 |
| 130 | 130 | 10 |
| 150 | 134 | 10 |
| 170 | 142 | 12 |
| 190 | 147 | 12 |
| 210 | 154 | 13 |
| 230 | 157 | 14 |
| 250 | 159 | 15 |
| 270 | 164 | 16 |
| 290 | 165 | 16* Noted VT |
| 310 | 166 | 17 |
| 330 | 169 | 19 |
| 350 | 170 | 19 |
| 370 | | |
| 390 | | |
| 410 | | |
| 430 | | |
| 450 | | |
| 470 | | |
| 490 | | |
| 510 | | |
| 530 | | |
| 550 | | |
| 570 | | |

| ZONE | RPE | BREATHING |
|---|---|---|
| 1 | 6–9 | Hardly noticeable |
| 2 | 10–12 | Slight |
| 3 | 13–14 | Aware of breathing a little harder |
| 4 | 15–16 | Starting to breathe hard |
| 5a | 17 | Breathing hard |
| 5b | 18–19 | Heavy, labored breathing |
| 5c | 20 | Maximal exertion noted in breathing |

Notes about bike set-up, current training status, how you feel:

1) BG felt good and well-rested

2) VT seemed to occur at 290 watts

FIGURE A.1   LTHR Test Data Sheet

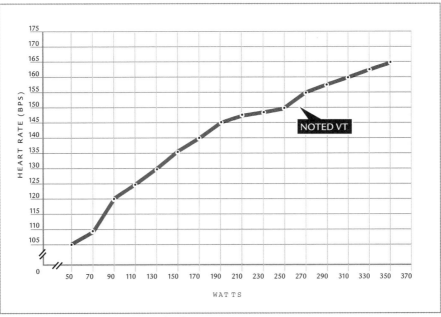

FIGURE A.2    Heart Rate Data Plot for BG

5.  Continue until you can no longer hold the power level (for at least 15 seconds) or feel you can't go on.

6.  The data should look similar to that shown in Figure A.1. VT heart rate and power is usually comparable to an RPE in the range of 15 to 17, and is usually a close estimate of LTHR; athletes are seldom able to go more than three to five minutes beyond their lactate threshold on this test.

7.  Create an XY graph with the vertical coordinate representing heart rate and the horizontal coordinate representing wattage. Plot the data points from the test onto a chart and connect them, as shown in Figure A.2. Lactate threshold can be estimated by using three references:

    *a) Note the heart rate at which breathing becomes labored (ventilatory threshold), which can be subjective.*

    *b) Lactate threshold is usually between 15 and 17 on the RPE scale.*

c) *Lactate threshold is usually no more than three to five data points from the end of the test—that is, when the test subject wishes to stop.*

If the ventilatory threshold found in (a) does not agree with (b) and (c), disregard it.

*8.* Now that you have an estimate for your LTHR, use Table A.2 to calculate your training zones. Find your LTHR in the "5a Zone" column (in bold). Read across, left and right, for training zones. The training zones will need to be confirmed: Compare the heart rates and perceived exertion you achieved during the test with the exertion levels and heart rates you experience during workouts and races. Based on training and racing information, the zones may need slight modification. Be aware that LTHR can change with improved fitness, particularly for beginners.

## OUTDOOR TEST FOR ESTIMATING CYCLING LACTATE THRESHOLD HEART RATE FOR FIT ATHLETES

Find an eight-mile course you can ride where there are no stop signs and there is limited traffic. After a good warm-up, do a time trial on the course. This means all out, as fast as you can go for eight miles. You will need to either mentally notice the average heart rate during the time trial or use a heart rate monitor with an average function. It is best to have the averaging function. Do not use the maximum heart rate you saw during the test as the average. After the test, recall your average heart rate for the eight miles. This average heart rate is approximately 101 percent of LTHR. For example, if your average heart rate for the test was 165, 165 divided by 1.01 equals 163 for LTHR.

If you happen to do an eight-mile time trial during a race, use 105 percent as your multiplier. In the example mentioned in the last paragraph, you would calculate your LTHR as follows:

*165 ÷ 1.05 = 157*

## TABLE A.2: CYCLING HEART RATE ZONES

| Zone 1 Recovery | Zone 2 Aerobic | Zone 3 Tempo | Zone 4 Sub-Threshold | Zone 5a Super-Threshold | Zone 5b Aerobic Capacity | Zone 5c Anaerobic Capacity |
|---|---|---|---|---|---|---|
| 90–108 | 109–122 | 123–128 | 129–136 | **137–140** | 141–145 | 146–150 |
| 91–109 | 110–123 | 124–129 | 130–137 | **138–141** | 142–146 | 147–151 |
| 91–109 | 110–124 | 125–130 | 131–138 | **139–142** | 143–147 | 148–152 |
| 92–110 | 111–125 | 126–130 | 131–139 | **140–143** | 144–147 | 148–153 |
| 92–111 | 112–125 | 126–131 | 132–140 | **141–144** | 145–148 | 149–154 |
| 93–112 | 113–126 | 127–132 | 133–141 | **142–145** | 146–149 | 150–155 |
| 93–112 | 113–127 | 128–133 | 134–142 | **143–145** | 146–150 | 151–156 |
| 94–113 | 114–128 | 129–134 | 135–143 | **144–147** | 148–151 | 152–157 |
| 95–114 | 115–129 | 130–135 | 136–144 | **145–148** | 149–152 | 153–158 |
| 95–115 | 116–130 | 131–136 | 137–145 | **146–149** | 150–154 | 155–159 |
| 97–116 | 117–131 | 132–137 | 138–146 | **147–150** | 151–155 | 156–161 |
| 97–117 | 118–132 | 133–138 | 139–147 | **148–151** | 152–156 | 157–162 |
| 98–118 | 119–133 | 134–139 | 140–148 | **149–152** | 153–157 | 158–163 |
| 98–119 | 120–134 | 135–140 | 141–149 | **150–153** | 154–158 | 159–164 |
| 99–120 | 121–134 | 135–141 | 142–150 | **151–154** | 155–159 | 160–165 |
| 100–121 | 122–135 | 136–142 | 143–151 | **152–155** | 156–160 | 161–166 |
| 100–122 | 132–136 | 137–142 | 143–152 | **153–156** | 157–161 | 162–167 |
| 101–123 | 124–137 | 138–143 | 144–153 | **154–157** | 158–162 | 163–168 |
| 101–124 | 125–138 | 139–144 | 145–154 | **155–158** | 159–163 | 164–169 |
| 102–125 | 126–138 | 139–145 | 146–155 | **156–159** | 160–164 | 165–170 |
| 103–126 | 1267–140 | 141–146 | 147–156 | **157–160** | 161–165 | 166–171 |
| 104–127 | 128–144 | 142–147 | 148–157 | **158–161** | 162–167 | 168–173 |
| 104–128 | 128–142 | 143–148 | 148–158 | **159–162** | 163–168 | 169–174 |
| 105–129 | 130–143 | 144–148 | 149–159 | **160–163** | 164–169 | 170–175 |
| 106–129 | 130–143 | 144–150 | 151–160 | **161–164** | 165–170 | 171–176 |
| 106–130 | 131–144 | 145–151 | 152–161 | **162–165** | 166–171 | 172–177 |
| 107–131 | 132–145 | 146–152 | 153–162 | **163–166** | 167–172 | 173–178 |
| 107–132 | 133–146 | 147–153 | 154–163 | **164–167** | 168–173 | 174–179 |
| 108–133 | 134–147 | 148–154 | 155–164 | **165–168** | 169–174 | 175–180 |
| 109–134 | 135–148 | 149–154 | 155–165 | **166–169** | 170–175 | 176–181 |
| 109–135 | 136–149 | 150–155 | 156–166 | **167–170** | 171–176 | 177–182 |
| 110–136 | 137–150 | 151–156 | 157–167 | **168–171** | 172–177 | 178–183 |
| 111–137 | 138–151 | 152–157 | 158–168 | **169–172** | 173–178 | 179–185 |
| 112–138 | 139–151 | 152–158 | 159–169 | **170–173** | 174–179 | 180–186 |
| 112–139 | 140–152 | 153–160 | 161–170 | **171–174** | 175–180 | 181–187 |
| 113–140 | 141–153 | 154–160 | 161–171 | **172–175** | 176–181 | 182–188 |
| 113–141 | 142–154 | 155–161 | 162–172 | **173–176** | 177–182 | 183–189 |
| 114–142 | 143–155 | 156–162 | 163–173 | **174–177** | 178–183 | 184–190 |
| 115–143 | 144–156 | 157–163 | 164–174 | **175–178** | 179–184 | 185–191 |
| 115–144 | 145–157 | 158–164 | 165–175 | **176–179** | 180–185 | 186–192 |
| 116–145 | 146–158 | 159–165 | 166–176 | **177–180** | 181–186 | 187–193 |
| 116–146 | 147–159 | 160–166 | 167–177 | **178–181** | 182–187 | 188–194 |
| 117–147 | 148–160 | 161–166 | 167–178 | **179–182** | 183–188 | 189–195 |
| 118–148 | 149–160 | 161–167 | 168–179 | **180–183** | 184–190 | 191–197 |
| 119–149 | 150–161 | 162–168 | 169–180 | **181–184** | 185–191 | 192198 |
| 119–150 | 151–162 | 163–170 | 171–181 | **182–185** | 186–192 | 193–199 |
| 120–151 | 152–163 | 164–171 | 172–182 | **183–186** | 187–193 | 194–200 |
| 121–152 | 153–164 | 165–172 | 173–183 | **184–187** | 188–194 | 195–201 |
| 121–153 | 154–165 | 166–172 | 173–184 | **185–188** | 191–195 | 196–202 |
| 122–154 | 155–166 | 167–173 | 174–185 | **186–189** | 190–196 | 197–203 |
| 122–155 | 156–167 | 168–174 | 175–186 | **187–190** | 191–197 | 198–204 |
| 123–156 | 157–168 | 169–175 | 176–187 | **188–191** | 192–198 | 199–205 |
| 124–157 | 158–169 | 170–176 | 177–188 | **189–192** | 193–199 | 200–206 |
| 124–158 | 159–170 | 171–177 | 178–189 | **190–193** | 194–200 | 201–207 |
| 125–159 | 160–170 | 171–178 | 179–190 | **191–194** | 195–201 | 202–208 |
| 125–160 | 161–171 | 172–178 | 179–191 | **192–195** | 196–202 | 203–209 |
| 126–161 | 162–172 | 173–179 | 180–192 | **193–196** | 197–203 | 204–210 |
| 127–162 | 163–173 | 174–180 | 181–193 | **194–197** | 198–204 | 205–211 |
| 127–163 | 164–174 | 175–181 | 182–194 | **195–198** | 199–205 | 206–212 |

Why use a different multiplier if the time trial was an actual race compared to a workout? Because we are typically able to push ourselves much harder in a race than in a workout.

If your optimal course is shorter than eight miles, can that be used? Yes. A list of time trial distances and their various multipliers are listed in Table A.3. If you are in the beginning stages of improving your cycling, you might be better off to use one of the shorter time trial distances, such as a 5K (3.1 miles). As you improve season after season, increase the time trial distance or continue to use a distance in the 3.1- to 4-mile range.

### TABLE A.3: PREDICTING LACTATE-THRESHOLD PULSE RATE FROM AN INDIVIDUAL TIME TRIAL AVERAGE HEART RATE

| Distance of ITT | As Race | As Workout |
|---|---|---|
| 5K | 110% of LT | 104% of LT |
| 10K | 107% of LT | 102% of LT |
| 8–10 miles | 105% of LT | 101% of LT |
| 40K | 100% of LT | 97% of LT |

NAME_____

DATE_____

BIKE AND RIDER WEIGHT _____

| WATTS | HEART RATE | RATE OF PERCEIVED EXERTION |
|---|---|---|
| 50 | | |
| 70 | | |
| 90 | | |
| 110 | | |
| 130 | | |
| 150 | | |
| 170 | | |
| 190 | | |
| 210 | | |
| 230 | | |
| 250 | | |
| 270 | | |
| 290 | | |
| 310 | | |
| 330 | | |
| 350 | | |
| 370 | | |
| 390 | | |
| 410 | | |
| 430 | | |
| 450 | | |
| 470 | | |
| 490 | | |
| 510 | | |
| 530 | | |
| 550 | | |
| 570 | | |

| ZONE | RPE | BREATHING |
|---|---|---|
| 1 | 6–9 | Hardly noticeable |
| 2 | 10–12 | Slight |
| 3 | 13–14 | Aware of breathing a little harder |
| 4 | 15–16 | Starting to breathe hard |
| 5a | 17 | Breathing hard |
| 5b | 18–19 | Heavy, labored breathing |
| 5c | 20 | Maximal exertion noted in breathing |

**Notes about bike set-up, current training status, how you feel:**

_____

_____

_____

_____

_____

_____

_____

_____

FIGURE A.3   Blank LTHR Test Data Sheet

# APPENDIX B
## FIELD TESTS FOR ESTIMATING LACTATE THRESHOLD HEART RATE ON THE RUN

## 10-MINUTE TIME TRIAL FOR BEGINNERS

See Appendix A.

## INDOOR TEST FOR ESTIMATING RUNNING LACTATE THRESHOLD HEART RATE

This test involves running on a treadmill. You and your assistant should be familiar with the operation of the treadmill you will use and you must have experience running on a treadmill. This test has some risks associated with it; be responsible for your own safety. If you begin to feel dizzy or light-headed during the test, stop the test before the treadmill shoots you off the back.

### EQUIPMENT, SETUP, AND ASSISTANCE

*1.* A treadmill with a top speed of at least 10 mph is necessary. If your treadmill has a slower max speed, it should have a variable grade mode.

*1.* Also needed is an assistant, a heart rate monitor, a clipboard, paper, and a pencil. The assistant holds the heart rate monitor wrist receiver during the test.

## PROCEDURE

*1.* With the assistant, read all of the instructions before starting.

*2.* Warm up for 10 to 15 minutes, gradually elevating heart rate to a comfortable and easy effort.

*3.* Once the test begins, the assistant will operate the treadmill. He or she should stand so he or she can easily reach the stop control button.

*4.* Begin the test at 6 mph on a level treadmill (if it has 10 mph as the max speed) or at 6 mph on a 2 percent grade (if the treadmill has less than 10 mph max speed).

*5.* Every minute, your assistant increases the speed by 0.2 mph.

*6.* Just before each of these speed increases, the assistant records your heart rate, rate of perceived exertion (RPE), and the current speed in mph. The data will look something like this:

| Speed | Heart Rate | RPE |
|-------|------------|-----|
| 6.0 | 130 | 8 |
| 6.2 | 133 | 9 |
| 6.4 | 134 | 11 |
| 6.6 | 137 | 13 |

*7.* Both you and the assistant should pay close attention to your breathing. When it becomes labored for the first time (when there's a lot of air being moved), the assistant should note the heart rate at that point on the data sheet. This data point is your VT or ventilatory threshold heart rate.

*8.* The test stops when you decide you have gone far enough. Tell the assistant to stop the treadmill or stop it yourself. Decide ahead of time how this will be done.

*9.* Create an XY graph with the vertical coordinate representing heart rate and the horizontal coordinate representing speed cubed.

## TABLE B.1: RUNNING HEART RATE ZONES

| Zone 1 Recovery | Zone 2 Extensive Endurance | Zone 3 Intensive Endurance | Zone 4 Sub–Threshold | Zone 5a Super–Threshold | Zone 5b Anaerobic Endurance | Zone 5c Power |
|---|---|---|---|---|---|---|
| 93–119 | 120–126 | 127–133 | 134–139 | **140–143** | 144–149 | 150–156 |
| 94–119 | 120–127 | 128–134 | 135–140 | **141–144** | 145–150 | 151–157 |
| 95–120 | 121–129 | 130–135 | 136–141 | **142–145** | 146–151 | 152–158 |
| 95–121 | 122–130 | 131–136 | 137–142 | **143–146** | 147–152 | 153–159 |
| 96–122 | 123–131 | 132–137 | 138–143 | **144–147** | 148–153 | 154–160 |
| 96–123 | 124–132 | 133–138 | 139–144 | **145–148** | 149–154 | 155–161 |
| 97–124 | 125–133 | 134–139 | 140–145 | **146–149** | 150–155 | 156–162 |
| 97–124 | 125–134 | 135–140 | 141–146 | **147–150** | 151–156 | 157–163 |
| 98–125 | 126–135 | 136–141 | 142–147 | **148–151** | 152–157 | 158–164 |
| 99–126 | 127–135 | 136–142 | 143–148 | **149–152** | 153–158 | 159–165 |
| 99–127 | 128–136 | 137–143 | 144–149 | **150–153** | 154–158 | 159–166 |
| 100–128 | 129–137 | 138–144 | 145–150 | **151–154** | 155–159 | 160–167 |
| 100–129 | 130–138 | 139–145 | 146–151 | **152–155** | 156–160 | 161–168 |
| 101–130 | 131–139 | 140–146 | 147–152 | **153–156** | 157–161 | 162–169 |
| 102–131 | 132–140 | 141–147 | 148–153 | **154–157** | 158–162 | 163–170 |
| 103–131 | 132–141 | 142–148 | 149–154 | **155–158** | 159–164 | 165–172 |
| 103–132 | 133–142 | 143–149 | 150–155 | **156–159** | 160–165 | 166–173 |
| 104–133 | 134–143 | 144–150 | 151–156 | **157–160** | 161–166 | 167–174 |
| 105–134 | 135–143 | 144–151 | 152–157 | **158–161** | 162–167 | 168–175 |
| 105–135 | 136–144 | 145–152 | 153–158 | **159–162** | 163–168 | 169–176 |
| 106–136 | 137–145 | 146–153 | 154–159 | **160–163** | 164–169 | 170–177 |
| 106–136 | 137–146 | 147–154 | 155–160 | **161–164** | 165–170 | 171–178 |
| 107–137 | 138–147 | 148–155 | 156–161 | **162–165** | 166–171 | 172–179 |
| 108–138 | 139–148 | 149–155 | 156–162 | **163–166** | 167–172 | 173–180 |
| 109–139 | 140–149 | 150–156 | 157–163 | **164–167** | 168–174 | 175–182 |
| 109–140 | 141–150 | 151–157 | 158–164 | **165–168** | 169–175 | 176–183 |
| 110–141 | 142–151 | 152–158 | 159–165 | **166–169** | 170–176 | 177–184 |
| 111–141 | 142–152 | 153–159 | 160–166 | **167–170** | 171–177 | 178–185 |
| 111–142 | 143–153 | 154–160 | 161–167 | **168–171** | 172–178 | 179–186 |
| 112–143 | 144–154 | 155–161 | 162–168 | **169–172** | 173–179 | 180–187 |
| 112–144 | 145–155 | 156–162 | 163–169 | **170–173** | 174–179 | 180–188 |
| 113–145 | 146–156 | 157–163 | 164–170 | **171–174** | 175–180 | 181–189 |
| 114–145 | 146–156 | 157–164 | 165–171 | **172–175** | 176–182 | 183–191 |
| 115–146 | 147–157 | 158–165 | 166–172 | **173–176** | 177–183 | 184–192 |
| 115–147 | 148–157 | 158–166 | 167–173 | **174–177** | 178–184 | 185–193 |
| 116–148 | 149–158 | 159–167 | 168–174 | **175–178** | 179–185 | 186–194 |
| 117–149 | 150–159 | 160–168 | 169–175 | **176–179** | 180–186 | 187–195 |
| 117–150 | 151–160 | 161–169 | 170–176 | **177–180** | 181–187 | 188–196 |
| 118–151 | 152–161 | 162–170 | 171–177 | **178–181** | 182–188 | 189–197 |
| 118–152 | 153–162 | 163–171 | 172–178 | **179–182** | 183–189 | 190–198 |
| 119–153 | 154–163 | 164–172 | 173–179 | **180–183** | 184–190 | 191–199 |
| 120–154 | 155–164 | 165–173 | 174–180 | **181–184** | 185–192 | 193–201 |
| 121–154 | 155–165 | 166–174 | 175–181 | **182–185** | 186–193 | 194–202 |
| 121–155 | 156–166 | 167–175 | 176–182 | **183–186** | 187–194 | 195–203 |
| 122–156 | 157–167 | 168–176 | 177–183 | **184–187** | 188–195 | 196–204 |
| 123–157 | 158–168 | 169–177 | 178–184 | **185–188** | 189–196 | 197–205 |
| 123–158 | 159–169 | 170–178 | 179–185 | **186–189** | 190–197 | 198–206 |
| 124–159 | 160–170 | 171–179 | 180–186 | **187–190** | 191–198 | 199–207 |
| 124–159 | 160–170 | 171–179 | 180–187 | **188–191** | 192–199 | 200–208 |
| 125–160 | 161–171 | 172–180 | 181–188 | **189–192** | 193–200 | 201–209 |
| 126–161 | 152–172 | 173–181 | 182–189 | **190–193** | 194–201 | 202–210 |
| 126–162 | 163–173 | 174–182 | 183–190 | **191–194** | 195–201 | 202–211 |
| 127–163 | 164–174 | 175–183 | 184–191 | **192–195** | 196–202 | 203–212 |
| 127–164 | 165–175 | 176–184 | 185–192 | **193–196** | 197–203 | 204–213 |
| 128–165 | 166–176 | 177–185 | 186–193 | **194–197** | 198–204 | 205–214 |
| 129–165 | 166–177 | 178–186 | 187–194 | **195–198** | 199–205 | 206–215 |
| 129–166 | 167–178 | 179–187 | 188–195 | **196–199** | 200–206 | 207–216 |
| 130–167 | 168–178 | 179–188 | 189–196 | **197–198** | 199–207 | 208–217 |
| 130–168 | 169–179 | 180–189 | 190–197 | **198–201** | 202–208 | 209–218 |
| 131–169 | 170–180 | 181–190 | 191–198 | **199–202** | 203–209 | 210–219 |
| 132–170 | 171–181 | 182–191 | 192–199 | **200–203** | 204–210 | 211–220 |

*10.* Plot the data points from the test onto this chart and connect them. As with the cycling test, if there is a point at which the line deflects or bends sharply, the heart rate associated with this deflection is assumed to be LT pulse. Confirm this by comparing it with the VT heart rate and your heart rate when perceived exertion was the range of 15 to 17. (Be aware that you may not have a deflection point on the graph.)

*11.* Use your lactate threshold heart rate (LTHR) and Table B.1 to determine your training zones. Notice the run and bike percents are slightly different. These zones were based on the work done by Peter Janssen and his book *Training Lactate Pulse Rate*.

## OUTDOOR TEST FOR ESTIMATING RUNNING LACTATE THRESHOLD HEART RATE

Find a three-mile course you can run where there are no stop signs and limited traffic. A track can be used. As with the cycling time trial, after a good warm-up, do a running time trial on the course. This means "all out," as hard as possible, as if it were a race. You will need to either mentally notice the average heart rate during the time trial (which is highly inaccurate) or use a monitor with an average function. It is best to have the averaging function. After the test, recall average heart rate for the test. That average heart rate is approximately 101 percent of LTHR.

For example, if average heart rate for the test was 172, 172 divided by 1.01 equals 170 for LTHR. If you happen to do a 5K running race, use 105 percent as your multiplier. In the example mentioned in the last paragraph, you would determine your LTHR as follows:

$$172 \div 1.05 = 164$$

This difference is because we tend to push ourselves much harder in a race than in a workout.

# APPENDIX C
## TRAINING WITH POWER

If you own a power meter, you can use it with some of the intensive endurance and lactate threshold endurance workouts in this book. Ironman-distance racing, for example, uses intensive endurance training. For Olympic-distance events, lactate threshold endurance or improved power output at lactate threshold heart rate is the long-term goal. To use power measurements for some of the heart rate intervals given in this book, use the guidelines that are covered in the paragraphs that follow.

### COMPUTRAINER OR OTHER INDOOR POWER METERS THAT CAN BE CALIBRATED

When you tested for lactate threshold on the CompuTrainer, lactate threshold heart rate (LTHR) was achieved at a particular power output. This value is lactate threshold power (LTP). When a training plan in this book designates a particular number of intervals or minutes at Zones 4 to 5a, you can use LTP plus or minus 5 percent—instead of LTHR—as the goal. For example, if lactate threshold power is 300 watts, the interval power range is 285 to 315 watts. If the workout calls for four sets of 6-minute intervals in Zones 4 to 5a, instead of shooting for a heart rate, aim for 285 to 315 watts. Typically, you'll find that the first interval or two seem too easy and that it takes a good deal of time for your heart rate to climb into Zone 4. By the last interval, however, heart rate is well into Zones 4 to 5a and it is a challenge to maintain power until the end of the designated time.

It's best to start with a low wattage of power and increase or build to the end of the interval. If power fades at the end of a given set, or heart rate climbs over Zone 5a early in the set, the goal power level is too high and needs to be adjusted.

Some intervals may be designated in Zone 3. The best way to determine Zone 3 power is by conducting an aerobic time trial (ATT) and then using the average power produced during the time trial, plus or minus 5 percent. Instructions for conducting an ATT are in Chapter 20.

## TESTING FOR POWER ZONES

Whether indoors or outdoors, power meters have made training with power on the bicycle much more affordable. Each power meter design has advantages and limitations. For instance, some power meters are not as accurate when used on an indoor trainer, compared with outdoor use. Do your homework to decide which power meter is best for your particular needs.

One method for testing for power zones comes from Joe Friel's work, *Training with Power*. Most applicable to this discussion is the average power, called critical power by Friel, produced in an all-out 30-minute time trial or CP30. After a good warm-up, zero your power meter and conduct an all-out time trial for 30 minutes. Do this test in a location with minimal traffic and no stops.

When intervals in this book are designated in Zones 4 to 5a, use the results from the critical power test for 30 minutes (CP30). Use CP30 plus or minus 5 percent. For example, if CP30 is 300 watts, the interval power range is 285 to 315 watts. If the workout calls for four sets of 6-minute intervals in Zones 4 to 5a, aim for 285 to 315 watts instead of shooting for a heart rate. Typically, you'll find the first interval or two seem too easy and that it takes a good deal of time for heart rate to climb into Zone 4. By the last interval, however, heart rate is well into Zones 4 to 5a, and it is a challenge to hold power constant to the end of the designated time.

For athletes who have multiple power meters, it is important to note that power output on one system is relative to that particular system. For example, CompuTrainer is relative to CompuTrainer and power output on PowerTap or SRM is relative to PowerTap or SRM. This means that power output compared between systems may not match.

As for Zone 3 intervals, an aerobic time trial is the best way to determine the power range to shoot for. The aerobic time trial is described in Chapter 20.

## WHY USE POWER AND NOT HEART RATE?

I have found that using heart rate as a tachometer for high-end speed training (Zones 4 to 5) can be inaccurate and difficult to monitor. In fact, for short sprints, a heart rate monitor is useless. For longer intervals, many athletes ride the first couple of intervals too fast and end up with fading speed at the end of the set. A power meter allows the athlete to be more consistent with energy and speed, aiming for a strong finish.

# APPENDIX D
## HEALTH QUESTIONNAIRE

## INSTRUCTIONS

The health questionnaire is intended to help you record health risks related to heredity and your current health condition. This information will need to be updated as more information becomes available about family members and as your personal health changes.

Sometimes athletes unwittingly put the goal to be thin ahead of the goal to be healthy. Severely restricting calories will affect current health and will certainly affect future health if wellness does not become the number-one priority.

Each question has been designed to prompt thoughts about personal health and genetic risks and to convey the idea that nutrition affects several areas of overall health. These areas can be used as markers to determine if a change in nutrition habits should be considered. Physical well-being, athletic performance, mental attitude, and nutrition are synergistic. They each need to be optimized in order for the athlete to perform at peak capability. The questionnaire appears in condensed form later in this appendix; first, here's a bit more detail about what information each question should elicit.

*1.* Knowing your family health history is important when making decisions about nutrition and any type of supplementation. Record any major health problems among your grandparents, parents, and siblings in this section.

*2.* Record the history of any health problems you have had in past years.

*3.* Do you currently have any health problems? Is your overall health improving or declining?

*4.* Describe your current diet. It is best to have a food log with details, but you can also describe how you eat. Do you eat highly processed foods? Do you eat out? If so, how many times each week? How many times each day do you eat? Do you eat because you are hungry, tired, stressed, or nervous? Do you eat a wide variety of foods or do you tend to eat the same things each day?

*5.* Has your diet always been like it is now or have you made recent changes? Why did the changes happen? Have the changes improved how you feel?

*6.* What does your blood chemistry work say? Are there any items that are outside the recommended ranges? If so, can the answers to questions 1 through 5 yield any help to correcting the problem?

Questions 1 through 6 are intended to stimulate thoughts about overall health over a period of time. The answer to any one of the questions may not yield valuable information, but the answers to all the questions together may help you and your health-care providers to flesh out solutions to any problems.

Questions 7 through 14 are subtle questions. The answers may suggest something is wrong with your health. These small details, again, when examined in total, may tell a tale of good health or impending trouble. When seeking the help of a physician, take the answers from this questionnaire along, as they can give a small snapshot of your health.

## HEALTH QUESTIONNAIRE

Questions 1 through 6 give you a health snapshot, including hereditary health issues.

*1.* What is my family history of health disorders?

2. What is my personal health history? What problems have I had in past years?

3. What health problems do I currently have?

4. What is my diet currently like?

5. Have I made recent changes to my diet?

6. What does my most recent blood chemistry work say about my health?

If you answer yes to several of the following questions, your diet may not be serving your needs. Chapter 3 can help you modify your diet; alternatively, consider seeking the help of a registered dietitian specializing in sports nutrition.

7. Am I frequently awake throughout the night?

8. Does my hair grow slowly? Is it dry or brittle?

*9.* Do I have acne, or wounds that heal slowly?

*10.* Are my nails weak and brittle?

*11.* Am I frequently ill or injured?

*12.* Am I often tired or have low energy?

*13.* Do I often have to skip training or reduce the intensity because I have no energy?

*14.* (Women) Are my periods irregular, often skipping months?

# APPENDIX E
## SAMPLE SWIM WORKOUTS

The workouts in this appendix are examples for some of the codes used in the plans. All workouts are freestyle and two levels are given for each workout, an "A" level and a "B" level. The A level is more advanced. Depending on your personal speed, the workouts take around 45 to 60 minutes to complete. More workouts are available in *Workouts in a Binder®: Swim Workouts for Triathletes* and *Workouts in a Binder® for Swimmers, Triathletes, and Coaches* (VeloPress).

The values in the "workouts" section will not specify meters or yards, as the two can be used interchangeably. For reading ease, yards are referenced in the "definitions" section.

## DEFINITIONS

*W/U.* Warm-up segment, with gradually increasing speeds throughout. All workouts in this appendix have the same warm-up for both A- and B-level swimmers.

*C/D.* Cool-down segment; Zone 2 finishing with Zone 1 rate of perceived exertion (RPE).

*T1 pace.* The pace you held in the time trial (T1 for swimming). For example, if T1 pace was 01:20 per 100 meters, then T1 pace for 200 is 02:40 and T1 pace for 50 meters is 00:40.

*Rest Interval.* Some swim sets will have a designated rest interval, such as (00:25 RI), which means a 25-second rest after each swim or repetition. For example:

200 (00:20 RI)
300 (00:25 RI)
200 (00:20 RI)

In this set, the swimmer would swim 200 meters, rest 20 seconds, swim 300 meters, rest 25 seconds, swim 200 meters, rest 20 seconds, and continue with the set. Once you begin rolling on the main set of the workout, the idea is to take only the amount of rest designated on the workout.

*Swim Interval.* Some workouts will have a designated swim interval, which includes the swim time and the rest time. A swim interval may be designated by a code such as "(T1 pace + 00:25 SI)." For example, assuming a T1 pace of 01:20 again, 4 × 100 (T1 pace + 00:25 SI) means swim 4 × 100 on a 01:40 interval. If the 100 is swum at a 01:20 pace, there will be 20 seconds of rest. If the 100 is swum at a 01:18 pace, there will be 22 seconds of rest. Typically, the idea behind this type of set is to swim at T1 pace or slightly—one to three seconds—faster.

The second way a swim interval may be designated is with a code such as "(01:00 SI)," which means the swim and rest must be completed within a minute. For example, 10 × 50 (01:00 SI) means to swim 10 repeats of 50 meters, starting every 60 seconds.

*No Rest Interval Designated.* Rest as long as you please.

*Rt. Arm.* This drill is freestyle with only one arm working—the right arm. With the left arm at your side (not out front), a moderate kick and normal body position and roll, the right arm performs a perfect stroke for the designated distance. That distance is typically 25 meters.

*Lt. Arm.* This drill is freestyle with only one arm working—the left arm. With the right arm at your side (not out front), a moderate kick and normal position and roll, the left arm performs a perfect stroke for the designated distance. That distance is typically 25 meters.

*Pull.* The swim is done with pull buoys, and paddles are optional. Paddles are used when working on force.

*Kick.* No arms, kick only; can be done with or without a kickboard. If kicking without a kickboard, try to simulate normal swimming body position and keep arms streamlined. Arms can be streamlined along the body or in front. Either way, they should be quiet. In other words, if your arms are in front of the body, do not do a breast stroke pull, short or long, to get a breath. A slight press with locked hands and a quick breath will do. Or keep your arms at your sides and roll the body to the side for a breath.

*DPS.* Distance per stroke; work on maximizing the distance each arm can propel the body. Count the number of strokes per 25 meters.

*Cruise.* A moderate pace; a Zone 3–type effort.

*Max Speed.* All-out fast, no holding back.

*Build.* Get faster within the designated swim. For example, "25 Build" means to get faster throughout the entire 25 meters. The last 5 meters should be the fastest swimming of that particular 25.

*Easy.* Zone 1 RPE.

*B-3.* Breathe every third stroke.

# WORKOUTS

## ENDURANCE FORM—E (FORM)

*W/U:* 200 swim, 200 kick, 200 pull; 6 × 75 (25 Rt. arm, 25 Lt. arm, 25 DPS)

| *Main Set:* | *A Level* | *B Level* |
|---|---|---|
| | 200 (00:15 RI) | 200 (00:20 RI) |
| | 300 (00:15 RI) | 300 (00:25 RI) |
| | 400 (00:20 RI) | 200 (00:20 RI) |
| | 400 (00:20 RI) | 300 (00:25 RI) |
| | 300 (00:15 RI) | 200 |
| | 200 | |

*C/D:* 200 (A level); 100 (B level)

*Total:* 3,050 – 2,350

## ENDURANCE SPEED—E (SPEED)

*W/U:* 300 swim, 200 kick, 100 pull

| *Main Set:* | *A Level* | *B Level* |
|---|---|---|
| | 600 (00:30 RI) | 300 (00:25 RI) |
| | 300 (00:20 RI) | 300 (00:25 RI) |
| | 300 (00:20 RI) | 200 (00:20 RI) |
| | 150 (00:15 RI) | 200 (00:20 RI) |
| | 150 (00:15 RI) | 150 |

*Speed Set:* 6 × 75: 25 cruise, 25 strong build, 25 easy (00:25 RI)

*C/D:* Your choice

*Total:* 2,550+ – 2,350+

## FORCE

*W/U:* 2 × (100 swim, 100 kick, 100 pull), 300 build

| *Main Set:* | *A Level* | *B Level* |
|---|---|---|
| | 200 (00:20 RI) | 100 (00:20 RI) |
| | 4 × 100 (00:15 RI) | 4 × 50 (00:15 RI) |
| | 50 (00:30 RI) | 50 (00:30 RI) |

*Tip:* Increase speed each time. The fourth set should produce faster speeds than the first set. Do not take additional rest after the 50—rest only 30 seconds and roll right back into the first long swim. Paddles are optional and recommended for working on force.

*C/D:* 300 easy swim

*Total:* 2,600 – 2,300

## MUSCULAR ENDURANCE—M

*W/U:* 2 × (150 swim, 75 kick, 75 build)

| *Main Set:* | *A Level* | *B Level* |
|---|---|---|
| | 6 × 100 @ (T1 pace + 00:25 SI) | 4 × 100 @ (T1 pace + 00:25 SI) |
| | 100 easy | 100 easy |
| | 6 × 100 @ (T1 pace + 00:20 SI) | 4 × 100 @ (T1 pace + 00:20 SI) |
| | 100 easy | 100 easy |
| | 6 × 100 @ (T1 pace + 00:15 SI) | 4 × 100 @ (T1 pace + 00:15 SI) |

*Tip:* The swims should be at T1 pace, at least for the first set. A slight increase in speed (1 to 2 seconds per 100) can be attempted on the second and third sets, but do not increase the rest time. The 100 swims are active recovery and easy, but not enough time for coffee!

*C/D:* 200 easy

*Total:* 2,600 – 2,200

## ANAEROBIC ENDURANCE—A (FORM)

*W/U:* 3 × 200 (swim, kick, pull); 3 × 100 (swim, kick, pull); 3 × 50 (swim, kick, pull)

| *Main Set:* | *A Level* | *B Level* |
|---|---|---|
| | 2 × 100 (01:00 RI) | 2 × 100 (01:00 RI) |
| | 2 × 75 (00:45 RI) | 2 × 75 (00:45 RI) |
| | 2 × 50 (00:30 RI) | 2 × 50 (00:30 RI) |
| | 4 × 25 (00:30 RI) | 4 × 25 (00:30 RI) |

*Tip:* Every swim listed above is all-out fast—no holding back. Both groups intentionally swim the same distances.

*C/D:* Your choice

*Total:* 2,050+

# APPENDIX F
## GENERAL INSTRUCTIONS
## FOR PLYOMETRIC WORKOUTS

The words *plyo* and *metric* are Latin for "measurable increases." Plyometric (plyo) workouts enhance the results of your regular training program by developing and improving your power. These workouts should be performed on jumping surfaces such as a sprung floor, dry grass, or an athletic track (avoid damp or concrete landings). Wearing a pair of crosstraining or court shoes will help you stay on the balls of your feet rather than landing on the sides of your feet or heels; flat-footed landings are also okay.

Warm up with 10 to 20 minutes of biking or running followed by stretching, especially of the legs, before starting your plyo workout. To make a portable square, tape two pieces of athletic tape together, sticky side to sticky side. A square can be made on the floor by simply taping the pattern on flat carpeting or a wooden floor, or you can use the lines on a basketball court. To count on the four-square, if the pattern calls for square 1 to 2, a count of "one" is when your feet return to square 1.

As you begin your workout, imagine that energy is stored in your legs like a giant spring. Remember, when jumping on the four-square plyos, accuracy is first, then speed. Rest between jumps until fully recovered—about 1 to 3 minutes. When doing single leg jumps, alternate right leg then left leg. Do not do all right leg sets before going to the left leg. Rest 2 or 3 minutes after both legs have completed one set. Record the number of jumps completed in the given time on the line provided. For example, square 1 to 2, 20 seconds, both legs: 22 jumps.

Beginner or advanced athletes new to plyometrics should start with the lower number of sets indicated. An additional option for beginners is to cut the time in half, jumping 10 seconds instead of 20.

Week 3 includes an optional set of advanced jumping using 6-inch by 2-foot foam blocks, which can be obtained at an upholstery shop. Beginning plyometric athletes may want to do the workout series a few times before opting to use the foam block.

Week 4 adds light weights. The weights should not limit your movements, which should remain quick, powerful, and smooth. Be sure you have mastered the movements without weights before adding resistance.

# SAMPLE WORKOUTS FOR PLYOMETRIC FLOORWORK

Figure F.1   Four-Square Pattern

*WEEK 1*

*Both legs*

*Set 1:* 2–4 × 20 sec. of square 1 to 2
Record number of jumps:            ____    ____

*Set 2:* 2–4 × 20 sec. of square 1 to 4
Record number of jumps:            ____    ____

*Set 3:* 2 × square 1 to 2 to 3 to 4,
then 3 times around
Record time:            ____    ____

*Set 4*: 2 × square 1 to 2 to 3 to 4,
then 3 times around
Record time: _____   _____

## WEEK 2
*Both legs*
*Set 1:* 2–4 × 20 sec. of square 1 to 2
Record number of jumps: _____   _____

*Set 2:* 2–4 × 20 sec. of square 1 to 4
Record number of jumps: _____   _____

*Set 3:* 2–4 × 20 sec. of square 1 to 3
Record your number of jumps: _____   _____
*Tip:* Be sure to jump diagonally,
keeping hips and toes pointed forward.

*Set 4:* 2–4 × 20 sec. of square 4 to 2
Record your number of jumps: _____   _____
*Tip:* Be sure to jump diagonally,
keeping hips and toes pointed forward.

*Single leg*                          *Right*   *Left*
*Set 1:* 2 × 10 sec. of square 1 to 2
Record your number of jumps: _____   _____
                             _____   _____

*Set 2:* 2 × 10 sec. of square 1 to 4
Record your number of jumps: _____   _____
                             _____   _____

## WEEK 3
*Both legs*
*Set 1:* 2–4 × 20 sec. of square 1 to 2
Record your number of jumps: _____   _____

*Set 2:* 2–4 × 20 sec. of square 1 to 4
Record your number of jumps: _____  _____

*Set 3:* 2–4 × 20 sec. of square 1 to 2
Record your number of jumps: _____  _____
*Optional:* Jump over a 6-inch foam block.

*Set 4:* 1–2 × 10 sec. of square 1 to 4
Record your number of jumps: _____  _____
*Optional:* For more of a challenge,
jump over a 6-inch foam block.

| *Single leg* | Right | Left |
|---|---|---|

*Set 1:* 1–2 × 5 sec. of square 1 to 2
Record your number of jumps: _____  _____
*Optional:* Jump over a 6-inch foam block. _____  _____

*Set 2:* 1–2 × 5 sec. of square 1 to 4
Record your number of jumps: _____  _____
*Optional:* Jump over a 6-inch foam block. _____  _____

*Both legs*
*Set 1:* 1–2 × 20 sec. of square 1 to 2
Record your number of jumps: _____  _____
*Tip:* All-out effort, especially if you
chose the foam the previous week.

*Set 2:* 1–2 × 20 sec. of square 1 to 2
Record your number of jumps: _____  _____
*Tip:* All-out effort, especially if you
chose the foam the previous week.

## WEEK 4

*Both legs*

*Set 1:* 1–2 × 20 sec. of square 1 to 2
Record your number of jumps: _____ _____

*Set 2:* 1–2 × 20 sec. of square 1 to 4
Record your number of jumps: _____ _____

*Set 3:* 1–2 × 20 sec. of square 1 to 2,
hold a set of 5- to 10-pound dumbbells.
Record your number of jumps: _____ _____

*Set 4:* 1–2 × 20 sec. of square 1 to 4,
hold a set of 5- to 10-pound dumbbells.
Record your number of jumps: _____ _____

| *Single leg* | *Right* | *Left* |
|---|---|---|
| *Set 1:* 2 × 10 sec. of square 1 to 2, hold a set of 5- to 10-pound dumbbells. Record your number of jumps: | _____ _____ | _____ _____ |
| *Set 2:* 2 × 10 sec. of square 1 to 2, hold a set of 5- to 10-pound dumbbells. Record your number of jumps: | _____ _____ | _____ _____ |
| *Set 3:* 2 × 10 sec. of square 1 to 2, no weights—go fast! Record your number of jumps: | _____ _____ | _____ _____ |

*Set 4:* 2 × 10 sec. of square 1 to 2,
no weights—go fast!
Record your number of jumps:　　　　　　＿＿＿　　＿＿＿
　　　　　　　　　　　　　　　　　　　　＿＿＿　　＿＿＿


*Both legs*
*Set 1:* 2 × 20 sec. of square 1 to 2,
no weights—go fast!　　　　　　　　　　＿＿＿　　＿＿＿
Record your number of jumps:　　　　　　＿＿＿　　＿＿＿


*Set 2:* 2 × 20 sec. of square 1 to 2,
no weights—go fast!　　　　　　　　　　＿＿＿　　＿＿＿
Record your number of jumps:　　　　　　＿＿＿　　＿＿＿

# APPENDIX G
## INSTRUCTIONS FOR TREADMILL WORKOUTS

Always warm up for 10 to 20 minutes to begin a treadmill workout (TM). Start out with a speed that keeps you in Zone 1 for 5 to 10 minutes, and then gradually increase your speed into Zone 2 for another 5 to 10 minutes of steady running. Note that the treadmill speed that allows you to comfortably run in Zone 2 is your "2-zone." Keep this speed the same for all of your workouts. For example, if your 2-zone speed is 6.5 mph, on TM#1 do 3 to 6 20-second intervals of 6.5 mph at a 7.5-percent incline. See Table G.1 for the treadmill workouts.

After each workout interval, get off of the treadmill, walk around, and stretch before moving onto the next. This recovery interval (RI) should take about 1 to 2 minutes; don't worry if heart rate drops below Zone 1. These workouts are for form and neuromuscular effect. One of the biggest mistakes athletes make is to continue running between workout intervals, not allowing themselves a full recovery. This may not be the type of running workout you are used to, but just trust me—at least for the first workout— so you'll have the opportunity to experience the effects for yourself.

After doing 3 to 6 sets, increase the elevation to 10 percent and run 3 to 6 repetitions of 20 seconds at the new incline. Change the incline once more, this time running only 2 to 4 repeat intervals.

The final run is at 1 mph faster than your 2-zone speed. Run at this speed until your heart rate reaches the end of Zone 3. Running at this new speed should feel very easy and relaxed, as if running downhill. If you don't feel as described, you did something wrong (I suspect you ran during your rest intervals). Get off the treadmill and walk 5 to 10 minutes to cool down and stretch. Remember to record your efforts in a training journal.

When you do TM#2, use the same warm-up routine and the same 2-zone speed that was used in TM#1, but increase your speed a bit more with each elevation change.

TM#3 builds on TM#2, while TM#4 builds on TM#3. On the third set of TM#4, run for 8 to 10 seconds, hop off the treadmill for just 10 seconds, and then back on for another 8 to 10 seconds. The final run for TM#4 should be the fastest of all the workouts.

Please be cautious when mounting and dismounting the treadmill. There's plenty of rest time between intervals and sets not only to allow for ample recovery, but to also avoid rushing back onto the treadmill. Take your time and be safe, especially toward the end of your workout when the legs are more tired. If you have problems getting on and off of a moving treadmill, these workouts may not be not be the best fit for your training plan.

## TABLE G.1: INSTRUCTIONS FOR TREADMILL WORKOUTS

### Treadmill Workout 1 (TM#1)

| Set | Speed | Elevation | Time | Interval |
|---|---|---|---|---|
| 1 | 2-zone | 7.5 | 20 sec. | 3–6 |
| 2 | 2-zone | 10 | 20 sec. | 3–6 |
| 3 | 2-zone | 12.5 | 20 sec. | 2–4 |
| 4 | 2-zone + 1.0 mph | 0 | Until heart rate exceeds Zone 3 | 1 |

### Treadmill Workout 2 (TM#2)

| Set | Speed | Elevation | Time | Interval |
|---|---|---|---|---|
| 1 | 2-zone + 0.5 mph | 7.5 | 20 sec. | 3–6 |
| 2 | 2-zone + 0.5 mph | 10 | 20 sec. | 4–8 |
| 3 | 2-zone + 0.5 mph | 12.5 | 20 sec. | 2–4 |
| 4 | 2-zone + 1.0 mph | 0 | Until heart rate exceeds Zone 3 | 1 |

### Treadmill Workout 3 (TM#3)

| Set | Speed | Elevation | Time | Interval |
|---|---|---|---|---|
| 1 | 2-zone + 0.5 mph | 7 | 20 sec. | 3–6 |
| 2 | 2-zone + 0.5 mph | 11 | 15 sec. | 4–8 |
| 3 | 2-zone + 1.0 mph | 11 | 12-15 sec. | 2–4 |
| 4 | 2-zone + 1.0 mph | 13 | 12-15 sec. | 2–4 |
| 5 | 2-zone + 1.5 mph | 10 | 10 sec. | 2–4 |
| 6 | 2-zone + 1.0 mph | 0 | Until heart rate exceeds Zone 3 | 1 |

### Treadmill Workout 4 (TM#4)

| Set | Speed | Elevation | Time | Interval |
|---|---|---|---|---|
| 1 | 2-zone + 1.0 mph | 7 | 20 sec. | 3–6 |
| 2 | 2-zone + 1.0 mph | 11 | 15 sec. | 4–8 |
| 3 | 2-zone + 1.5 mph | 11 | 10sec./10sec./10sec.* | 2–4 |
| 4 | 2-zone + 1.5 mph | 13 | 10 sec. | 2–4 |
| 5 | 2-zone + 2.0 mph | 10 | 12–15 sec. | 2–4 |
| 6 | 2-zone + 1.5 mph | 0 | Until heart rate exceeds Zone 3 | 2 |

*8 to 10 seconds running, 10 seconds off, 8 to 10 seconds running

# APPENDIX H
## INSTRUCTIONS FOR TREADMILL TRACK WORKOUTS

When looking at the workouts in this section (see Tables H.1–H.5), perhaps the thought crosses your mind, "Why are the interval times so strange? Why not nice round numbers?" These workouts were originally designed for a runner with an open-10K speed of approximately 50 minutes. The times listed are approximate values for the time it would take such a runner to accomplish standard track distances. That design is where the name for the workouts came from, Treadmill Track. For your own use, the values in the chart—as is—will work. If you need nice round numbers to be at ease, feel free to round the run time up or down by 1 to 10 seconds. For example, in the second set of Table H.1: Treadmill Track Workout 1, rounding 02:35 to 02:30 is fine.

## TABLE H.1: TREADMILL TRACK WORKOUT 1 (TM#1)

Name: _____

Date: _____

W/U 20–30 min.: _____

**Description:** Treadmill speed is 8% faster than open 10K pace or 8% faster than lactate threshold speed. Heart rate should climb into 5b–c, PostHR. Rest interval equals the work interval.

C/D 10–15 min.: _____

| Set | Speed | Elevation | Run Time | No. | PreHR | PostHR | Comments |
|-----|-------|-----------|----------|-----|-------|--------|----------|
| 1 | | 0 | 03:30 | 1 | | | |
| | | 0 | 03:30 | 2 | | | |
| | | 0 | 03:30 | 3 | | | |
| 2 | | 0 | 02:35 | 1 | | | |
| | | 0 | 02:35 | 2 | | | |
| | | 0 | 02:35 | 3 | | | |
| 3 | | 0 | 01:44 | 1 | | | |
| | | 0 | 01:44 | 2 | | | |
| | | 0 | 01:44 | 3 | | | |
| 4 | | 0 | 00:50 | 1 | | | |
| | | 0 | 00:50 | 2 | | | |
| | | 0 | 00:50 | 3 | | | |

## TABLE H.2: TREADMILL TRACK WORKOUT 2 (TM#2)

Name: _____

Date: _____

W/U 20–30 min.: _____

**Description:** Treadmill speed is 8% faster than open 10K pace or 8% faster than lactate threshold speed. Heart rate should climb into 5b–c, PostHR. Rest interval equals the work interval.

C/D 10–15 min.: _____

| Set | Speed | Elevation | Run Time | No. | PreHR | PostHR | Comments |
|-----|-------|-----------|----------|-----|-------|--------|----------|
| 1 | | 0 | 04:18 | 1 | | | |
| | | 0 | 04:18 | 2 | | | |
| 2 | | 0 | 03:27 | 1 | | | |
| | | 0 | 03:27 | 2 | | | |
| 3 | | 0 | 02:35 | 1 | | | |
| | | 0 | 02:35 | 2 | | | |
| 4 | | 0 | 01:44 | 1 | | | |
| | | 0 | 01:44 | 2 | | | |
| 5 | | 0 | 00:55 | 1 | | | |
| | | 0 | 00:55 | 2 | | | |

## TABLE H.3: TREADMILL TRACK WORKOUT 3 (TM#3)

Name: _____

Date: _____

**W/U 20–30 min.:** _____

**Description:** Treadmill speed is 8% faster than open 10K pace or 8% faster than lactate threshold speed. Heart rate should climb into 5b–c, PostHR. Rest interval equals the work interval.

**C/D 10–15 min.:** _____

| Set | Speed | Elevation | Run Time | No. | PreHR | PostHR | Comments |
|-----|-------|-----------|----------|-----|-------|--------|----------|
| 1 |  | 0 | 05:10 | 1 |  |  |  |
| 2 |  | 0 | 04:18 | 1 |  |  |  |
|   |  | 0 | 04:18 | 2 |  |  |  |
| 3 |  | 0 | 03:27 | 1 |  |  |  |
|   |  | 0 | 03:27 | 2 |  |  |  |
| 4 |  | 0 | 02:35 | 1 |  |  |  |

## TABLE H.4: TREADMILL TRACK WORKOUT 4 (TM#4)

Name: _____

Date: _____

**W/U 20–30 min.:** _____

**Description:** Treadmill speed is 8% faster than open 10K pace or 8% faster than lactate threshold speed. Heart rate should climb into 5b–c, PostHR. Rest interval equals the work interval.

**C/D 10–15 min.:** _____

| Set | Speed | Elevation | Run Time | No. | PreHR | PostHR | Comments |
|-----|-------|-----------|----------|-----|-------|--------|----------|
| 1 |  | 0 | 05:10 | 1 |  |  |  |
| 2 |  | 0 | 04:18 | 1 |  |  |  |
|   |  | 0 | 04:18 | 2 |  |  |  |
| 3 |  | 0 | 03:27 | 1 |  |  |  |
|   |  | 0 | 03:27 | 2 |  |  |  |
| 4 |  | 0 | 02:35 | 1 |  |  |  |

Each treadmill workout can be copied and taken to the gym. It is best to record workout particulars on a copied sheet if you plan to use the appendix workouts in the future. These workouts are anaerobic endurance workouts versus the sessions designed to improve form in Appendix G.

An explanation of each column follows:

*Set:* Includes time-specified repetitions.

*Speed:* Record the speed you set the treadmill at. Start with a speed that is 8 percent faster than your open 10K time (a 10K run without swimming and cycling first). This speed is roughly 20 seconds per mile faster than the 10K speed at the end of an Olympic-distance triathlon.

*Elevation:* Set elevation at zero to approximate a track elevation. Some people prefer a 1- to 2-percent grade, which will work as well.

*Time:* The time you run on the treadmill at the designated speed.

*No.:* The repetition number within a given set.

*PreHR:* Heart rate prior to stepping on the treadmill for each repetition.

*PostHR:* Heart rate immediately after stepping off the treadmill for each repetition.

*Comments:* How did you feel?

Warm up for 10 to 20 minutes before all treadmill workouts. If you are doing the workout correctly, heart rate should be close to Zone 5b by the end of the first repetition of the first set. If heart rate is low, say, barely making Zone 4, increase the treadmill speed by 10 seconds per mile. For example if you begin at an 8-minute pace per mile and it was too slow, increase the treadmill speed to a 7:50 pace per mile. Be cautious not to increase speed too much. If you are unable to stay on the treadmill for the designated time (in other words, if you get spit off the back), the speed is too fast.

Record PostHR after each repetition and between repetitions; jog easy in Zone 1 for a time that is equal to the previous interval. Hence, rest interval equals work interval.

The overall goal of each workout session is to run the final repetitions of the final set faster than the repetitions of the first set. This is accomplished by gently increasing the speed on the second repetition of subsequent sets. An example follows.

## TABLE H.5: SAMPLE TREADMILL TRACK WORKOUT 1 (TM#1)

Name: _____

Date: _____

W/U 20–30 min.: _____

**Description:** Treadmill speed is 8% faster than open 10K pace or 8% faster than lactate threshold speed. Heart rate should climb into 5b–c, PostHR. Rest interval equals the work interval.

C/D 10–15 min.: _____

| Set | Speed | Elevation | Run Time | No. | PreHR | PostHR | Comments |
|-----|-------|-----------|----------|-----|-------|--------|----------|
| 1 | 08:00 | 0 | 03:30 | 1 | 130 | 171 | Felt hard |
|   | 08:00 | 0 | 03:30 | 2 | 120 | 172 | Felt easier |
|   | 08:00 | 0 | 03:30 | 3 | 135 | 175 | Got in a rhythm |
| 2 | 08:00 | 0 | 02:35 | 1 | 130 | 170 | Time went fast |
|   | 07:50 | 0 | 02:35 | 2 | 115 | 173 | Steady |
|   | 07:50 | 0 | 02:35 | 3 | 120 | 175 | Okay |
| 3 | 07:50 | 0 | 01:44 | 1 | 120 | 169 | Feeling good |
|   | 07:40 | 0 | 01:44 | 2 | 125 | 173 | Okay |
|   | 07:40 | 0 | 01:44 | 3 | 130 | 173 | Okay |
| 4 | 07:40 | 0 | 00:50 | 1 | 130 | 170 | I'm faster! |
|   | 07:30 | 0 | 00:50 | 2 | 135 | 175 | Good |
|   | 07:30 | 0 | 00:50 | 3 | 130 | 175 | Good |

# APPENDIX I
## TRAVEL AND RACE DAY CHECKLIST

A race day checklist can be an extremely helpful item to have when traveling to races. The guide that I prepared for you (see Table I.1) should be modified to meet your personal needs. It will keep you organized when packing for your trip and on the morning of your race. Some athletes have found this list to be helpful for non-race-related travel, as well.

Keep in mind that you cannot travel with $CO_2$ cartridges on an airplane. Remove these from your repair kit before getting to the airport. Airlines can charge a hefty fee for bicycle transportation; be sure to check with your airline for exact pricing.

In the last-minute check section of the list, notice "Shoes lubricated and powdered." For athletes racing without socks, spreading a lubricant such as Body Glide on "hot spots" where blisters can potentially form may keep you blister-free on race day. Some athletes prefer lubricant on hot spots and a light coating of powder in each shoe to help them slip on easily and prevent blisters.

For athletes racing in a swim suit, a thin layer of body lubricant on the seat and a small stash under the seat can help prevent a friction sore from forming on race day. This lubricant, when applied to wrists and ankles, can make wetsuit removal go faster.

| BACKPACK | GENERAL BAG | SWIM BAG | BIKE/RUN BAG |
|---|---|---|---|
| ☐ House keys | ☐ Toothbrush/paste | ☐ Heart rate monitor | ☐ Running shoes |
| ☐ USA Triathlon card | ☐ Contact supplies | ☐ Goggles (2) | ☐ Number pinned to: |
| ☐ Driver's license | ☐ Underwear | ☐ Defog |    elastic band or singlet |
| ☐ Cash + coin | ☐ Extra clothes | ☐ Age-group swim cap | ☐ Hat |
| ☐ Charge Card | ☐ Extra shoes | ☐ Extra swim cap | ☐ Small First Aid |
| ☐ Airline Tickets | ☐ Hair ties (bands) | ☐ Wetsuit | |
| ☐ Passport | ☐ Alarm | ☐ Wetsuit bag | |
| ☐ Bike boarding pass | ☐ Sweats | ☐ Body Glide | |
| ☐ Race instructions | ☐ Tights | ☐ Swimsuit | **FINISH LINE BAG** |
| ☐ Town Maps | ☐ T-shirts | ☐ Tri-shorts | ☐ Towel |
| ☐ Sunglasses | ☐ Jeans | ☐ Sports gra | ☐ Shower items |
| ☐ Workout log | ☐ Shorts | ☐ Sunscreen | ☐ Clothes for post race |
| ☐ Music | ☐ Workout clothes | | ☐ Sunscreen, lip balm |
| ☐ Travel food | ☐ Energy drink powder | **SWIM/BIKE BAG** | ☐ Sandals |
| ☐ Travel $H_2O$ bottle | ☐ Energy bars | ☐ Helmet | ☐ Towelettes |
| ☐ Camera | ☐ Safety pins | ☐ Bike Shoes | ☐ Hair dryer |
| ☐ Video | ☐ Waterproof tape | ☐ Sunglasses | ☐ Hat |
| ☐ Memory sticks | ☐ Black marker | ☐ Clear Lenses | |
| ☐ Medications | ☐ Scissors | ☐ 2 Towels | |
| ☐ Vitamins | ☐ Use tape to mark your | ☐ 2 $H_2O$ bottles | |
| |    race number on your | ☐ Wind jacket | |
| |    bags, shoes, helmet. | ☐ Bike | |
| ☐ Change phone message | | ☐ Spare tire | |
| ☐ Phone and charger | | ☐ Quickfill $CO_2$ cartridge | |
| ☐ Computer & plug-in | | ☐ Floor pump | |
| | | ☐ Disk attachment | |
| | | ☐ Bike tools | |
| | | ☐ Lock & cable | |
| | | ☐ First aid | |
| | | ☐ Towelettes | |

**LAST-MINUTE CHECKS**

| | |
|---|---|
| Water bottles full? | Brakes centered, wheels spun? |
| Energy drink in race bottle? | Chain lubricated? |
| Number pinned on shirt or elastic? | Bike number on? |
| Shoes in bike pedals? (Right feet?) Or laid out correctly? | Bike stripped to the bare minimum? |
| Shoes lubricated and powdered? | Heart rate monitor set and on? |
| Body Glide under seat? | Body Glide wrists, ankles, neck? |
| Gears set for start of the bike? | Did you warm-up? |
| Computer zeroed? | Sunscreen on? Lip sunscreen? |
| Tires inflated? | Goggle defog? |

**Everything is going right. You are prepared. This is fun and challenging. You are a Winner!**

TABLE I.I    The List

# REFERENCES

## CHAPTER 1

Bernhardt, G. *The Female Cyclist: Gearing Up a Level.* Boulder, CO: VeloPress, 1999.

——. *Triathlon Training Basics.* Boulder, CO: VeloPress, 2004.

Burke, E. R. *Serious Cycling.* Champaign, IL: Human Kinetics, 1995.

Edwards, S. *The Heart Rate Monitor Book.* Finland: Polar Electro Oy, 1992.

Friel, J. *The Cyclist's Training Bible.* Boulder, CO: VeloPress, 1996.

——. *The Triathlete's Training Bible.* Boulder, CO: VeloPress, 1998.

Janssen, P. G. J. M. *Training Lactate Pulse-Rate.* Finland: Polar Electro Oy, 1987.

Martin, D. E. and Coe, P. N. *Better Training for Distance Runners.* 2nd ed. Champaign, IL: Human Kinetics, 1997.

McArdle, W. D., et al. *Exercise Physiology, Energy, Nutrition, and Human Performance.* 5th ed. Malverne, PA: Lea & Febiger, 2001.

## CHAPTER 2

American Council on Exercise. *Research Matters,* May 1995.

Anderson, O. "Are Women Better Than Men in the Long Run?" *Running Research News,* November–December 1994.

——. "Question and Answer Section." *Running Research News,* 11, No. 4 (May 1995).

——. "Dad, Mom, and You: Do Your Genes Determine Your Performances?" *Running Research News,* October 1995.

Bernhardt, G. *The Female Cyclist: Gearing up Up a Level.* Boulder, CO: VeloPress, 1999.

McArdle, W. D., et al. *Exercise Physiology, Energy, Nutrition, and Human Performance.* 5th ed. Malverne, PA: Lea & Febiger, 2001.

Seiler, S. "Gender Differences in Endurance Performance Training." March 1998. http://home.hia.no/~stephens/gender.htm MAPP.

## CHAPTER 3

Armstrong, L. E., "Caffeine, Body Fluid–Electrolyte Balance, and Exercise Performance." *International Journal of Sport Nutrition and Exercise Metabolism* 12 (2002): 189–206.

———. *Performing in Extreme Environments*. Champaign, IL: Human Kinetics, 2000.

Balch, J. F., and P. A. Balch. *Prescription for Nutritional Healing*. Garden City Park, NY: Avery, 1997.

Barr, S. "Women, Nutrition, and Exercise: A Review of Athletes' Intakes and a Discussion of Energy Balance in Active Women." *Progress in Food and Nutrition Science* 11, no. 3–4 (1987): 307–361.

Book, C. Interview by Gale Bernhardt, July 7, 1998.

Burke, L. *The Complete Guide to Food for Sports Performance*. New York: Allen & Unwin, 1995.

Coleman, E. *Eating for Endurance*. Palo Alto, CA: Bull, 1997.

Colgan, M. *Optimum Sports Nutrition*. Ronkonkoma, NY: Advanced Research Press, 1993.

Correll, D. "Young Girls Attempt to Mimic Model Bodies." *Sunday Loveland Reporter-Herald,* June 21, 1998.

Cox, G. R., et al. "Effect of Different Protocols of Caffeine Intake on Metabolism and Endurance Performance." *Journal of Applied Physiology* 93, no. 3 (2002): 990–999.

Coyle, E. F. "Substrate Utilization During Exercise in Active People." *American Journal of Clinical Nutrition* Supplement (1995): 968S–979S.

Davis, J. M., et al. "Central Nervous System Effects of Caffeine and Adenosine on Fatigue." *American Journal of Physiology* 284, no. 2 (2003): R 399–404.

Eades, M. R., and M. Eades. *Protein Power*. New York: Bantam, 1996.

Frentosos, J. A., and J. T. Baer. "Increased Energy and Nutrient Intake During Training and Competition Improves Elite Triathlete's Endurance Performance." *International Journal of Sports Nutrition*, March 1997, 61–71.

Friel, J. *The Cyclist's Training Bible*. Boulder, CO: VeloPress, 1996.

Graham, T. E., "Caffeine And and Exercise: Metabolism, Endurance, and Performance." *Sports Medicine* 31, no. 11 (2001): 785–807.

Janssen, G. M., et al. "Marathon Running: Functional Changes in Male and Female Subjects During Training and Contests." *International Journal of Sports Medicine* 1989 supplement, October 10, 1989, 118–123.

Klesges, R. C. "Changes in Bone Mineral Content in Male Athletes: Mechanisms of Action and Intervention Effects." *Journal of the American Medical Association* 276, no. 3 (1996): 226–230.

Lampert, E. V., et al. "Enhanced Endurance in Trained Cyclists During Moderate Intensity Exercise Following Two Weeks of Adaptation to a High-Fat Diet." *European Journal of Applied Physiology* 69, no. 4 (1994): 287–293.

Liebman, B. "Avoiding the Fracture Zone. Calcium: Why Get More?" *Nutrition Action,* April 1998.

———. "Three Vitamins and a Mineral: What to Take." *Nutrition Action,* May 1998.

Lutter, J. M., and L. Jaffee. *The Bodywise Woman,* . 2nd ed. Champaign, IL: Human Kinetics, 1996.

McArdle, W. D., et al. *Exercise Physiology, Energy, Nutrition, and Human Performance.* 5th ed. Malverne, PA: Lea & Febiger, 2001.

———. "The Big Jolt: Mountain Biking's Love Affair with Coffee." *Mountain Biker,* February 1998.

Norager, C. B., et al. "Caffeine Improves Endurance in 75-Year-Old Citizens: A Randomized, Double-Blind, Placebo-Controlled, Crossover Study." *Journal of Applied Physiology* 99, no. 6 (2005): 2302–2306.

Paluska, S. A. "Caffeine and Exercise." *Current Sports Medicine Reports* 2, no. 4 (2003): 213–219.

Roberts, A. T., et al. "The Effect of an Herbal Supplement Containing Black Tea and Caffeine on Metabolic Parameters in Humans." *Alternative Medicine* Review 10, no. 4 (2005): 321–325.

Ryan, M. "Less Is More, : Taking the Sensible Approach to Shedding Weight." *Inside Triathlon,* July 1998.

———. *Sports Nutrition for Endurance Athletes.* Boulder, CO: VeloPress, 2002.

Sabo, D., et al. "Modification of Bone Quality by Extreme Physical Stress. Bone Density Measurements in High-Performance Athletes Using Dual-Energy X-Ray Absorptiometry." *Z. Orthop Ihre Grenzgeb* 143, no. 1 (1996): 1–6.

Sears, B. *The Zone.* New York: HarperCollins, 1995.

Sharkey, B. J. *Fitness and Health.* Champaign, IL: Human Kinetics, 1997.

Shulman, D. Exercise Physiologist. Interviews by Gale Bernhardt, July 1998.

Ulene, A. *The NutriBase Nutrition Facts Desk Reference.* Garden City Park, NY: Avery, 1995.

*USA Cycling Elite Coaching Clinic Manual.* Colorado Springs, CO: USA Cycling, 1997.

Yeo, S. E., et al. "Caffeine Increases Exogenous Carbohydrate Oxidation During Exercise." *Journal of Applied Physiology* 99, no. 3 (2005): 844–850.

## CHAPTER 20

Bernhardt, G. *The Female Cyclist: Gearing Up a Level.* Boulder, CO: VeloPress, 1999.

Friel, J. *The Triathlete's Training Bible.* Boulder, CO: VeloPress, 1998.


## CHAPTER 21

Bernhardt, G. *The Female Cyclist: Gearing Up a Level.* Boulder, CO: VeloPress, 1999.

Friel, J. *The Triathlete's Training Bible.* Boulder, CO: VeloPress, 1998.


## CHAPTER 22

Alter, M. J. *Sport Stretch.* Champaign, IL: Human Kinetics, 1998.

American Council on Exercise. *Personal Trainer Manual.* San Diego, CA: The American Council on Exercise, 1992.

Anderson, B. *Stretching.* Bolinas, California: Shelter, 1980.

Anderson, J. C. "Stretching Before and After Exercise; Effect on Muscle Soreness and Injury Risk." *Journal of Athletic Trainers* 40, no. 3 (2005): 218–220.

Bell, F. Interview by Gale Bernhardt, July 1998.

Bernhardt, G. *The Female Cyclist: Gearing Up a Level.* Boulder, CO: VeloPress, 1999.

Friedlander, A. L., et al. "A Two-Year Program of Aerobics and Weight Training Enhances Bone Mineral Density of Young Women." *Journal of Bone and Mineral Research* 10 (1995): 574–585.

Friel, J. *The Triathlete's Training Bible.* Boulder, CO: VeloPress, 1999.

Gremion, G. "Is Stretching for Sports Performance Still Useful? A Review of the Literature." *Review of Medicine Suisse,* July 27, 2005, 1830–1834.

Handel, M., et al. "Effects of Contract-Relax Stretching Training on Muscle Performance in Athletes." *European Journal of Applied Physiology* 76, no. 5 (1997): 400–408.

Hickson, R. C. "Potential for Strength and Endurance Training to Amplify Endurance Performance." *Journal of Applied Physiology,* 65, no. 5 (November 1988): , 2285–2290.

Ingraham, S. J. "The Role of Flexibility in Injury Prevention and Athletic Performance: Have We Stretched the Truth?" *Minnesota Medicine,* May 2003, 58–61.

Kerr, D., et al. "Exercise Effects on Bone Mass in Postmenopausal Women Are Site-Specific and Load-Dependent." *Journal of Bone and Mineral Research,* February 1996, 218–225.

Kraemer, W. J., and S. J. Fleck. "Exercise Technique: Classic Lat Pull-Down." *Strength and Health Report* 1, no. 6 (1997).

——. "Exercise Technique: Machine Standing Calf Raise." *Strength and Health Report* 2, no. 1 (1998).

——. "Exercise Technique: Seated Cable Row." *Strength and Health Report* 1, no. 3 (1997).

LaRoche, D. P., et al. "Effects of Stretching on Passive Muscle Tension and Response to Eccentric Exercise." *American Journal of Sports Medicine* 34, no. 6 (2006): 1000–1007.

Marcinik, E. J., et al. "Effects of Strength Training on Lactate Threshold and Endurance Performance." *Medicine and Science in Sports and Exercise* 23, no. 6 (1991): 739–743.

McArdle, William D., et al. *Exercise Physiology, Energy, Nutrition, and Human Performance.* 5th ed. Malvern, PA: Lea & Febiger, 1991.

McCarthy, J. P., et al. "Compatibility of Adaptive Responses with Combining Strength and Endurance Training." *Medicine and Science in Sports and Exercise* 27, no. 3 (1995): 429–436.

Nelson, A. G. "Acute Muscle Stretching Inhibits Muscle Strength Endurance Performance." *Journal of Strength and Conditioning Research* 19, no. 2 (2005): 338–343.

Nelson, A. G., et al, . "Chronic Stretching and Running Economy." *Scandinavian Journal of Medicine and Science in Sports* 11, no. 5 (2001): 260–265.

Newton, R. U., et al, . "Kinematics, Kinetics, and Muscle Activation During Explosive Upper Body Movements: Implications for Power Development." *Journal of Applied Biomechanics* 12, no. 1 (1996): 31–43.

O'Connor, D. M., et al., "Effects of Static Stretching on Leg Power During Cycling." *Journal of Sports Medicine and Physical Fitness* 46, no. 1 (2006): 52–56.

Paavolainen, L., et al. "Explosive-Strength Training Improves 5-km Running Time by Improving Running Economy and Muscle Power." *Journal of Applied Physiology* 5, no. 86 (1999): 1527–1533.

Pearl, B., and G. T. Morgan. *Getting Stronger.* Bolinas, CA: Shelter, 1986.

Puhl, J., et al. *Sport Science Perspectives for Women.* Champaign, IL: Human Kinetics, 1988.

Shrier, I. "Does Stretching Improve Performance? A Systematic and Critical Review of the Literature." *Clinical Journal of Sports Medicine* 14, no. 5 (2004): 267–273.

Tanaka, H., and T. Swensen. "Impact of Resistance Training on Endurance Performance: A New Form of Crosstraining?" *Sports Medicine* 25, no. 3 (1998): 191–200.

Thacker, S. B. "The Impact of Stretching on Sports Injury Risk: A Systematic Review of the Literature." *Medicine and Science in Sports and Exercise,* March 2004, 371–378.

Wallin, D., et al. "Improvement of Muscle Flexibility. A Comparison Between Two Techniques." *American Journal of Sports Medicine* 13, no. 4 (985): 263–268.

Witvrouw, E., et al. "Stretching and Injury Prevention: an Obscure Relationship." *Sports Medicine* 34, no. 7 (2004): 443–449.

# GLOSSARY

*Aerobic; aerobic metabolism.* Requiring oxygen for energy transfer.

*Aerobic capacity.* A term used in reference to $VO_2max$. Aerobic capacity training is in the range of 90 to 100 percent of $VO_2max$ pace, or 95 to 98 percent of maximal heart rate in women (90 to 95 percent in men).

*Anaerobic; anaerobic metabolism.* Describes energy transfers that do not require oxygen.

*Arteries.* Blood vessels rich in oxygen that conduct blood away from the heart to the body.

*ATP—adenosine triphosphate.* Molecules where potential energy is stored for use at the cellular level.

*Atherosclerosis.* The accumulation of fat inside the arteries.

*Circulatory.* Refers to blood flow throughout the body.

*Concentric contraction.* Process during which a muscle contracts, exerts force, shortens and overcomes a resistance. For example, concentric contraction occurs in the quadriceps muscles when lifting the weight in a knee extension exercise.

*DNA—deoxyribonucleic acid.* The molecules that determine our heredity; the units of heredity are the genes on our chromosomes. Each gene is a portion of the DNA molecule.

*Eccentric contraction.* Process during which a muscle contracts, exerts force, lengthens and is overcome by a resistance. For example, eccentric contraction occurs in the quadriceps muscles when lowering the weight in a knee extension exercise.

*Economy.* When referenced in exercise, this term usually means the highest level of exercise achievable at the lowest energy cost.

*Extension.* Movement about a joint that increases the angle between the bones on either side of the joint.

*Fartlek.* Swedish for "speed play." It is intervals at a fast pace, inserted into a workout at the athlete's will or desire. Full recovery follows each fast bout.

*Flexion.* Movement about a joint that brings the bones on either side of the joint closer together.

*HDL.* High density lipoprotein, considered the "good" cholesterol, or that which helps prevent atherosclerosis.

*Hemoglobin.* The oxygen-transporting component of red blood cells.

*Interval.* A specified amount of time between events. Workouts that contain intervals typically have a series of work bouts (work intervals) where the athlete is attempting to achieve a specific exercise intensity. The work intervals are separated by specified rest periods (or, rest intervals).

*Isometric contraction.* A muscular contraction where the muscle exerts force but does not change in length.

*Lactate.* A salt of lactic acid formed when lactic acid from within the cells enters the bloodstream and lactate ions separate from hydrogen ions.

*Lactate threshold.* The point during exercise where increasing intensity causes blood lactate levels to accumulate.

*Lactic acid.* An organic acid produced within the cell from anaerobic carbohydrate metabolism.

*LDL.* Low density lipoprotein, considered the "bad" cholesterol, or that which contributes to atherosclerosis.

*Mitochondria.* Organelles within the cells responsible for ATP generation for cellular activities.

*Myoglobin.* Oxygen-binding matter in muscle.

*Negative-split.* A workout or interval that is split in half, with the second half executed faster than the first half.

*Plasma.* The nonliving fluid component of blood. Suspended within the plasma are the various solutes and formed elements.

*Torque.* A measure of a force that rotates the body upon which it acts about an axis. It is commonly expressed in pound-feet, pound-inches, kilogram-meter and other similar units of measure.

*Triglycerides.* Often called "neutral fats," these are the most plentiful fats in the body—more than 95 percent of the body fat is in the form of triglycerides. They are the body's most concentrated source of energy fuel.

*Veins.* Blood vessels returning blood from the body to the heart.

*Ventilation.* The circulation of air through—in this context—the lungs. Ventilatory threshold is the rate of exercise where the relationship between ventilation and oxygen consumption deviates from a linear function. Breathing rate at ventilatory threshold becomes noticeably labored.

*$VO_2max$.* A quantitative measure of an individual's ability to transfer energy aerobically. The value is typically expressed in terms of (ml $\Sigma$ kg-1 $\Sigma$ min-1), or milliliters of oxygen consumed per kilogram of body weight, per minute. The maximum value can be measured in a laboratory, where resistance is incrementally increased on a bicycle ergometer and the test subject's oxygen consumption is constantly measured. As the workload increases, there is a point where the test subject's oxygen consumption no longer increases to meet the increasing demand of the workload. The maximum oxygen consumption value achieved is considered $VO_2max$.

*Work-to-Rest Ratio.* The ratio of fast swimming, running, or cycling to easy recovery in the same sport. For example, a 4:1 work-to-rest ratio could be 4 minutes of fast running followed by 1 minute of easy jogging.

# INDEX

# ABOUT THE AUTHOR

Gale Bernhardt traveled to Athens, Greece, as the 2004 USA Triathlon Olympic Coach for both the men's and women's triathlon teams. This honor was in addition to the selection by USA Triathlon as the 2003 Pan American Games Coach for both the men's and women's teams. But her first Olympic experience was as a personal cycling coach at the 2000 Sydney Olympic Games.

Gale has instructed or coached athletes since 1974. She has a Bachelors of Science from Colorado State University and is certified as a Level I Coach by USA Cycling, and a Level III Coach by USA Triathlon; both certifications are the highest levels awarded in both organizations. She has served on the USA Triathlon National Coaching Committee since 2000 and held a leadership role for five consecutive years. She continues to serve as one of a select few USA Triathlon World Cup coaches.

Gale uses her education and experience to help endurance athletes meet their race-related goals. Athletes utilizing her personal guidance include Olympic and professional cyclists, top national-level masters road racers, ultra-endurance cyclists, runners and multisport racers. Her athletes have placed on Olympic National levels, and she has coached multisport athletes to podium finishes at world championship events and Hawaii Ironman competition.

Gale's legendary and proven training plans are available in her books, *The Female Cyclist: Gearing Up a Level* and *Training Plans for Multisport Athletes* and *Triathlon Training Basics*.

She created the Workouts in a Binder® book series and co-authored its first edition of swim workouts for triathletes, which quickly became a best-seller. This product line expanded in 2005 and further editions in the series lie ahead.

She is a regular columnist for several print and online magazines, such as *Triathlete*, the Active.com newsletters, Inside Triathlon, Rocky Mountain Sports and Fitness and the *VeloNews* gear guide. Interviews with Gale have appeared in *Outside, Runner's World, Bicycling, Her Sports, USA Today, Muscle and Fitness HERS for Women, Newsday,* and *Cooking Light,* to name a few.

Gale lives and trains in Loveland, Colorado, with her husband, Delbert, and is available for a limited number of personal coaching engagements. She is also available for custom designed seminars addressing athletic and business subjects. She can be reached through her Web site, www.galebernhardt.com.